FROM BORDEAUX TO THE STARS

FROM BORDEAUX TO THE STARS

THE REAWAKENING OF A WINE LEGEND

JEAN-MICHEL CAZES

Foreword and Translation by
JANE ANSON

ACADEMIE DU VIN LIBRARY

Published 2023 by Académie du Vin Library Ltd
academieduvinlibrary.com
Founders: Steven Spurrier and Simon McMurtrie

Publisher: Hermione Ireland
Editorial Director: Susan Keevil
Designer: Martin Preston
Art Director: Tim Foster
Translation: Jane Anson
Index: Hilary Bird

ISBN: 978-1-913141-48-6
Printed and bound in the EU

© 2023 Académie du Vin Library Ltd. All rights reserved. No parts of this publication may be reproduced, stored in a retrieval system or transmitted, in any form or by any means, electronic, mechanical, photocopying, recording or otherwise, without the prior permission of the publishers.

Contents

Foreword 7

1. Introduction 9
2. To the Médoc 11
3. From Domaine de Bages to Lynch-Bages 20
4. The War Years 28
5. The Lavinal House 39
6. From Latin Quarter to Lone Star State 43
7. From the Air Force to Big Blue 52
8. Back to My Roots 63
9. La Place de Bordeaux 75
10. First Harvest 79
11. The Collapse 87
12. Making it Through 93
13. Tourism and Gastronomy 99
14. Loudenne, a British Enclave 107
15. Daniel LLose 113
16. The Conquest of the West 120
17. The Oenological Revolution 131
18. The Beginnings of AXA-Millésimes 151
19. Pichon-Longueville 157
20. Robert Parker 167

21	Cordeillan-Bages	173
22	In the East, Something New	186
23	Blanc de Lynch-Bages: Villa Bel-Air	200
24	Saint-Emilion, Margaux, Pomerol, Sauternes and Pauillac	209
25	Quinta do Noval	217
26	The Hungarian Parenthesis	225
27	Chess and Success	244
28	The Call of the Languedoc	256
29	Return to the Douro	265
30	Shipping to Châteauneuf-du-Pape	270
31	Château Haut-Batailley	278
32	In Pursuit of Quality, 1995–2021	287
33	A Family Affair	301
34	And Then	307
	Index	313
	Acknowledgements	319

Foreword

JANE ANSON

ONE OF THE MOST DOG-EARED BOOKS on my shelves is a two-volume, closely typed history of the Médoc vineyards from the Middle Ages to the mid-20th century. Written by French geography professor René Pijassou in 1980, it is a major contribution to Bordeaux history that is still not particularly well known, as it was published as a thesis with only a limited number of copies.

My copy was given to me by Jean-Michel Cazes, during one of our first meetings, in his offices at Château Lynch-Bages. He barely knew me at the time, but told me: 'You are here to write about Bordeaux, so you should read this book.'

It was obvious then that this was a kind and generous gesture – but today I know just how typical it was of a man who has spent much of his professional life welcoming wine lovers into the world of Bordeaux. I was back in his office recently and saw a small collection of the Pijassou books on the top shelf of his bookcase. Waiting, I like to imagine, to help the next person get hooked on the beauty of these wines.

His own autobiography will achieve much the same result, but without the dry academic text. Instead, these pages are full of insider stories and personal histories told with warmth, humour and honesty. You'll learn about the impact of an Allied bombing raid on Pauillac towards the end of World War II, when Jean-Michel's mother hid in a shelter in her friend's garden, while Jean-Michel and his sister Jacqueline ('Jacotte') sat on a wall in their garden a few kilometres away to watch the local oil refinery burning, creating a 'fireworks display' for the two young children. And about the poverty of the postwar years, when it was impossible to earn a living from a wine estate alone, and Jean-Michel's father tried to persuade him to stay away from the industry, meeting him in Paris to discuss selling Lynch-Bages, and replying, 'You're crazy!' when he tentatively suggested moving back to Pauillac to keep the estate in the family.

Later, we follow him into the United States in the 1970s and 1980s, then to Hong Kong, Shanghai and Beijing in the early 1990s, as Bordeaux wines gain ground globally. He meets with legendary characters from Robert Mondavi to

Vincent Cheung and Johnny Chan, and heads to a wine fair in 1993 Beijing where he tells us, 'red wine makes people grimace... Sauternes is better received'. He leaves China at the time believing Bordeaux will manage to sell a few bottles of sweet wine, 'but for the reds there is no significant market'.

Unlike many of the aristocratic owners of the great châteaux of the Médoc, the Cazes family emigrated to the region in 1875 from the Ariège region of southwest France, after spending decades as seasonal workers around Pauillac during the winter months, as was typical for migrant workers at the time.

In many ways this makes them the perfect owners of this 1855 Fifth Growth, as Lynch Bages was created not by a Parisian banker or industrialist, but by local Pauillac merchants and notaries from the Déjean family. They slowly bought plots of high-quality land around the small hamlet of Bages, and planted the first vines here in the 17th century, constructing an estate that would be handed over to Irishman Michel Lynch, who also spent much of his life in Pauillac on the land he loved. Jean-Michel Cazes has followed this tradition, still one of the few owners of a classified estate who lives full-time on the property, and has done so since he moved back to the area on July 13th 1973, as we find out in the opening pages of the book.

It's a tradition now carried on by his son, Jean-Charles Cazes, the latest generation of a family that has grown Lynch-Bages from a scattered collection of farm buildings in the early years of the 20th century to today's stunning architectural treasure – and has, in 1985, literally seen it sent into space, on the STS-51-G Discovery rocket alongside French astronaut Patrick Baudry.

The memoir offers a front row seat on more than wine, as Jean-Michel spent his early career in Paris, part of a team at IBM that built and sold the first personal computers into businesses worldwide. It was a time when the word *informatique* (computer science) was invented and entered into the dictionary of the French academy in 1966, and the job took him over to the United States as well as placing him in Paris during the time of the 1968 student uprisings.

We should all be grateful that Jean-Michel Cazes has shared with us these memories of a life well lived, alongside a family that is both rooted in Bordeaux and yet open and welcoming to the rest of the world. His recounting of his life is a rare treat, inviting us both into his world and into the rich tapestry of 20th-century wine history. Both prove to be never less than entertaining.

Jane Anson – Bordeaux, January 2023

1 Introduction

FRIDAY JULY 13TH 1973. The eve of the French national holiday, the weather is gloomy and it's Friday 13th… a bad omen?

I leave Paris in the early morning, driving our brown Renault 16 that is bursting at the seams with luggage. My Portuguese father-in-law, João-Maria, who is spending a few days in France, follows me at the wheel of our green English Austin Cooper. We are off to the Médoc to join my wife Thereza and our three children – Anne-Christine, known as Kinou, born in 1969, Marina who was born on Christmas Eve 1970 and the youngest, Catherine, born in Boulogne, a one-month-old baby comfy in her bassinet – who have made the trip by train ahead of us.

It will be good for our family to be together again in the Médoc. We are waiting to find a permanent home; until then, we move into the apartment my parents built for their friends in the old Duhart-Milon barrel cellars on the quays of Pauillac. It's a beautiful modern house built around 15 years earlier on the site of the old 'château'; a building of little character that was threatening to fall into ruin.

I have just turned 38 years old. We have chosen this weekend of July 14th to reverse the journey I took from Pauillac to Paris 20 years earlier. I thought at the time that I would never return. My university career in Paris finished in the United States in 1960 with a degree in petroleum geology, followed by a dozen years as an engineer in a new discipline, for which the word *informatique* (computer science) was invented and entered the dictionary of the French Academy in 1966. I know that a new chapter in my family and professional life is opening today, and, despite some nerves, I am looking forward to it.

Once back in Pauillac, the second half of July is marked by incessant rain. This distinctly unfriendly welcome sums up the oceanic climate of the Gironde and puts my sun-loving wife Thereza immediately on edge, but the summer of 1973 passes quickly, fortunately.

I am now a partner in the insurance agency André and Jean-Michel Cazes in Pauillac; we are the local representatives of the La Providence insurance company. I work hard at my new role, while familiarizing myself with the daily life of Château Lynch-Bages, our family property, where Roger Mau is in charge – he is an experienced cellarmaster who also acts as head of the vineyard.

The wine market, in freefall during decades of slump, has begun to recover. Bordeaux has come a long way.

For a long time 'all the Médoc was for sale', as my father used to say. There was a slight improvement after the frost of February 1956, which destroyed large parts of the vineyard, especially on the Right Bank. The coldest parts, invariably the areas that always struggled to ripen, had been most affected, which meant a decrease in production but an overall improvement in quality. The 1956 catastrophe also gave a small boost to wine prices, the effects of which were gradually felt in the 1960s, despite the disastrous quality of the 1963, 1965 and 1968 vintages.

American demand is growing, led by New York importers Austin Nichols and Dreyfus Ashby. The Bordeaux trade is in full swing. In the vineyards, people are starting to believe again. Henri Martin, president of the *Conseil Interprofessionnel des Vins de Bordeaux* (CIVB), mayor of Saint-Julien and Grand Master of the Commanderie du Bontemps, gives his opinion. He proclaims loud and clear: 'The years of misery in Bordeaux are over!'

It all seems to underline my father's words that the last three years had been getting better and better – first slowly with the 1969 and 1970 harvests, then more markedly with the 1971 and especially the 1972, for which the En Primeur release prices in the spring of 1973 reached unprecedented levels.

With all of this good news, we begin plans to buy a house… but soon give up the idea when we see the wheel of fortune turn… in the wrong direction.

Barely two months after our arrival, the oil crisis of September 1973 hits. The price of a barrel of crude oil rises dramatically in a few days from US$3 to US$30, causing a sudden rise in interest rates and widespread credit restrictions which lead to a series of bankruptcies in the Bordeaux trade and the great wine crisis of 1974–80.

But let's not get ahead of ourselves… Let's start at the beginning.

2 To the Médoc

I AM OFTEN ASKED where our surname comes from. I reply that Cazes is a family name found regularly in southwest France, meaning *casa*, the house… It's used either on its own, as ours is, or joined with another word such as Cazabonne or Cazeneuve. There are Catalan Cazes', like my talented winemaking friends in Rivesaltes in the Roussillon, or in the Auvergne, like Marcellin Cazes who moved to Paris in the early 1900s aged 14 and worked his way up from pot boy to infamous owner of Brasserie Lipp.

I've found Cazes' in Canada, Chile, even Louisiana where my namesake, Mike Cazes, works tirelessly as the active – signed in for a fifth term in 2019 – sheriff of a small town in Cajun county. It's a name that belongs to travellers and emigrants. My own Cazes ancestors came from Couserans, near to Saint-Girons, in the Ariège region of southwest France. Leaving behind their mountains, their goats and their pastures, they emigrated to the Médoc in 1875. There they found the work that was lacking in their picturesque but poor

The Ariège landscape of southwest France. My great-grandfather, Jean Cazes, was born here in Montégut-en-Couserans in 1837.

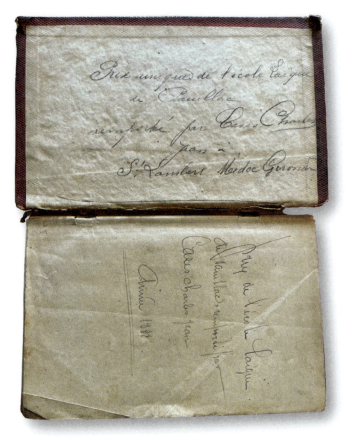

Lessons from Natural History, *the red-bound book awarded to my grandfather Jean-Charles Cazes for passing his school certificate in 1888.*

valleys. These workers, dismissed by many as *montagnols*, or country hicks, came in their thousands, sometimes even entire villages at a time, and began to clear and plant the Médoc. When phylloxera invaded the region, destroying its vines, it was these men who were essential to the fight. Hardworking and tough as boots, they kept the disease at bay where they could, and replanted vines when they were not able to fight it any more. By the time the phylloxera louse had been contained, they had earned their place on the land.

My great-grandfather Jean Cazes was one of them. He had nine brothers and sisters. In the dialect of his childhood, he was called 'Lou Janou'. He was born in Montégut-en-Couserans in 1837, where his family made a living from mountain agriculture and raised a few goats. Like many of his neighbours, he worked as a seasonal worker in the Médoc during the winter.

In 1875, at the age of 38, he decided to stop going back and forth to Ariège and settled a stone's throw from Pichon-Longueville, in the hamlet of Saint-Lambert near Pauillac. With his wife Angélique, whose family was also from Ariège, they owned a house and an adjoining vineyard of a few acres. Lou Janou was a good man, who liked to joke – often teasing his wife.

They had three children. The first two were born in Ariège, the third was Jean-Charles, my grandfather, who was born in 1877 in Pauillac. Lou Janou became a team leader and worked by recruiting workers from his native village on behalf of local châteaux owners. He paid them himself and provided them with basic lodging (meaning sleeping on the floor) and food in his house. Angélique was the cook. The house in Saint-Lambert was cramped, especially during the winter, when the couple had to accommodate half a dozen Montagnols. Later on, Lou Janou also became a gardener, no doubt to improve the food they could offer. Grandma Angélique sold her fruits and vegetables in Pauillac on market days, when she travelled in a cart pulled by a donkey.

My grandfather, Jean-Charles, didn't become a labourer as his father had been. An excellent student, he passed his school certificate with flying colours and, at the age of 11, in 1888, won the school prize for best pupil – a small, red-bound, eight-inch book, *Lessons from Natural History*, which is now carefully and proudly preserved in the family archives.

But his parents did not have the means – or, no doubt, the idea – of sending their son to study in the city. While waiting for his military service, Jean-Charles became apprentice to an influential local banker, Paul Alibert, a very distinguished man who proudly sported a neat beard. With his brother Marcel Alibert, he also owned the vineyards of Ormes de Pez in Saint-Estèphe, Belgrave in Saint-Laurent, Valrose on the island of Patiras and a few others.

At the Alibert Bank, Jean-Charles was first a messenger, then learned to keep accounts and to handle financial management tools: cheques, drafts, deadlines. At the age of 18, he was two years ahead of the call-up and joined the army – he 'marched', as it was called then, with the class of 1875. During five years of military service, he earned his first stripes.

At the turn of the century, when he was a *sergeant-fourrier* (quartermaster) in the 144th regiment, he married the daughter of another Montagnol from Saint-Girons called Eychenne, who became a baker on rue Victor Hugo in Pauillac. When his father-in-law died, he quickly took over the bakery and made it the family home. Antoinette Eychenne gave him two children, Henri and Marcel, before dying prematurely in 1904, shortly after the birth of the second.

JEAN-CHARLES WAS NOW 30, with two children and a demanding job. He decided to start a new life with Andréa Gimbert, an assistant in a dressmaker's shop in Pauillac, also from a modest background. Her father Gimbert was a worker from Creuse who helped build the railway line that crossed the Médoc and brought the first leisure trains from Bordeaux to the beaches of Soulac. He worked as a foreman, and on his retirement was given a small house in Pibran a few hundred metres from Pauillac's train station, on the spot where marshland separates the vineyards of Pontet-Canet and Mouton d'Armaillacq from those of Lynch-Bages. This is where Andréa grew up with her six older brothers and sisters.

Andréa sometimes told how, in her youth, she was impressed by a family of aristocrats who owned the nearby Château Grand-Puy-Lacoste, the Saint-Girons. When they went hunting in the marshes of Pibran, the men rode their horses over the railway line. The ladies, in crinolines, followed in carriages. It was the end of the 19th century, the twilight of the Médoc's heyday. After mildew, phylloxera attacked the vineyards, kicking off the great wine crisis of the following decades. For the great Médoc families of the time, who did not yet know it, it was the beginning of the end…

At the age of 22, Andréa changed jobs. She followed her husband and moved to the bakery on rue Victor Hugo. Someone had to run the shop. Located less than a hundred metres from the river, the shop overlooked the street; set behind it was a large kitchen and living room where the family spent most of their time.

The house was located at the corner of a private alleyway closed by a gate, along which the flour loft and the stables for the four horses required to deliver the bread were lined up. This alleyway was reserved for the children, who played with those of the owner of the beautiful house opposite, a wealthy notary.

The street itself, sloping towards the Gironde, was paved with enormous cobblestones on which the carts of the neighbouring shopkeepers rolled with a clatter. The river lay at the bottom of the road, with a small, lively dock where people embarked for the islands in yoles, the small open boats equipped with a short mast and small sail.

A little further on, perfect lines of single-mast cutters would wait at anchor before setting off for the Cordouan lighthouse to meet the large steamships which they then guided through the dangerous currents of the river Garonne. In autumn, the port came alive in spectacular fashion when the *terre-neuvas* (the Newfoundlander fishermen) anchored in front of Pauillac to refuel before

Jean-Charles Cazes and his family on the eve of the Great War.

heading up to Bordeaux city to deliver their cargo of cod. Their boats were large, ocean-going sailing ships with imposing masts.

After months of fishing, the sailors went ashore in their *dories*, flat-bottomed boats shaped like pointed spindles, and wandered from bar to café in the streets of Pauillac, in heavy boots that would pound the ground.

Two more sons, Gilbert and André, were both born on rue Victor Hugo on the eve of World War I. For all four boys, Andréa was an exemplary mother, authoritarian and ambitious. She pushed her children to study, seeing education as key to getting on in life.

Every day, Jean-Charles harnessed the cart and delivered the bread – each morning covering the northern section of Pauillac and Pouyalet village. After changing horses, he headed south in the afternoon to Bages and Saint-Julien. At each stop he jumped off the cart, knocked on the door and shouted '*le boulanger*' or '*el panadero*' depending on the nationality of the inhabitants. He liked to have one of his children with him so he could stay in the cart while they handed

The portraits of my uncles Marcel Cazes (left) and Gilbert Cazes wearing the uniforms of the prestigious Ecole Polytechnique in Paris. I know that my grandmother longed for me to follow their example, but life took a different turn.

Above: *My grandfather, Lieutenant Jean-Charles Cazes, in 1915. Like many, he came back from the Great War a changed man.*

Right: *Jean-Charles Cazes c1930, now head of a new insurance agency in Pauillac. Business progressed quickly, from the first policies written on the bakery kitchen table…*

over the freshly baked *boules*. It saved time. Sometimes, in the afternoon, grandmother Gimbert ran the shop and looked after the children. Andréa then did the rounds. She liked it and knew how to handle the horse perfectly.

Recalled to the army in 1914, Jean-Charles then went to war. He returned from the battlelines a decorated captain. He took part in the fighting at Ypres and the battle of Verdun where his unit suffered heavy losses. In his role as head of supplies for his regiment, he demonstrated real organizational skill, and in spite of hard times, was proud of his achievements. For him, as for so many soldiers, the war meant a profound intellectual, geographical and social upheaval. He came back a changed man.

The family's destiny turned upside down again in 1925. That day, Henri, Jean-Charles and Andréa's eldest son, returned from Morocco where, having joined the French army, he took part in the Rif War. At the bakery, it was an ordinary day. The routines ticked along just as they did every morning: the cart delivering its hot bread, Andréa attending customers in the shop. At four o'clock in the afternoon, the baker took the oak bundles used for heating out of the oven and placed them against the wooden staircase that led to the attic where the hay for the horses and the bags of flour were stored. At the end of the day, the family gathered around Henri to hear about his adventures.

At around 11 o'clock in the evening, there was a loud knock on the door: 'Fire! The bakery is burning!' Almost immediately, the siren sounded and people came running, lining up from the burning store to the banks of the river. Forming a human chain, the men passed canvas buckets filled with water from the estuary, which they emptied into a large tank to feed the hand pump. On a parallel chain, the women returned the containers along the hundred metres that separated the bakery from the river.

The fire was eventually extinguished, but the damage was considerable. Everything was burned except the shopfront. The flour was sorted out to try to save whatever was possible, and to satisfy customers who were waiting for deliveries, Jean-Charles bought bread from the other local bakers.

Someone lent him an old oven that had been retired 15 years earlier. He refurbished it and very quickly resumed baking his own bread. The rounds started again. Months passed. Business was tough. The bakery had been poorly insured; a large part of the flour stock had gone up in smoke. Jean-Charles began to wonder… should this be a turning point? He was now over 50 but he still felt full of energy. He decided to sell the business: a decision that changed his future, and that of his family.

Above all, Jean-Charles was a farmer. He had a taste for the land and was thrifty. In Pradina, on the southern outskirts of Pauillac, he had a meadow for his horses and a vineyard that a wine grower was looking after. He produced a little wine there. The vineyard interested him, but he was more naturally drawn towards cereals or even flour milling. He visited a farm in the Pas de Calais but it didn't work out. Then a flour mill in the Somme, with the same result. In the end, it was Pauillac. He approached Paul and Marcel Alibert who put him in touch with the absentee owners of Les Ormes de Pez in Saint-Estèphe, Ile Vincent in Patiras, Margaux, Lieujean in Saint-Sauveur, and others.

Jean-Charles was competent, respected, and gave sound advice. I was later told of this by Henri Martin, mayor of Saint-Julien, who Jean-Charles encouraged to buy vines in the Beychevelle area. This was the beginning of an estate that Henri later enlarged and which became Château Gloria, one of the best in the commune. Jean-Charles also suggested to the Aliberts that they take him on as a partner, but they wanted to remain alone.

At the same time, he began to be interested in the insurance business, perhaps as a result of the bakery disaster. The accounting knowledge he had learnt at the Alibert bank was an asset. He scoured the financial pages of newspapers and found the company with the highest share value listed on the stock exchange – at the time La Providence. The die was cast.

He sent a letter of application to the president of the company. 'If you need an agent in Pauillac, I'm your man.' He soon received a visit from an inspector who was delighted at the idea of setting up a new agency in the Médoc: 'Let me take a look at you, sir… I've been looking for an agent in Pauillac for 10 years and I've never found one!' The beginnings were modest, with the first policies written on the bakery's kitchen table on rue Victor Hugo.

The recession of the early 1930s was terrible and hit the wine economy hard. After the good years of 1924 and 1926 came the weaker vintages of 1927 and 1928. The stock market crisis broke out in 1929, and even though this was an exceptional year in the vineyards, there were no buyers to be found for the wine. The châteaux were drowning in debt, and among them, just a hair's breadth from Pauillac, Lynch-Bages. The property belonged to General Félix de Vial, a hero of the Great War, who lived between Paris and Saint-Jean-de-Luz. He had bankrupted himself with this estate, which he inherited from his Bordeaux wife, a Miss Cayrou.

Like many Médoc properties, Lynch-Bages was for sale but nobody wanted it. As a result, General de Vial was frequently at the Alibert bank and it was there that he met Jean-Charles. I was not witness to their conversations but I know that they concluded in a very unusual agreement: Jean-Charles became the tenant farmer of Lynch-Bages, without having to commit to a length of contract or even to pay any rent for the first year.

When Jean-Charles had completed his first harvest at Lynch-Bages in 1933, at the heart of the crisis, he found only one wine merchant in Bordeaux prepared to buy his wine: Cruse & Fils Frères, who took the entire harvest. The price offered enabled him to break even in the first year. He would remain grateful all his life to Emmanuel Cruse for having given him his start.

After this, he wrote to Félix de Vial, saying: 'General, I would like to try for another year, with a small rent.' To reduce his risk, he convinced his friend Georges Fortage, a local garage owner and Peugeot agent, to join him. The partnership lasted three years, with Jean-Charles continuing alone from 1937. Lynch-Bages was still for sale, and de Vial still unable to find a purchaser. With the help of the Crédit Agricole, Jean-Charles made a low offer, promising to pay over two years. The General resisted, but in the end had no other option but to accept.

The deed was finally signed in 1939, as France headed towards war. Jean-Charles refused to buy the stocks, including many excellent 1929s. The château itself was an empty shell, as the general had sold off everything inside for as much as he could get. My grandfather wanted to live in it, at least during the summer (there was no heating), to stop the Germans from moving in as they did at so many other properties, and so it had to be furnished. He was able to buy the furniture of neighbouring Château Croizet-Bages, also for sale without the vines – including the paintings of its former owner, Julien Calvé, a talented local artist.

The following year, Jean-Charles bought Château Ormes de Pez in Saint-Estèphe from Marcel Alibert, an estate that had seen a succession of owners since the beginning of the financial crisis. He knew the vineyard well and had been farming the land for several years – and his sister Marie was married to Guillou, the estate's master winemaker, and already lived there.

3 From Domaine de Bages to Lynch-Bages

FOR THE FAMILY, the purchase of Lynch-Bages meant they were now writing a new chapter in an estate with an ancient history. This château is one of the 18 Pauillac châteaux that were classified in 1855 and one of the oldest.

Unlike most of the big Médoc wine properties, the first stirrings of Domaine de Bages did not come about from outside investment but were born through the work of several generations of a local family, called Déjean. They were notaries, judges and merchants in Pauillac and the surrounding areas. It was this family that began patiently, from the early years of the 17th century, piecing together, either through purchase or exchange, small plots of good-quality agricultural fields, vines and woodland around the small hamlet of Bages. The exact make up of the Déjean family is not easy to establish. Names seem to endlessly swap between Jean, Pierre, Bertrand, Marie, Isabeau, Catherine. The older members are known by familiar monikers that reflect the peasant origin of the clan: 'Camarade' (friend), 'Chic' (chic), 'Nadau' (giver)…

In the fourth generation we find the only Bernard of the family, for whom I have a particular affection. Born in Bages around 1680, he left home at the age of 23 to open a store selling Médoc wines in the Saint-Michel area of Bordeaux. I imagine him dressed in the fashion of the time in a vest, *justacorps* (a single-breasted long coat), frilled shirt and breeches tied with drawstrings to the knee, strolling through the streets of Bordeaux, or flying up and down dusty Médoc roads in a horse and carriage or stagecoach. The wines of the family estate, first created by his great-grandparents and by now well-established, took pride of place among his wine stocks. He quickly expanded, establishing a commercial base in the port of Saint-Malo from where he could send inventory to wine merchants in northern France and along the Brittany coast. His merchant businesses diversified into eaux-de-vies and liqueurs, but also into selling different goods, such as tallow for candles, and weapons.

Bernard Déjean's dynamism was noticed by the Drouillard family, originally from the Ile d'Yeu, who had made their fortune in Bordeaux in the banking, trade, insurance and shipping industries. Pierre Drouillard, then treasurer general of Guyenne, gave him the financial support he needed to develop his business.

The incessant maritime wars that marked the end of the 17th century made life difficult for the merchants of Bordeaux. The seas of Europe abounded with English and Dutch privateers who did all they could to upset commercial relations between the Channel ports and those of the North Sea. Déjean's ships, the *Dauphin*, the *Suzanne*, the *Catherine de l'Ile d'Yeu*, the *Marie* and the *Perle*, among others, were attacked, losing valuable cargo – bringing their owner to his knees. Pierre Drouillard was called in to help, but the liabilities proved to be too heavy and, riddled with debts, Bernard had to sell him the Bages estate in 1728. In order not to damage Bernard Déjean's reputation, it was agreed that the agreement would remain secret and that he would continue to manage the estate on behalf of the buyer.

Shortly afterwards, Bernard found himself at the centre of a vicious family drama. He still owed his three sisters Marie, Anne and Catherine their part of the inheritance that he received in 1728, and they were running out of patience. They asked for the seizure of their brother's property. Then the truth came out: Bernard owned nothing. His exasperated family showed him no sympathy, and instead the poor man was soon languishing in prison.

Yet again, it was Drouillard who came to his rescue, paying 'one hundred and eighty-three pounds, twelve sols' for his food and board during eight months in a Bordeaux jail.

As soon as he was released, Bernard Déjean was reinstated as farmer-manager of the Domaine de Bages by Pierre Drouillard, who clearly still had faith in him. A loyal 'man of business' (a title that had long been used to describe the Médoc managers reporting back to their far-flung bosses), he set about enlarging the estate and improving the methods used in the vineyards and cellars. Able to make use of his former professional network, he succeeded in improving both the reputation and distribution of the wine. When he died, a little before 1750, he had been dedicated to the task for almost 50 years.

In the course of a life rich in events, he was the driving force behind the development of the Bages estate, which owes much to his vision and perseverance. From the disparate plots of vines assembled by his ancestors, he had created one of the leading properties of the Médoc.

AND THEN IT WAS LYNCH TIME… It was Pierre Drouillard's daughter who was key to the next stage of the Domaine de Bages story, when she fell in love with Thomas Lynch, a handsome Irish merchant.

John, Thomas' father, came to Bordeaux from Galway at the end of the 17th century. His story is emblematic of Irish immigration which dates back to the end of the 11th century, when William, Duke of Normandy, known as William the Conqueror, led his 15,000 men and 3,000 horses to battle, and dispatched the Saxon King Harold at the Battle of Hastings.

After his victory, he was crowned King of England at Westminster Abbey. Many of his Norman compatriots, meanwhile, continued their murderous campaign and crossed the Irish Sea, where they set about ravaging the country. The only thing that stopped their rout was the Atlantic Ocean, and when they could go no further, they founded Galway, creating a fortified city that was capable of resisting the reprisals of the Irish locals, the 'terrible O'Hara clan'. These Norman knights were the forefathers of 14 merchant families who became known as the Tribes of Galway. History tells us their names were D'Arcy, Athy, Ffrench, Kirwan, Morris, Martin… and, probably the most famous and respected of the lot, Lynch, who legend has it – although there is precious little proof – come from the city of Linz in Austria and were descended from the same line as Charlemagne himself.

A few centuries later, the descendants of the Tribes rallied to the cause of the Catholic King James II, who had been chased from the throne by the Protestant William of Orange. Crushed at the Battle of the Boyne in 1690, many young Irish Catholics had no other way out than to flee the land and to emigrate.

This was the infamous Flight of the Wild Geese, which would see a generation of Irish disperse across the world, not just to La Rochelle and Bordeaux, cities that had long and active commercial ties with Ireland, but also Paris, where they would concentrate around their exiled king in Saint-Germain-en-Laye.

Others went further still, to New York or Buenos Aires, where I met, a few years ago, an Argentinean Lynch who was a winemaker in Mendoza and an accomplished tango dancer. He told me that his aunt Ana Lynch, originally from Galway, married an Argentinean doctor called Guevara. Together they had a bouncing baby boy called Ernesto, who would one day grow long hair and a beard, and take to wearing a beret. Better known by the nickname Che, he became legendary worldwide. His father would say: 'In my son's veins flows the blood of Irish rebels…'

Back to Bordeaux, where John Lynch, a young Catholic officer, took refuge in 1691, just one year after the defeat of his king, and began exporting wine to Galway, Belfast and Limerick. From the Irish ports, he brought back salt, tallow and wool that he sold in Bordeaux or shipped to the colonies. He became 'Jean' Lynch, married a Guillemette from Bordeaux, integrated brilliantly into local society and had his Irish titles of nobility officially recognized by the King of France.

Settled in the Chartrons neighbourhood, Lynch was one of those foreign merchants who drove the Bordeaux trade in the 18th century. Jean Lynch knew Pierre Drouillard, General Treasurer of Guyenne, one of the pivotal financial agents in the city. He gained his confidence and established fruitful business relations with him and, no doubt, a solid friendship. Their children Thomas and Isabeau-Pétronille met many times in the salons of the Pavé des Chartrons but waited until their 30s to conclude a marriage that consecrated the alliance of two great Bordeaux families. From their union six children were born, two of whom, Jean-Baptiste (1749) and Michel (1754), would later play an important role in the formation of Lynch-Bages.

On June 9th 1750, at the death of her father, Isabeau-Pétronille Drouillard and Thomas bought the domain of Bages from her siblings. A merchant, like his own father, Thomas was an active owner. In Pauillac, he continued the work begun by Bernard Déjean, growing the estate and putting down roots in the village of Bages, where he bought barns, houses and various buildings.

He died on the eve of the French Revolution, leaving two sons. The eldest, Jean-Baptiste, inherited an old and beautiful property from the Drouillard family, the Dauzac estate, located five leagues from Bordeaux. This closeness to the city undoubtedly helped his brilliant political career. He was mayor of the capital of Guyenne from 1805 to 1819. Raised by Napoleon to the rank of Count Lynch, he faithfully served the interests of the emperor... at first.

In 1814, encouraged by Bordeaux merchants who were tired of the economic stagnation caused by the Napoleonic wars, he was the first magistrate of a major French city to take the plunge and pledge allegiance to Louis XVIII. Putting his money where his mouth was, he opened the gates of his city to the English troops who were heading north after having driven the imperial armies out of Spain, and welcomed Marshal Beresford with great pomp.

To thank him, Louis XVIII, when restored to the throne, made him a peer of France. For the same reason, in 1823, the king gave his own grand-nephew Henri, Count of Chambord, the title of Duke of Bordeaux. A somewhat forgotten character, Henri lived his whole life outside his country. For a time, he embodied the hopes of the House of France under the name of Henri V, but his push to replace the republican Tricolour flag of France with the white fleur-de-lys of royalty swung public opinion away from him. But this is another story... of which there remains the fleur-de-lys on the label of Lynch Bages in memory of the Lynch family's loyalty to the crown, and the memory of the Lynch-Bages wine that the Duke of Bordeaux liked to serve to his guests in his Austrian exile at the Schloss Frohsdorf.

JEAN-BAPTISTE LYNCH, mayor of Bordeaux, may have had a greater place in French history than his brother Michel, but he left little trace in Pauillac, unlike his younger brother who spent most of his life there. When his father died, Michel had to make do with the Bages estate, which was the furthest from Bordeaux of all the family properties.

The Revolution, which started in Paris, reached the Médoc well before the end of the century, and Michel Lynch showed flexibility and diplomacy. As of 1789, he gave up his noble title inherited from his Irish ancestors (Knight Lynch) and became colonel of the National Guard of Pauillac. According to the documents of the time, he abandoned both lofty titles and external signs of nobility to become a simple 'farmer'. This did not prevent him from appearing third on the list of 'suspects' of the commune of Pauillac published in 1793 by the local Committee of Public Safety. His name appeared just after that of the priest Nicolas Mercier and his neighbour Joseph de Pichon-Longueville – ex-baron, also recently turned ordinary 'grower' – who was described as having an 'aquiline nose and a cleft chin'. Their listing earned all three an enforced stay of several weeks on the straw of the 'national house' of Meyrac in Vertheuil-Médoc.

Throughout this period, chaos reigned and there was a chronic lack of supplies for ordinary citizens. Many Pauillac inhabitants, desperate with hunger, committed numerous crimes: ransacking boats that were headed towards Bordeaux with provisions, stealing sheep, raiding crops, vegetable gardens and even vines when heavy with grapes. But the storm eventually subsided. Food crops improved, the fevered atmosphere began to slowly calm down. A free man, Michel Lynch returned to his land. Forgiven by his peers, he was soon-after nominated – truly brought back from the dead – president of the Pauillac municipal administration.

Top: *A tower constructed by the powerful Lynch family in southern Ireland. The Lynches were one of 14 merchant families to dominate Galway life from the 13th to the 19th centuries.*

Above left: *Tracing our Lynch-Bages heritage – a visit to Mrs Loïs Blosse-Lynch, Galway, 1985.*

Above right: *Welcoming Henry Blosse-Lynch, Colonel of the Irish Guards, on a visit to Lynch-Bages.*

He clearly did all he could to show willing, even if through gritted teeth, as he swore 'hatred to the king, and proclaimed (his) love and (his) unshakeable attachment to the Republic'. He must have been convincing, as, a few years later, he left the local town hall to head to Paris and join the Council of Five Hundred, one of two legislative bodies brought in after the Revolution.

On '27 germinal V' (April 16th 1797), he eloquently and succinctly explained his decision: 'Having been nominated by the General Assembly of the Gironde to this legislative body, and having accepted the commission, I am bound by my decision. Please accept therefore my resignation, as well as my deepest regret to be leaving, and know that I will remember for the rest of my life the kindness and friendship that you have shown me.'

In the early years of the 19th century, Michel Lynch returned to the Médoc and devoted himself to the management of his estate. He extended the vineyard to the neighbouring hamlet of Cordeillan, to the west to the Madrac farmhouse and into the Moussas area. Work in both the vineyards and cellars was evolving rapidly at the time, and Michel Lynch played a key part in its development. The manager of Lafite even wrote in his diary of his surprise at seeing the de-stalking of the harvest that his neighbour was carrying out in order to bring down the high acidity levels in the grapes.

It is also likely that Lynch was the first to sort the harvest into two qualities of grapes intended for a first and second wine. He pulled up vines in certain areas and planted in others, suggesting that he understood the impact of terroir in improving quality. He either discovered or learned the technique of barrel ageing that was being carried out in the warehouses of Chartrons' buyers, and began to top up, rack and fine his wines in his cellars at Bages, something that was almost unheard of at the time.

It didn't last. The Bordeaux trade was once again paralyzed by war and the Continental Blockade imposed by Napoleon. In retaliation for Napoleon's blockade, the English enacted a naval blockade across the French coast. Unable to survive the financial blow this caused, Michel Lynch was eventually forced to rent out his estate. A farm lease dating from 1808 bestows the property to a Mr Jean Lafon, a doctor in Bordeaux, and is a mine of information of the state of the property at the time.

The inventory is precise and detailed. It gives us an astonishingly complete picture of Bages, comprising numerous buildings for housing workers and family, a winery, cellars, stable, pigsty, barn, sheep pen, large wooden vats and smaller ones encircled by bands of iron or wood, harvest tools, baskets and wooden crates, funnels, new and old barrels, taps and pipes for racking wine, and wooden bowls. Every item is carefully listed, from the cart to the wheelbarrow, the copper pans to the cooking pots, the dishes to the bedding, the cooking utensils to the vast array of pottery. A full picture is drawn, sharply in focus, as if they are setting about their daily lives right before our eyes.

In 1819, Michel Lynch turned 65. He finally set about finding a wife and chose a local Pauillac woman, of English origin, called Elizabeth Davies. A few years later, times were clearly still hard, as he sold almost 220 hectares of his estate. He kept 180 hectares of forests, fields and vines around Madrac and

Moussas where he spent his last years in an attractive house that he had built there. He continued to make wine from the 40 hectares of vines he had kept – a vineyard on fine terroir, close to the village of Bages, that would one day form the heart of the Lynch-Bages estate. In 1824, Lynch finally sold up entirely, to a Swiss wine négociant called Sébastien Jurine.

Bordeaux is often given the reputation of a city closed in on itself, ruled by an inner circle that is impenetrable to outsiders. But the history of the Lynch family, and indeed countless others, proves the exact opposite. Grandsons of immigrants, the Lynch brothers were welcomed with open arms and elected to the heads of their communities by their own contemporaries. But just as with Bernard Déjean, Michel Lynch was the last of his line. And as his brother Jean-Baptiste also had no male heirs, the name Lynch of Bordeaux died with them.

THE SWISS MERCHANT never set foot in Pauillac. He entrusted the management of the estate to a talented local businessman, Léonard Pouyalet, who was born in Vertheuil and died in Bages. He ran the estate for 40 years and continued the work of Michel Lynch. In order to make his mark on the wine, Sébastien Jurine had the absurd idea of putting his name on the label, even though it had little commercial significance. That was how the Bages estate came to be known for a while as 'Jurine-Bages' – and why it was classified in 1855 under this name

Family events led to a new sale of the estate in 1865. This time, the purchasers were two cousins, Jérôme-Maurice and Henri Cayrou, tallow- and candle-makers in Bègles, a suburb of Bordeaux. The first thing they did was to change the name of the property, which finally at this point became Lynch-Bages. The name had its first official mention in the second edition of the celebrated *Cocks & Féret* guide, in 1868.

Jérôme Cayrou modernized the installations, enlisting the help of Théophile Skawinski, the famous manager of the Cruse estates. He built the magnificent vat room in 1866, which you can still find at the estate today, next to our new installations. Cayrou faced mildew, oidium and finally phylloxera and left his heirs to deal with the successive crises that affected the vineyard in the first half of the 20th century. His widow, his daughter and finally his son-in-law, General Félix de Vial, faced an increasingly difficult financial situation. On the eve of World War II, the general finally gave up and sold his property in Pauillac to Jean-Charles Cazes.

4 The War Years

DESPITE THEIR MODEST ORIGINS, two of my father's brothers, Marcel and Gilbert, went to one of the most prestigious universities in France, the Polytéchnique. For the children of a baker in Pauillac during the inter-war period, this was no mean feat. André, my father, initially followed the same path: boarding school at the Lycée de Talence from the age of 11, then extra studies at Michel Montaigne in Bordeaux.

After initially failing the Polytéchnique exam, he signed up to Lycée Louis-le-Grand in Paris, where the chances of success were higher. Unfortunately, he fell ill after a few months. Suffering from tuberculosis and a serious case of pleurisy, he was forced to abandon his studies and had to be rushed back to Pauillac in February 1933. He was bedridden for several months.

During his convalescence, André worked with his father Jean-Charles in the creation of the Médoc wine cooperatives. Starting with the one in Pauillac, which was launched in 1933, the same year that Jean-Charles took over as manager of Lynch-Bages. At the cooperative, Cazes senior became the treasurer while his son André acted as secretary. The cooperatives sprung up out of a great need – the financial crisis was raging and small producers were ill-equipped to deal with it effectively. Pooling resources to modernize equipment and help sales was essential.

Back on his feet, André resumed his studies, and this time, aged 20, enrolled in the Faculty of Law in Bordeaux. There he met up with a former school friend Claudine Lavinal, who was studying for a degree in physics. By November 1934 they were married.

I don't have many details about their romance. One thing is certain, it can't have been easy. On the one hand, a Pauillac Catholic family from peasant farming stock. On the other hand, a city family whose head was a teacher, a free thinker, upholding the beliefs of the 'black hussars' teaching spirit of the Republic. As a result, I never knew where the wedding ceremony was held and

I have no photo of the event. I still regret not asking them more about it when they were alive and I had the chance.

I was born in Lavalance, the biggest maternity hospital in Bordeaux at the time. My parents, both still students, lived in Caudéran, a chic suburb of Bordeaux near the Parc Bordelais.

We were living in the Lavinal family house, and soon joined by my sister Jacqueline, who we call 'Jacotte'.

Arthur Lavinal, my grandfather, was born at the end of the 19th century, in Rueyres, a rural commune in the Lot, into a family of farmers. He was the youngest of four children. His parents also ran a café-grocery in the centre of the village. His brother Jules, who everyone called 'Godfather', became a teacher, as did his sister Sidonie. His other sister, Maria, became a nurse. All three remained single and on retirement also moved to the house in Caudéran. They lived there until their death, leading a quiet life.

Arthur, the youngest of the four, was a man of medium height, authoritative, as lively in his movements as in his words. Like his brothers and sisters, he became a teacher, and when working in the public school system in Villeneuve-sur-Lot met a beautiful girl with bright red hair, Berthe Delbrel, also a teacher, whose parents owned – coincidentally – a café on the Avenue d'Eysses, in the suburbs of Villeneuve.

They got married in the early 1910s and settled near Bordeaux, in Saint-Laurent d'Arce, where they had two children, Claudine and Claude. World War I interrupted his career. He was mobilized and became an officer in the medical services. He returned with the rank of lieutenant, and took up his career where he left off, moving to Bordeaux as head of the school on rue David Johnston, and soon setting his sights on a beautiful house in Caudéran at 22 rue Raymond Bordier, a stone's throw from the Parc Bordelais.

It was here my young parents took up residence with their two babies. Living together in Caudéran was not easy. For, in addition to seven Lavinal family members, the house also housed Berthe's widowed mother Léonie Delbrel. If I count correctly, that makes 12 residents in total.

It was in this house in Caudéran that my grandfather, Arthur, tired of public education, decided on the eve of the war to create his own private school. He resigned and founded what would become known throughout Bordeaux as the 'Cours Lavinal'.

Arthur specialized in helping children from good families who were failing at school. He was an excellent teacher, if traditional – slaps were handed out regularly, and he had his own very effective way of pulling the hair or ears of distracted pupils. No matter what, he quickly got results and people flocked to rue Raymond Bordier, where they met the heirs of Bordeaux's bourgeois families: Marly, Secousse, Nadal, Bonnal, Sanz, and some of the great names of the Chartrons wine district.

As the city became more dangerous when World War II threatened, my sister Jacotte and I headed for Pauillac to the small house my parents had bought with the help of their respective parents. This was without my father, who was doing his military service and was then mobilized in the first hours of the conflict as an officer in the 196th artillery regiment.

I was four years old at this point, and I barely have any memory of it. My first real memories are of being told that he was taken prisoner in 1940. During the 'Phoney War', he had been waiting for the Germans on the Rhine but the Wehrmacht bypassed the French through the Ardennes. The 196th regiment found itself on the Seine, near Rouen, without having fired a single shot. He was almost amused later to remember: 'The Germans were advancing so fast that they did not have time to take us prisoners. They told us to stay there, they would come back later!'

He ended up in a camp in Laval, without guards. There he received a visit from his brother Gilbert, who was still free, who advised him to put on a raincoat over his uniform and to run away. Convinced that they would be freed very quickly and not wanting to abandon his fellow soldiers, he decided to stay. In the end, they were all loaded into cattle cars, heading for Nuremberg, Oflag XIII-A: where things were immediately less funny.

My father was transferred to Oflag IV-D in Elsterhorst near Hoyerswerda on the Saxon-Silesian border, between Dresden and the Polish border. He was able to send us short, regulated letters, often redacted by the censor. To answer him, we received blank, pre-stamped letter forms. I was six or seven years old. In our little house in Pauillac, every night when we went to bed, my mother brought us a framed photograph of our father and we kissed Papa. These are sad memories.

I remained in Pauillac for the whole of the war. The winter in town, the summer at Lynch-Bages along with my grandparents, who spent every June to October at the château.

Sundays with the family were sacrosanct: we had lunch with the Cazes grandparents. We listened to the news on the radio in the dining room, with the speeches of Pétain and Laval… and also Radio London with its famous scrambling of personal messages for which I did not understand the meaning or purpose. We respected Pétain, who ensured schoolchildren across France ate vitamin-enriched biscuits, and proclaimed himself the friend of prisoners-of-war.

We had no contact with the German soldiers, who inspired in us a slightly dull fear. '*Gott Mit Uns*', we read on the buckles of their leather belts. God is with us. Sometimes we saw them on the street, in their impeccably kept uniforms, marching to the swimming pool in Trompeloup, towel folded over their shoulder, singing '*Heili, Heilo, Haila*' at the top of their voices to the rhythm of their boots. We imagined the tune was a war song but I learned much later that it was actually a drinking song. The Kommandantur was set up on the quays of Pauillac, at Château Grand Puy Ducasse, a building next to the town hall.

We went everywhere by bicycle or on foot. To go further, such as to Ormes de Pez in Saint-Estèphe, we harnessed our donkey, Aliboron, to the cart that my grandmother expertly drove.

Vineyard work was carried out by a dozen vigorous horses, looked after mostly by Basque or Spanish workers. There were, of course, ration coupons, but the hardships were more bearable in the countryside than in the big cities: in Bages we had a vast vegetable garden, fruit trees, a field of potatoes, alfalfa, a farmyard with chickens, ducks and rabbits and a herd of 25 cows – meaning vegetables, fruit, eggs, milk and cream. An excellent cook, Andréa churned her own butter and acquired a machine for crimping cans so she could preserve as much produce as possible.

Every summer we moved to Bages. In June, Andréa and Jean-Charles loaded their weapons and luggage into a horse-drawn cart (later, a few years after the war, into the first truck of the estate, a gleaming American GMC), and moved to Lynch-Bages, where they stayed until after the harvest.

Farm life was busy. Jean-Charles only took off his boots in the evening to put on his slippers that were stored during the day in a drawer at the bottom of the stove. I often went with him to feed the animals, and sometimes he took me to the winery, especially during the busy harvest.

He was a very good winemaker. He had little scientific knowledge of oenology, which was typical at the time, but plenty of common sense, and was a good taster, especially of young wines – and this despite the pipe he often smoked, including while tasting. He liked to say: 'I am a baker, I know yeast!' He was one of the first to produce more powerful, higher alcohol wines because he knew how to take risks and harvest later than the others. 'Eight days after

Latour', he used to say. Thirteen degrees alcohol or even more did not scare him, even at a time when many other wines barely reached 12. To ensure stability and balance, and to fix a good colour, the acidity of the wine was high, probably often boosted with tartaric acid.

After the war, he made a string of great vintages: '47, '48, '49, '52, '53, '55 and '59; it was he who made the reputation of Lynch-Bages, which was beginning to be said to be 'better than its classification' as a Fifth Growth, an opinion duly reported in *Cocks & Féret*, the Bordeaux wine Bible.

We drank a little wine with meals, always watered down. Sunday was the day to take out a bottle 'with a label', often an Angludet 1929. In the early 1930s, the owner, a Pauillac man, was on the verge of bankruptcy and Jean-Charles bought a *tonneau* (1,200 bottles) from him. They needed to be drunk.

My mother suffered a little from having her mother-in-law control what she did and the way she spent her money. It wasn't just the generational differences that put them at odds; she was a city girl, raised in Bordeaux, used to doing things differently. In Pauillac, she befriended refugees, industrialists from Strasbourg whose company had been relocated to Pauillac after the Germans invaded Alsace. She also met an unlikely couple, a Dutch painter and a Swiss musician who gave children lessons in flute and rhythmic gymnastics under the suspicious eyes of Andréa…

I went to the local school, which had many children of Spanish migrants who had fled the Civil War. They arrived by boat in 1937 and 1938 at the port of Trompeloup and were housed in a camp that was once a military hospital and served as barracks for the American Expeditionary Force during World War I. There were also plenty of children of Basque immigrants, who played *pelota* and spoke a strange language that we didn't understand. They were tough and tightly knit, and we were fascinated by them.

We spent summers in Bages with kids our age, running around the vineyards, exploring the hayloft and climbing on the roofs. Ignace Béhéretche was my best friend, the son of a local vigneron and a bit – a lot – of a drinker.

The Béhéretche family lived in Bages where several Basque families had settled. Ignace was agile and quick-witted, funny and intelligent. The children of Bages rarely wore shoes and their parents gave them a lot of freedom. I liked to join them and run barefoot through the village streets. My family disapproved but that just made it all the sweeter. We formed clans: those from Bages against those from Pauillac. Armed with slingshots, we confronted each other at the 'Barreyre pass', where the supermarket is today, the border of our territories.

Above: *The Wehrmacht lost no time installing themselves in the Médoc, as here, in Saint-Estèphe.*

Below: *Happily, Jean-Charles Cazes survived to tell the tale – here he is as an old man, at Bages.*

The War Years 33

The echoes of war reached us, but as children we paid little attention. My grandmother called us in one day to tell us about the Allied landings in Italy, which she had heard about on the radio from London. With an air of mystery, she gathered us in the room where Julien Calvé's billiard table was located, closed the doors and took us in her arms. She had tears in her eyes and we understood, perhaps for the first time, how much she had hardly dared hope for the nightmare to end and our father to return home.

One day in August 1944, around noon, the sky suddenly darkened; it was a vast squadron of planes, so tight together they looked like a huge roaring metal roof over our heads. I would later learn that this Anglo-American raid involved nearly 500 aircraft. They targeted the oil refinery and the port facilities of Pauillac where some German ships were anchored.

That day, my mother was in town and she found refuge in the shelter that her Alsatian friends had dug in their garden. I don't know where my grandmother was, but my sister Jacotte and I were alone at Lynch-Bages. Left to ourselves, we climbed the garden wall for a better view. Less than a kilometre away, as the crow flies, in Pauillac, a fireworks display was unfolding before our eyes. The refinery burned, sending monstrous clouds of black smoke into the sky… the ships at anchor fired back with all their machine guns before being sunk by the British dive bombers.

Terrified locals came running towards us in the rows of vines and took refuge at the foot of the wall – including a few German soldiers in uniform. The same thing happened the next day, another ferocious raid that finally destroyed the port and the oil installations. Once the bombing was over, we spent hours outside catching the ribbons of reflective paper that had been dropped by the planes to deceive enemy radars. Caught by the wind, they took ages to reach the ground.

The toll of these two days was heavy: 300 died; their coffins were gathered in the market place a few days later. A quarter of the city was reduced to ashes. Many homeless families found refuge in the surrounding châteaux, most of which had been uninhabited since the economic crisis of the 1930s.

Two of the refugees came to live in Lynch-Bages in unused rooms above the barrel cellar, a place we called 'the liner' because the long corridor that ran through it resembled a ship's gangway. The many empty rooms of the imposing Château Pichon-Longueville were home to several families. For the first time in 20 years, it was inhabited from the cellar to the attic, and it was there that, a few months later, when visiting friends staying at Pichon with my mother, I witnessed the departure of the German occupiers. Before our eyes, trucks loaded with helmeted soldiers followed each other on the road towards Bordeaux. They did not look much like those I had seen parading in town a few years previously. No more marching, no more songs…

In the autumn of 1944, the last Germans were entrenched in the north of the Médoc and around the mouth of the Gironde, in a strongly fortified pocket. The local French Forces of the Interior appeared and took possession of the town hall. They requisitioned our old Peugeot 202 from the garage where, without access to petrol, it had spent the war years. We saw it from time to time, driving like crazy in the streets of Pauillac, loaded with young people with armbands brandishing machine guns. I remember my grandmother saying: 'You realize, so-and-so has seen our car. It was driving through the town at 80 kilometres an hour!'

My grandfather spent a fortnight under lock and key at the Souge camp near Bordeaux because of his role as deputy mayor. He was accused of a lack of fairness when giving out milk from his cows. He was quickly released though, to the great relief of Andréa and the whole family, but it was an indication that temperatures all over the region were running high.

In Pauillac, throughout the winter of 1944–45, we watched the Allied troops move up the line towards Saint-Vivien and Soulac. They were accompanied by terrifying artillery and tanks. Aircraft with cockades flew low over the vineyards. The first friendly GIs introduced us to chewing gum, which very quickly became a sought-after currency at school. In the spring of 1945, the town of Royan was pulverized, and the final pocket of German resistance eradicated. Everywhere in the Médoc, it was the Liberation.

May 1945: the end of hostilities meant my father's return, more than a year since we had last heard from him. As the Red Army approached, the inmates of Elsterhorst Oflag were kicked out onto the roads of Silesia. For several weeks, thousands of malnourished, exhausted and sick prisoners shuffled along broken roads through burning villages. Held at gunpoint by the Hungarian SS guards, they zigzagged between the remnants of the Nazi defenses and the hardly reassuring Soviet vanguard.

Finally turned loose, they made their way home, surviving by looting abandoned houses and shooting game in nearby forests with machine guns. Weakened by four years of detention, my father became seriously ill. Scarlet fever. Unmovable. Two of his friends refused to abandon him, and by staying with him, saved his life.

A few weeks later the three of them managed to get to Berlin, then to Paris, where they were welcomed and given a medical examination. André weighed just 42 kilograms. From Paris, he let us know he was coming home. This was the end of June 1945, six weeks since hostilities had ended on May 8th.

Jean-Charles, accompanied by my mother, went to meet him by car at Bordeaux station. My grandmother, having learned that he was ill and fearing contagion, forbade us to approach him when he arrived. Jacotte and I stood at the entrance to Lynch-Bages at a respectful distance, under a large plane tree. Under orders, we waved to him from afar, but it wasn't long before he gathered both of his nervous children onto his knees. At 10 years old, I finally got to know my father.

All he brought back from Germany was a small notebook. I still have it. A few years ago, on a wine-tasting trip to Dresden with a German buyer, I went to Hoyerswerda. It's a medium-sized town, near the Polish border today. Elsterhorst is a village, four or five kilometres from the centre of the city. The name was changed by the Russian occupiers in 1945. When we asked for directions in the main street of Hoyerswerda, no one could give us any information. No doubt the memories had to be erased. We finally thought to ask an elderly woman, whose memories might go back that far. It worked. She was surprised: 'It was a long time ago…', but she gave us the information we needed, with rather bad grace. When we arrived in the village, I asked the same question of the postman, but he also claimed no knowledge of Elsterhorst. Eager to forget the past.

BACK TO PAUILLAC. After more than six years of separation, my parents decided to go to the mountains, to the Pyrenees, to spend time together. On their return, my father got down to work. Jean-Charles had been running Lynch-Bages since 1933, but before the war he had also built up a modest insurance portfolio under the name La Providence. My father made this his priority. He visited customers by bicycle. After a few months, he mounted a small VAP engine on the rear hub of his bike and began criss-crossing the Médoc at a more significant speed. An excellent lawyer and a great insurer, he inspired confidence and his reputation grew.

At Lynch-Bages, in the immediate aftermath of the war, it was hard to find people to help in the vineyards. The authorities assigned us a dozen German prisoners, who were put up in abandoned houses in Bages village, in the place that has now become the Lavinal café. They worked with us for a little more than

The entire Cazes family in 1948. André, my father, standing in the back row on the left, had returned from Germany three years earlier. In the front row, my sister Jacotte and I are sitting left and second left.

a year and bent over backwards to be helpful. Most of them worked in the vineyard, but my grandmother engaged two to serve the house: Hans and Erwin.

As she did not speak a word of German, to make herself understood, she spoke to them in pidgin French. 'You wash salad, you fetch rabbit…' We became friends. Hans, an architect in civilian life, in his early 40s, bald, distinguished, skilful with his hands, made boats for us out of tree bark. Erwin was 18 years old, tall, strong, blond, friendly. Sent to the Eastern front at 16, a Russian bullet pierced his lungs almost as soon as he arrived. Repatriated to Germany, his strong constitution meant he quickly recovered and he was reassigned to the Western Front. He knew exactly how lucky he was to have been captured by the Americans and not by the Cossacks. I believe that Hans, originally from East Germany, was never reunited with his family. I never heard from Erwin again after the war.

Café Lavinal, the cradle of my maternal family, in the village of Rueyres, Lot, southwestern France.

My maternal grandfather, Arthur Lavinal, was a teacher of French, arithmetic, algebra and geometry, who ran a school from the family home in Caudéran.

5 The Lavinal House

IN OCTOBER 1945, I entered secondary school. The curriculum at the local school in Pauillac ended at 11, so I had no choice: if I wanted to pass my *baccalauréat*, I had to go to Bordeaux. It was to be the Lycée de Longchamp, now the Lycée Montesquieu. I would not be a boarder like the children of the generation before me. My father, who had terrible memories of his boarding school years, decided to send me to live with the Lavinals in Caudéran.

The rue Raymond Bordier became my world, and I remember it well. The cellar was full of coal, firewood, and some good bottles locked in metal racks. On the ground floor, there was a living room on the street, a windowless dining room, a kitchen and a veranda overlooking a small garden at the back where we raised chickens. Outside, a place to scrub clothes clean. On the first floor, three bedrooms, a small bathroom – the only bathroom in the house. On the second floor, one large room and another tiny one that was mine, next to an attic filled with provisions such as dried vegetables, packets of sugar, Marseille soaps and bottles of oils. Marked by wartime shortages, my grandfather Arthur kept a permanent stock on hand in case of difficult times. And finally, a large attic, full of books up to the roof. There were books covering every wall of the house. Arthur was very cultured and read a lot. He gave me a taste for it.

Every morning, and again in the afternoon, I took the tram from the Saint-Médard stop or from the Parc Bordelais to go to the high school located in front of the Jardin Public. At the time, the local public lycée was the essential path to success, and the place where all the best teachers taught. If you didn't get into high school, you went to the Jesuit school called Tivoli. If you weren't clever enough for Tivoli, you headed to Grand Lebrun and the Marianists. The hopeless cases were sent to the Lasallian Brothers of Saint-Genès. Today, everything has changed, it is rather the opposite. National education is not what it was.

At the end of the afternoon, when I came back from school, I joined the classes at Cours Lavinal, where things were simple and efficient. The pupils often arrived by bicycle and their bikes were piled up on the pavement in front of the door at number 22. At the entrance, at the foot of the stairs, there was a wooden crate filled with felt-soled slippers because Mama Berthe was very fond of her wooden floors. The pupils were spread throughout the house: most would be in the dining room, around the large square table that took up the whole room, where a dozen could sit; in the living room, which became a bedroom in the evening, seven or eight pupils could be seated around Arthur's desk; on the veranda on the ground floor, another table seated four or six more children. At certain times of the day, two or three were in the kitchen, as well as upstairs in the room that Maria Lavinal shared with her brother Jules. On busy days we even used the bathroom where a maximum of one pupil could balance his notebooks on the corner of the sink.

Arthur taught French, arithmetic, algebra and geometry. Mama Berthe taught a little English, but her role was more that of general supervisor. She moved from one room to the next enforcing order and discipline with authority and a lot of benevolence. The other subjects, Latin, history, geography, German and English, were taught by students to make a little money. At around five o'clock in the afternoon, the regular students were replaced by others who'd spent the day at the high school or at the nearby Tivoli school. They came to Lavinal's for private lessons or to do their homework for the next day under supervision. They are the ones I met when I came back from school at the end of the afternoon.

A year later, my sister Jacotte started the Mondenard High School, reserved for girls, and joined me in Bordeaux. On Saturdays, we both returned to Pauillac by train, which we took at the Saint-Louis station in Bordeaux, a beautiful 1930s building that has now been transformed into a shopping centre. We often took advantage of the Peugeot 202 convertible belonging to Father Capdeville who spent the weekend with his doctor son-in-law and so would let us use his car while he was away. If I was allowed, I would go into Pauillac town to see my friends from the football team.

I hope I have made it clear that my grandfather, Arthur, was the boss at his house. After morning classes, he went shopping at the Barrière Saint-Médard: bakery, grocery store, butcher shop. He was solely responsible for the supplies. The clinking of his key in the lock announced his return and, with the door half open, a resounding '*à table! à table!*' gave the signal for lunch. Arthur served everyone personally.

In terms of ideas, he was a freemason, but this was something he did not talk about at home. He belonged to the Burdigala Lodge which apparently had roots in Scotland, something that he was very proud of. He liked to say that he had no link to the French freemasons – which only made us wonder what they had done wrong. Politically, he was a curious mixture of nationalism (as espoused by the counter-revolutionary author and politician Charles Maurras) and free thought.

Passionate about literature and French history, he knew the French Revolution and the Napoleonic epic by heart. Comic books – which we call '*illustrés*' – were banned from the house and only read under the covers at night. My favourites were *Coq Hardi* and the adventures of *Les 3 Mousquetaires du Maquis*.

Arthur was also a prodigious worker. To make a little extra income, he not only taught but also became a salesmen for a company in Mauléon that made berets and Basque linen. He never owned a car and didn't have a driving license, but visited his customers in Bordeaux on foot or by tram. Later, to keep the peace, I would sometimes drive him on his rounds to the more difficult-to-reach suburbs.

This was because communications were becoming strained at the Lavinal house. Everything worked out pretty well until the third grade. And then one day, in the cellar, I cut open a pipe and water flooded everywhere, which led to a couple of slaps from my grandfather… and disrespectful words from me. Following this, our relationship soured.

The next school year, my parents wisely decided to move to Bordeaux, at least for some of the time. It was a sacrifice for them and made life somewhat complicated. They rented a small house on rue du Haillan, near the Lycée Mondenard. My father brought the whole family to Bordeaux on Sunday evenings. On Monday he visited the Bordeaux clients of his insurance agency and returned alone at the end of the day to Pauillac where he lived during the week. We returned home on Saturday with my mother, who had passed her driving test. At the time, for a woman, this was a big deal.

In 1949 we went on our first beach holiday, to Saint-Palais-sur-Mer, near Royan. The following year we went to the Arcachon Basin, to Le Canon, and stayed in a wooden hut in the fishing village, which we rented from 'Nénette', a big guy and a local celebrity. We liked it very much and the Basin became our summer destination: Le Canon, Piraillan, and later Cap-Ferret were for years the setting for our summer holidays.

In addition to our holidays, my grandfather's connections allowed my sister and I to spend a few weeks in an English public school not far from London: The Royal Masonic Senior School, in Bushey for the boys, in Rickmansworth for the girls. At 15 years old, it was my first trip abroad.

I boarded the cargo ship *Grebe* in Bordeaux, hugged the coastline of Brittany, crossed the Cherbourg Peninsula and then sailed up the Thames. In London, Arnold Sewell, a teacher friend of my grandfather welcomed me on the quay and immediately took me to the college.

This British boarding school bore little resemblance to my high school in Bordeaux. For a French boy, the food was strange, as were the customs, traditions and discipline of school life. Even though this was a Masonic school, we had to attend Anglican mass every morning. A real culture shock. It was also my first serious exposure to the English language.

I graduated from high school in 1952. Having noted that the sons of doctors seemed to belong to a privileged social category (and no doubt also influenced by the novels of A J Cronin that I loved), I was tempted by medicine. But the Faculty of Medicine only opened its doors in November, whereas for the preparatory class at the high school, the start of the school year was October 1st at Michel Montaigne, cours Victor Hugo.

'If you don't like it, you can always go to university', said my father, who had not lost hope that one day his son would fulfil his dream of going to the Polytéchnique like his brothers had done.

Against all expectations, I took to the mathematics course given by Mr Gerbaud, an exceptional, authoritarian, haughty and elegant teacher. I have one particularly special memory of my father from that time: one Sunday evening, in rue du Haillan, I was trying to finish up a lesson on descriptive geometry, a discipline nowadays quite forgotten which combines geometry, algebra and drawing. The challenge was to position the sun on the horizon and shade the shadow areas with midnight-blue ink. A meticulous work that took at least two hours… Once the drawing was done, I looked at my board: Horror! The sunny area was in the shade and vice versa. I realized that I had reversed everything. Too bad, it's too late, I'm going to sleep…

The next morning, I found the shadows had returned to the right place. Before going back to Pauillac, while I was sleeping, my father had redone the whole layout. It was perfect.

I had long since given up thinking about medicine. But the prospect of studying further maths in Bordeaux from the same teacher my father had 20 years earlier was even less attractive. Instead, I decided to apply to Louis-le-Grand in Paris, and was lucky enough to be accepted. It meant that at the beginning of the school year in October 1953, I left Bordeaux and the cours Victor Hugo for the rue Saint-Jacques and the Latin Quarter.

6 From Latin Quarter to Lone Star State

I ARRIVED IN PARIS, not unhappy to leave Pauillac and the doldrums of the Médoc. But taking the maths classes up in Paris after Bordeaux was like suddenly pedalling in the middle of the Tour de France after cycling on country lanes. It went too fast!

My first year was painful. All the more so because for the first time, at 18, I found myself a boarder. A real barracks: 55 beds per dormitory, 55 washbasins, cold water… one hot shower per week. The Sorbonne clock, on the pavement opposite, punctuated our nights by ringing every quarter of an hour. School was difficult and morale was low. At the end of the year, I failed my exams and had to repeat the year… Fortunately, the summer holidays got me back on track.

It was my first long-distance trip. With three friends from the boarding school, I set off for Norway in the Citroën 2CV that my father had lent us, with a brand-new driving licence in my pocket, along with tents and sleeping bags in the trunk. We crossed Belgium, Holland, Germany, boarded the ferry to Denmark, visited Copenhagen and finally reached Norway at a volunteer youth camp where they broke rocks to build a road in the mountains. We didn't stay long. We then travelled to the fjords and Sweden, before retracing our steps. Two months in unknown countries was an incredible experience.

Back to Louis-le-Grand. With great effort, I just about caught up. It took me two years but in 1956, I was accepted by several engineering schools. Alas, not at the Polytéchnique… I never did attend that prestigious establishment, which was a great pity for my grandmother Andréa, whose prayers were not enough to get me over the last hurdle. She had reserved a place for me on the walls of her room, next to the photos of my uncles Marcel and Gilbert, proud of their beautiful uniforms, with their swords at their sides. It was the same spot that had been reserved for my father 20 years earlier, and I had always known that it was meant for me. Bad luck…

I had to choose between three schools – Centrale, Ponts et Chaussées and Mines de Paris, and finally picked the Mines. The school had a good reputation. There were only a little more than 50 students per class and the atmosphere was quite relaxed – at least that was the reputation.

It was located on Boulevard Saint-Michel, in an enclave of the Luxembourg Gardens, and the student house was on rue Saint-Jacques, 200 metres on foot from the classrooms. This was the deciding argument, because the Centrale school was close to the Gare de Lyon in a run-down area. I had no desire to leave the Latin Quarter.

I didn't even have to move. From Louis-le-Grand, I simply walked up rue Saint-Jacques to the Maison des Mines, a stone's throw from the Val-de-Grâce. I lived there for three years.

Once I passed the entrance exam, the hardest part was over. I took full advantage of my first year of freedom. Three years of specialized maths and boarding school meant that I was now ready to make up for lost time.

I was only really good at concentrating on the things that interested me – mechanics, law, economics, geology above all – rather than in maths and physics, which I had had enough of, or in chemistry, which I hated. I took up rugby seriously. At Louis-le-Grand, my gym teacher was Gérard Dufau, 'Zézé' to my mates, scrum half of the French team, who enlisted me into the main team of the lycée, and now in Paris I joined the team at Mines and then the Racing Club de France where I stayed for three years.

I had plenty of time for training, which took place in the evenings at the Colombes stadium under the floodlights. I played a few good matches, but I quickly realized that to keep playing at such a high level meant living a quasi-monastic life.

Mainly, I explored the Latin Quarter. The old cinema on rue d'Ulm was a five-minute walk away. The price of a ticket was practically nothing and I got into the habit of going there several times a week, thus completing the initiation to cinema that my father had begun with the private screenings organized for his children after the war. After Harold Lloyd, Charlie Chaplin, Buster Keaton, Max Linder, whom we had loved as a family, I discovered the classics of cinema: Fritz Lang, Julien Duvivier, FW Murnau, Luchino Visconti… and many others.

The student milieu was highly politicized at the time. Leftists of all persuasions held sway. The world was rewritten during long evenings. I preferred cinema to dialectics and the rue d'Ulm to meetings of the *Union des Grandes Ecoles* (UGE), as the student union was known.

The Hungarian rebellion of 1956 brought thousands of refugees to Paris fleeing the Soviet army. We took in some of them at the Maison des Mines. The Algerian War, which started in 1954, brought bloodshed to North Africa. Out of sympathy for my many *pieds-noirs* friends at Louis-le-Grand and the Ecole, I supported French Algeria. In 1958, we witnessed the return of Charles de Gaulle with amazement and scepticism. Our generation considered the General as a kind of dinosaur that had long since disappeared. We thought he was buried in the history of France, belonging to the past... And here he was in a few months, driven by a wind of revolt from Algeria, sweeping away an entrenched power that had suddenly run out of breath.

I began working in industry and did internships at Renault in Billancourt, at Usinor in the steelworks of Valenciennes and Montataire, and above all in the coal mines in France, Scotland and England. In Wales, they still used horses, poor harried beasts whose life at the bottom of the mine was hell.

I was fascinated by the earth sciences, especially geology. With our teacher, Jean Goguel, director of the Geological Map of France, an engaging personality and remarkable professor, we explored the Alps and the Boulonnais region. He oversaw my dissertation, and I studied hard, particularly the 'diapir' geological structures of the Triassic Era in Mérindol-les-Oliviers, Haute-Provence, of which I became one of the – very rare – specialists in the world!

On graduation, I finished without a spark in the middle of the ranking. It was 1959 and the Algerian War was raging. I was in no hurry to do my military service. With my engineering diploma in hand, I wanted to train for another year, abroad, to improve my knowledge of geology and specialize in oil research.

Thanks to the discovery of large oil fields in the Sahara, this industry was booming. I was tempted to go to the United States, but I had no contacts at the universities and I had to finance the trip and the tuition fees, which were high. I explored several possibilities and finally found a sympathetic ear with Rotary International. Thanks to Rotary, I left for Austin, capital of the state of Texas, a country of oil if ever there was one, where my French diploma was accepted – just – by the university.

I CAN STILL PICTURE the trip to the American continent on the liner *Liberté*. In the light of August, in the summer of 1959, I was 24 years old... An image of the arrival in New York: at sea in the early morning fog, the buildings of Manhattan suddenly appear, high in the sky above the mist. Then the Statue

At the Ecole des Mines in Paris I developed a passion for earth sciences, geology in particular. Here, I am on a geological expedition in the Alps.

of Liberty appears. What a shock! I think of Ferdinand Bardamu from *Journey to the End of the Night* exclaiming: 'New York is an upright city!'

We docked at the French Line pier. Luggage and passengers were lined up in a huge hangar where they were inspected by Immigration and Customs officials. I asked about cheap accommodation; an American passenger suggested the West Side YMCA at 63rd Street.

My New York days were full, everything surprised me: the numbered streets and avenues that intersected at right angles, the easy orientation, the gigantic advertisements in Times Square, the 'cops' on horseback on the public highway, the baseball in Central Park, the air conditioners that invaded the façades of the buildings, the humid heat of August, unknown in Europe.

I visited the Empire State Building, admired the Rockefeller Center and its Art Deco style, and Oscar Niemeyer's new UN headquarters inaugurated three years earlier. Picasso's *Guernica* was hanging in the MoMA, where I also discovered Douanier Rousseau's *Dream* and his *Sleeping Gypsy*. I explored Broadway, Greenwich Village, Chinatown, mostly on foot. In Harlem, I ended up in the bar of Ray 'Sugar' Robinson, a huge boxing star, who was very popular in France where he often fought. A mecca of jazz, the place was exclusively frequented by African-Americans. My Frenchness was an asset: everyone shook my hand. In broken French, the great Sugar Ray himself proclaimed his Francophilia… An unforgettable evening.

I then boarded a Greyhound bus to Evanston, a suburb of Chicago where Rotary International was headquartered. I spent a day or two there doing paperwork. Then I headed south: 36 hours of Greyhound, interrupted by brief overnight stops in Missouri and Oklahoma, until I reached my destination: Austin, the capital of Texas.

A LITTLE STUNNED by the journey, I disembarked at the bus station in the early hours of the morning where I was greeted by Maurice Acers, president of the local Rotary, who greeted me effusively and took me directly to his office in the Capitol, the seat of the state government, of which he was one of the 'commissioners'. After showing me around the place, with its incredible luxury, size and modernity, he sat me down, grabbed a microphone and said a few words of welcome. Then he opened his desk drawer, pulled out what looked like a floppy disk and handed it to me. He had recorded his speech. I'd landed on another planet…!

I discovered the American university system, so different from the French one, and enrolled in the geology and petroleum engineering departments. The pace was nothing like that of the Ecole des Mines. The exams followed one another without interruption, and the workload was made heavier by the language learning.

The first few weeks were difficult, but I hung in there and eventually adapted. My spirits quickly rose, along with my command of the language and the Texan accent that went with it. Everything was new to me. The university campus was gigantic: 19,000 students. I also discovered Segregation.

Texas is a southern state, and the University of Austin accepted black students for the first time the year that I arrived. Well, a few... There were only a dozen students, admitted to the classrooms but not to the cafeteria. For a French student, this racial separation was a shock. The cafés, restaurants and cinemas around the university were all forbidden to black students, who lived in a remote part of the city. At gas stations, there were three doors to the toilets: Gentlemen, Ladies, Coloured. It was not until a few years later and a Texan (!) president, Lyndon Johnson, that the wall between the races in the southern states cracked.

The students themselves all seemed to be bursting with health; big, strong, athletic and relaxed. Most were diligent in the library and worked hard. They were aware of the responsibility resting on their shoulders, and people were watching their every move.

It was a far cry from the atmosphere of Boulevard Saint-Michel in Paris, and the classes were not like those I had experienced in France either. There were rarely more than 10 students at a time and the relationship with our teachers was marked by a great freedom of tone and attitude. Many of the students were married and from a wide variety of geographical and social backgrounds. I became good friends with many of the South American students. My rather dark complexion helped, and we had a great time together. We hung out a lot in the black districts of Austin, where we discovered with shock and delight a strange and popular music, rock 'n' roll.

At the same time, I had to deal with Prohibition, because Texas, at least in some cities or neighbourhoods (the rules were dictated at the local level), was a 'Dry' state. No alcohol, no beer and, of course... no wine! That's not to say there wasn't plenty of hypocrisy: in Austin's bars, the customers brought their bottles out of sight in brown paper bags and were sold empty glasses for 25 cents, which they just had to fill, legally of course.

Above: *My welcome to Austin, Texas, by Maurice Acers, president of the local Rotary Club and state commissioner. Thanks to his support I was able to study petroleum engineering at the university there.*

Below: *Who says Texas says ranches and horses. At Hillsboro I sit clumsily on my mount…*

I made one new wine discovery though: in New Orleans, I heard the word Napa for the first time. My initial experiences didn't give me much desire to deepen my knowledge of California wine, however – at that time I was far from being an enlightened wine lover. Beer and 7Up were enough to quench my thirst.

There were few French wines on sale in Texas back then. The bottles of Bordeaux that I occasionally saw were all adorned with a sticker that caught my eye: 'An Alexis Lichine Selection'. I had often heard my father and grandfather talk about this Russian-born American wine merchant, author of the remarkable *Encyclopaedia of Wines and Spirits*[1] covering every wine country, who had been living in Bordeaux for a few years. His modern approach to promoting and selling wine had made him a household name. I would later meet him and we would become friends.

I had made a commitment to the Rotary authorities to participate as often as possible in meetings of its clubs and associations, where I was usually asked to speak about France. I would generally turn up in my puncture-proof 1951 Ford, or occasionally by plane for more distant destinations, in noisy old DC-3s.

I was scared to death of speaking in public, in English no less, to unknown audiences. To deal with my nerves, I would invariably write my text in advance and learn it by heart. These speeches required a lot of preparation, but the experience served me well throughout my professional life. I worked hard and was on Rotary duty once a week, sometimes twice. In May 1960, the reward came: I was invited to speak on behalf of the European fellows at the International Convention of Rotary Clubs in Miami Beach, in front of 2,000 people.

Rather than return to Austin, I switched my return ticket to a more exotic destination. I had the whole summer ahead of me and Pan Am and Cubana de Aviación DC-4s served all the Caribbean. My first stop was Cuba, where Castro and Che's *Barbudos* had taken over the previous year. Fidel had not yet discovered that he was a communist. There was a Rotary Club in Camagüey where I was staying. I felt like I had landed in a paradise on earth.

From Cuba, I headed for Kingston, Jamaica, where I met my first Rastas. Then I stopped over in Port-au-Prince, Haiti. The houses were miserable and dilapidated, with the exception of the 'Marché en Fer' and the spectacular presidential palace of the 'honourable' Dr François Duvalier.

In Ciudad Trujillo, formerly Santo Domingo, in the Dominican Republic, it was the end of the reign of Generalissimo Rafael Leonidas Trujillo. There

---

[1] *Encyclopaedia of Wines and Spirits* by Alexis Lichine, Editions Robert Laffont (France), 1972.

I found the heavy atmosphere of the dictatorship and… golf. After Santo Domingo, I landed in Puerto Rico… A stop in Christiansted, in the US Virgin Islands, then in Saint John's, Antigua, and finally I found myself in a French territory, on the island of Guadeloupe. It was time to go back – I'd burnt through all my savings anyway.

Small problem: the ticket for Europe that I had was valid on the liner Liberté for the trip from New York to Le Havre. It was of little use to me in Pointe-à-Pitre. Fortunately, I managed to exchange it with a banana boat captain on his way to Europe, in return for accommodation on board. Twelve days at sea, good weather, lazing around… We finally entered the mouth of the Seine on the morning of July 14th 1960.

Along the banks of the river, the Normandy villages were decked out with French flags for the national holiday, and I had an overwhelming feeling of coming home. The landing in New York had been striking, but the return to France was no less so… I jumped on the next train to Paris where I caught the first one back to Bordeaux… and Pauillac.

7 From the Air Force to Big Blue

IT WAS MY TURN to be drafted. I chose aviation and was signed up in the autumn of 1960 at the Carpiquet air base, near Caen.

I only flew once, in an old Nord Atlas, over Mont-Saint-Michel. I did my training in Normandy, in the freezing cold winter of 1960–61. Three months later, I was assigned to a Forward Command Post (FCP) in Algeria.

A few weeks before leaving for North Africa, during a leave weekend in Paris, I had met up with a classmate who had been posted to the operational research department of the Ministry of Aviation. From what he told me, this was clearly a more attractive proposition than the stint in Aurès, Algeria, that I had in store, and he suggested I apply. To my great surprise, my application was accepted, along with that of a friend no more familiar with the business of operational research than I was. As the department where we were to exercise our talents was integrated into the Air Force commissariat, we first had to become presentable Air Force commissioners. So, we set off for training in Aix-en-Provence, under the sun of Cézanne and Zola. It was early spring; the ski slopes of Serre Chevalier were not far away. Things could definitely have been worse.

My training earned me the title of *Commissaire de L'Air*, or air marshal, as a reserve of course. A few days' leave in Pauillac were granted before I headed into the Ministry on Boulevard Victor in Paris. I didn't really need to rest, but I took advantage of the modern and comfortable house that my parents had finished building on the Pauillac quays. They had moved in while I was in Texas.

I was nervous that my ignorance was going to be uncovered as soon as I got to Paris, but fortunately, a few days before the fateful date, a letter from the Ministry came asking me to 'present myself in civilian clothes' to a programming course in the Parisian premises of the IBM company.

There, I met up with some of the soldiers in the service. We bonded over our discovery of the world of computers, a new universe that made me forget sedimentary geology. I didn't know it yet, but I was going to spend the next 12 years of my life there. At the department, we cut our teeth on the last of the tube computers, the IBM 650, before receiving one of the first transistor machines, the famous and revolutionary IBM 1401.

I was back in the Latin Quarter, on the third floor of a furnished hotel on the rue de la Montagne Sainte-Geneviève. From my window I could see the vast door of the Ecole Polytechnique with its motto: 'For the homeland, science and glory'.

On summer evenings, a group of friends and I would meet on the steps of the Sacré-Cœur cathedral. Some of us took our guitars, and I would sing in Spanish… and busk for money on behalf of a friend who was studying to be a dancer. As I spoke English, performing for American tourists was my speciality. It all felt far, far away from the Médoc and its wine.

At the end of my military service, with the medal in my pocket, I became a geologist again and applied to oil companies. Algeria's independence in April 1962 had changed things. The most interesting roles were being given to the large numbers of older, more qualified men who returned from Algeria, and I didn't find a job.

On the other hand, my experience with computers, which most young engineers did not have, was an unexpected asset. I knocked on the doors of the two big names in the sector, IBM and Bull, both of whom were hiring like crazy. I had kept good contacts at IBM, and the training I had acquired in the army led to my direct entry into the development laboratory at La Gaude, near Nice, where I spent the winter of 1962–63 in Oscar Niemeyer's futuristic building. There I discovered teletransmission, modems, programming languages… A world opened up. And my office overlooked the snow-covered Alps. Life was beautiful.

At the beginning of the 1960s, IBM had nearly 20,000 employees in France. It was a young company, with an average age of 32. It was also in the middle of a transformation, from the punched card readers that had made its reputation and its wealth to 'data processing', a new technology that would soon be called *informatique* in French.

The computing wave was sweeping through companies in all sectors. In the spring of 1963, I left the Côte d'Azur and took up a commercial post in Paris. When I moved to IBM's Parisian offices near the Louvre, the traditional starch-collared shirt of the in-house salesmen was no longer compulsory… even if serious-looking neckties were still advised.

The 'Baou de Saint-Jeannet' seen from the IBM research centre in La Gaude, near Nice, where I spent the winter of 1962–63.

I discovered a company culture that was very different from the one I had known during my internships in industry: the meetings we attended were full of energy, team spirit and camaraderie between colleagues, and hierarchical relations were simple, open and direct. There was a strong emphasis on continuous training, not just in the technical field, and recruitment was diverse. There were almost as many self-taught engineers as there were holders of the best university degrees. Graduates of the Polytéchnique rubbed shoulders with former Social Security employees and lapsed jazz musicians.

Thanks to the experience I had acquired in the army and my time at La Gaude, I had a definite technical edge over my colleagues. At the beginning of the 1960s, in the nascent world of computing, one was quickly labelled an expert or a specialist. I worked at the national railways agency (SNCF), the radio and television office (ORTF), the Social Security, the electricity board (EDF) and the gas board (GDF), in Paris and in regional France… overall things went rather well.

At the end of 1963, I was given responsibility for the EDF and GDF accounts, IBM's biggest clients at the time. Over the next few years, I was part of the transformation of the management methods of these large companies. It was a difficult, new and exciting role to which I devoted all my energy for seven years.

My responsibilities changed over time. IBM entrusted me with what were then called 'special systems'. These were the first IT packages that could be supplied to customers on a turnkey basis. The offer had to integrate both hardware and software. Inevitably, the more my responsibilities increased, the greater was the weight of American supervision from our parent company, particularly as the systems we were working on were complex and their pricing complicated. Head office had little confidence and exercised strict, sometimes even crushing, control over our proposals – no doubt something that played a role in my decision to leave the company in 1971.

Since 1953 and my move to Paris, the link with the Médoc of my adolescence had grown weaker. Any news that was not directly concerned with my family reached me like the muffled echo of a conversation in a neighbouring room, which one hears without listening.

The vineyard remained a world of joyful memories and childhood friends, but it was also a miserable region and a fairly backward society where there was little future for a young man with even moderate ambition. I had little interest in what happened in the Médoc, and in our family independence and autonomy were key to maintaining harmony.

On his return from captivity, my father, André, had thrown himself wholeheartedly into developing the insurance agency. My three uncles had successfully built their careers far from Pauillac. Henri, the eldest, had settled in Dax where he was running a prosperous business. Marcel and Gilbert, both of whom joined the Crédit Lyonnais about 10 years before the war, had followed brilliant career paths, up to general management for the former. The four brothers therefore left their father to look after the two properties – Lynch-Bages and Ormes de Pez – that had been bought in 1939 and 1940. It was a situation that worked for everyone.

Some of my fellow IBMers were bon vivants. For the first time, I noticed that the name Lynch-Bages created a reaction in wine lovers, and many of them knew the wine better than I did. Notably, Jean-Pierre Engrand, a colleague who was both a hedonist and a man of taste. He knew how to use the pleasures of the table to deepen relationships with his customers, and shared his restaurant address book with me: Lort on quai de Jemmapes, Lucas Carton at the Madeleine, the delicious Madame Cartet on rue de Malte, Allard on rue Saint-André-des-Arts…

I also owe Jean-Pierre the revelation that good wine could be born outside Bordeaux. Together we explored the Beaujolais under the expert guidance of Léon Gouin, who had a shop on rue du marché Saint-Honoré called the Ruby Bar. At Georges Garin's – a talented Burgundian chef who left Nuits-Saint-Georges for the banks of the Seine – I took my first steps into the complicated world of burgundy wine. I discovered Bonnes-Mares, Musigny, Chambertin,

Volnay, Meursault and Corton-Charlemagne... all enhanced by a few studious visits to our IBM agency in Dijon, where the director had privileged access to the region's cellars. In this field, nothing beats practice.

One day, my father invited Jean-Pierre Engrand to lunch at a restaurant and ordered a bottle of Cheval Blanc. My friend's emotional reaction surprised me... I didn't know this Saint-Emilion wine that my father seemed to hold in such high esteem. That's how little I knew about Bordeaux at the time.

Thanks to my friends in Paris, this emerging interest in wine continued to grow. I enjoyed returning regularly to the Médoc. In Pauillac, the local branch of La Providence had grown, thanks to the ambition and hard work of my father since his return from Germany in 1945.

By this point it had 20 employees and managed nearly 8,000 clients, which, in a town of 5,500 inhabitants, was a real tour de force. The agency's influence extended throughout the Médoc and beyond, and was by far the most important in the wine world, occupying an important place in the local economy. My father was hard-working, intelligent, affable, and listened to people. In 1947, he was elected to the municipal council, succeeding the team that had been self-appointed at the Liberation.

The mayor, a Shell refinery executive, had to resign two or three years later when he was transferred away from the region, and a successor had to be appointed. My father remained mayor of Pauillac and general councillor of the commune for more than 40 years.

At Lynch-Bages, my grandfather Jean-Charles had remained firmly in charge for many decades, assisted by Roger Mau, the old-fashioned, solid cellarmaster, an excellent leader of men whose competence was based on tradition and experience. But in 1967, Jean-Charles was 90 years old. For a few years, following some haphazard vinifications in 1963 and 1964, my father had taken over the reins, with the agreement of his brothers Marcel and Gilbert and the help of Roger Mau.

Jean-Charles gave his instructions, but his cellarmaster did nothing without André's approval. Not a comfortable situation, but it kept the peace. Things carried on in this slightly haphazard way until my grandfather's death in 1972.

Mr Mau (or 'Monsieur Roger') was from a family of coopers and owned five hectares of vines in Bages from which he produced his own wine, lovingly aged in barrels and bottled under the label 'Grand Vin de Rosiers'. He was a prisoner during the war and Jean-Charles recruited him on his return from Germany. Together, they had produced splendid vintages throughout the

At an IBM training session in 1964… there were few women in the computer industry at that time.

1950s. Monsieur Roger had a tiny office between the vat room and the barrel cellar, and was assisted by a motley crew of Médoc natives, Spaniards, Basques and Portuguese: Gabriel Bérard, head of the vineyard, Jésus Nuñez in the cellar, Justino Nieto, cooper, Xavier Tibur, master winemaker, and Lilou Laforgue, cowherd, in charge of all the chores.

In the vineyards, my grandfather believed in getting the grapes as ripe as possible, even if it meant taking risks. 'I start harvesting eight days after Château Latour', he used to boast. He brought a personal touch to the winemaking process, abandoning certain traditional methods (such as plastering the top of the vats during fermentation to avoid oxidation) and taking care to pump the juice over the skins during fermentation to deepen the colour of the wine.

His wines were more colourful, less acidic, more robust and richer-textured than many of the traditional Médocs that were leading the market at the time. He also knew how to gain the confidence of the trade by intelligent and timely marketing. 'You always have to be a salesman and respond to demand,' he explained. That meant knowing the right moment to negotiate, and he almost always sold 'En Primeur', which at the time meant just a few weeks after harvest, and sometimes even when the bunches were still on the vine, as early as April or May when spring frosts threatened to affect the volume and quality of the vintage.

For the buyer, the speculation was an attraction in itself. Lynch-Bages began to be talked about, and gained the attention particularly of Alexis Lichine, that tireless promoter of wine. As a good American, he was shaking up the somewhat corseted world of great Bordeaux and often put Lynch-Bages in the spotlight in his 'blind' tastings – a clear indication of the great work my grandfather Jean-Charles had done in building up the image of his estate over the previous 30 years.

Jean-Charles and Andréa lived very modestly. From the 1960s onwards, as they grew older, they decided to live in Lynch-Bages year-round. Running water was installed, then heating. The sanitary installations were modernized.

Beyond that, my grandfather never wavered in his work ethic. He would dress in a beret, a string tie and a waistcoat that was often unbuttoned, crossed by the chain of his pocket watch. He rose at 6 o'clock in the morning to go to the stables and give the horses their oats. Then he poured the milk from the morning milking of our cows, which the cowherd had brought in at first light, into cans that had been left near the kitchen the night before.

The volume allocated to each family depended on the number of mouths to feed. Once this ritual was completed, Jean-Charles headed off into the cellar or the vineyard. Or to the insurance office, where he would sit at a table in the centre of the large reception room. Customers greeted him as they passed. I can still see him preparing the weekly pay, always in cash, which he distributed in envelopes carefully marked with the name of each employee.

He and my grandmother were never very social and they rarely received guests, beyond the occasional relative from the Ariège region or friends from World War I. They never took holidays. The only trip I remember is the one my grandmother made to Rome in 1950 to celebrate the Jubilaeum Maximum Holy Year. That kept her going for a long while.

AT THE BEGINNING OF 1968, with some remaining holiday allowance to take, I headed off with a friend to Val d'Isère in my Mustang convertible. After a week of intense skiing, we joined a group of Parisian friends in the Swiss mountains. I was told about a new arrival in the group. Originally from

Mozambique, she was spending a few days in the Valais with a friend she had met at school in Lucerne.

We arrived in Crans-sur-Sierre on March 12th 1968. I remember the date, because on that day everyone was celebrating the 25th birthday of this young woman from Africa. I celebrated along with them. I was nearly 33 years old at the time. She was lively, funny… we probably drank a bit too much that night…

Thereza was Portuguese. Her grandfather, Angelo Carregal Ferreira, was a lawyer who had emigrated from Lisbon to Mozambique at the end of the 19th century and became a prominent figure in the Portuguese community there. Thereza was born in Lourenço Marques (now Maputo) and her parents lived in Beira, 2,000 kilometres north of the capital, where her father, an aviation pioneer and former pilot with DETA (Mozambique's airline), ran the family brewery that produces Manica beer.

After working in travel agencies in Lourenço Marques and Johannesburg, Thereza had just been hired by the Paris office of TAP (Portuguese Air Transport). We saw each other often and lived through the tumultuous events of May 1968 together.

In the evenings, we went to the Sorbonne, to the Odéon, where we listened to the great speeches of the budding revolutionaries. We didn't really feel personally impacted by the subjects they were talking about, but it was fascinating to be a witness to history. On May 30th, we found ourselves in the huge crowd that marched down the Champs-Elysées to support General de Gaulle on his return from Baden-Baden – where he'd been to garner support from the French occupational forces there.

Even though we had only known each other since March, things moved fast. The mail service between France and East Africa was patchy, and there was no telephone link, so when I wanted to propose, I asked for her father's permission – in English – by radio Marconi between Paris and Beira, with a relay in London. The line was bad, and it was quite a challenge, but the answer was positive.

On November 9th 1968, André Cazes, mayor of Pauillac, married us in his town hall. Three weeks later, we embarked for Africa to hold the religious service on December 2nd in Lourenço Marques.

I braved the tropical climate wearing a frock coat and a waistcoat made from thick English cloth, rented in November at the Cor de Chasse on rue de Buci, Paris. Don Custódio Alvim Pereira, bishop of Lourenço Marques, gave the marriage blessing. Afterwards there was a photo session in the garden of

Thereza's grandparents' house, at 40°C in the shade, that made me curse my stupidity at the Parisian suit hire company…

After the ceremony, as the French side of the family began the journey home, Thereza and I flew to Durban, on the southeastern coast of South Africa. From there, we drove along the Garden Route from Margate to Capetown: 2,000 kilometres of road along the Indian Ocean. A journey in a still-wild country where the Apartheid reigned, unlike Mozambique where different races seemed to coexist peacefully. In South Africa, the landscapes were sumptuous, but human relations were difficult or non-existent.

December 1968 marked our return to Earth, or rather to Paris. I was asked to help in the company's recruitment drive. About once a month, I met with potential candidates. The events of May 1968 had left their mark. Young people had changed. Their values were different than ours had been just a few years earlier. They were less rigid, less traditional. Paris no longer seemed the only place to be for a successful professional career, and cities outside of the capital were growing in confidence and self-respect.

At the beginning of 1971, my father, who often came up to Paris to visit the headquarters of La Providence, asked me to have lunch with him. We met at the bistro Au Beaujolais, near La Trinité, in the insurance district.

As usual, we exchanged updates on our lives. Mayor since 1952, general councillor since 1955, he was busy looking after his increasingly important insurance agency, as well as Lynch-Bages and Ormes de Pez. Since the accidental death of his brother Henri, he also managed the insurance agency in Dax, in the Landes. He was overwhelmed and working himself to the bone, and seemed on the verge of depression.

There was one positive point, however: the 1970 harvest was good and the market was starting to slowly recover. To my amazement, my father concluded: 'Maybe it's the right time to get rid of the vines?'

Was he joking? I replied almost without thinking: 'I don't have to live in Paris any more. I am sure we could be happy in the Médoc with our children. Of course, who knows if we could make any money from it, but your insurance agency can easily feed two families now. If I just give you a hand, we'll be able to keep the vines in the family.'

My father's reaction was immediate: 'You're crazy! You're not going to come and live in Pauillac!'

It was true that when I left the Médoc 20 years previously I had never thought about returning one day. Unsure of myself, I didn't reply. Above all, I had

1968. Thanks to my good friends, I met Thereza Carregal Ferreira while on a skiing trip in the Swiss Alps. A few months later, my father, André Cazes, mayor of Pauillac, signs my marriage certificate.

to talk to Thereza, who had married an engineer from Paris and not an insurance agent from the provinces. It would be a radical change in our family life…

In the months that followed, I received several job offers. Joseph Dupin de Saint-Cyr, who had been an advisor at IBM 10 years earlier, offered me the chance to manage two computer companies with the Schneider group, one in Paris, the other near Châteauroux. It was hardly a promotion from my role at IBM, but I liked the thought of being entirely responsible for the running of a department. I had concentrated on the technical and commercial side of the business at IBM and had never had to deal with financial or legal management issues. Schneider's offer was an opportunity to gain new experience. It could be useful grounding if I decided to join the family business in Pauillac, and in the early summer of 1971, I left IBM.

For the next two years, I experienced the daily life of a large French company, and saw how different its corporate culture was from that of IBM. Relationships were more fraught, rivalries and jealousies more pronounced – and my own department was in great difficulty. It helped cement my decision.

My father and I soon set the date for my involvement in the family business: summer 1973. In mid-1972, I let the president of Schneider know that I had accomplished the job he had hired me to do, and that I would be leaving the company within the year.

My grandfather Jean-Charles died in 1972. I was travelling in Switzerland with Thereza and our children at the time, and was unable to attend his funeral. I had visited him a few days before our departure, at the hospital where he had been taken following a fall. I can still remember his hand gesture, as if to say goodbye; he could hardly speak.

The Parisian managers of La Providence agreed that I would begin working with my father, but I had to learn the trade, about which I knew almost nothing. I spent a few weeks at the company's headquarters, suddenly plunged into a new world. The offices were a little dusty and the atmosphere far removed from that of IBM. I went between departments, practising writing fire policies, drawing up multi-risk contracts, resolving delicate claims, and making a few friends who would be helpful later on. My express training came to an end at the beginning of July 1973. Everything was about to change.

8 Back to My Roots

THE 1973 HARVEST was approaching. Lynch-Bages was no longer the farm I knew as a child. At the end of the 1960s, Jean-Charles stopped feeding the horses and distributing the milk himself. My father André then took the decision to gradually abandon animal traction altogether and adopt the new high-performance tractors that were beginning to be seen in the vineyards. Within a year or two, the nine horses in the stable and the 20 or so cows in the cowshed disappeared, leaving the vast premises unoccupied.

The winery was still a patchwork of more or less dilapidated buildings, embedded in the village of Bages. Most of the houses were in ruins. You entered the property by passing between two small squat windowless houses which framed the entrance. The one on the left was used as a shelter when it rained. Wine growers spent the day there splitting the '*vîme*', which meant making the wicker ties which they used to tie up the vines' shoots to the trellises.

The house on the right was occupied by General de Vial's former estate manager, who by this point had turned into some kind of scrap-metal dealer and used the premises to store the products of his marauding.

This unimpressive entrance gave access to a vast inner courtyard shaded by several hundred-year-old plane trees. There were a few garages built by my grandfather on the site of the former farmyard, the *bûchère* where vine shoots and firewood were stored, the harvest kitchen (whose equipment had not changed for a century), and the main house, which had stood empty since the death of my grandmother. Next to the 'château' was the vat room, a sawmill and the manure pit. In a corner, wooden huts operated as the village's public toilets. Then there were the almost uninhabitable wine growers' lodgings, and finally the stable and the cowshed, two large adjoining buildings with haylofts on their upper floors.

The barrel cellars were located behind the vat house, cobbled together from several buildings. Once owned by small wine growers in the village, now almost all gone, they had been linked together, rebuilt or extended by my grandfather. Electricity was only available sporadically, and you had to use candlelight in the bottle cellar. The site was the fruit of the imagination of my grandfather's favourite mason, André Gimenez, from the nearby Pouyalet village, better known for his taste for thick concrete and indestructible frames than for elegant architecture.

An assortment of tools propped up in various corners stood witness to long-ago working methods. The whole thing was like a time capsule. 'Bottle-barrows' were still used in the cellars for the bottling process, which was carried out by filling bottles direct from the barrel using a small tube, followed by separate corking and capping.

Everything was done by hand. Drawing, corking and capping by men, while the women were in charge of the labelling. The labels were laid flat on a table that had been coated with glue, then affixed by hand, one by one.

The team was multi-skilled, dividing their time between vineyard and cellar work, meaning that it was extremely rare for the bottling of a vintage to be carried out without interruption, especially if the threat of oidium or mildew in the vineyard meant the vines needed immediate attention. The bottling process was instead spread out over several months, resulting in what the English euphemistically call 'bottle variation'.

We kept a weighing machine which worked on the principle of a Roman scale and was used to check the capacity of each barrel. Particularly important because, until 1970, most deliveries to the Bordeaux merchants were still being made in barrels. The buyer was often accused of supplying barrels that were bigger than average, while the estate's barrels were similarly accused of being a little smaller... the barrel scale allowed everyone to agree.

The bottles, transported by the famous bottle-barrows, were stacked in an assortment of cellars or garages on the estate, meaning they were everywhere. They were stored 'in rhyme', which is to say, one on top of the other, a sometimes precarious balance that caused memorable accidental breakages, as happened to us in 1975.

Pallet boxes were unknown, as were forklifts – and even if financially possible, these would have been unusable inside the buildings, as the floors of the wineries were almost all at different levels, accessed via sloping boards that had been placed to allow the wheelbarrows to roll between them.

The vat house dated from 1866. It was one of the few old winemaking facilities in the Médoc that had remained intact, and was housed in a building

Left: *Jean-Charles Cazes in the vineyard in around 1960.* **Right:** *My daughters Kinou and Marina on Father Celhay's cart at Bages, in 1973; horses were still part of vineyard life back then.*

The Lynch-Bages stable housed around 10 horses in 1970.

built over successive periods in the 18th and 19th centuries. The many crises of the 20th century had meant maintenance had been somewhat neglected.

There were 13 wooden vats of different sizes and ages that were used for fermenting the wine. The only way to get inside them was through a trapdoor on the top. Until quite recently, it had been customary, once the vat had been filled, to protect it (or so it was believed) from air that could lead to oxidation and spoilage by spreading a thick layer of plaster over the top of the vat. A small hole allowed the carbon dioxide to escape during fermentation.

The vats were filled, plastered, and then 'we went hunting and returned after All Saints' Day'. The vat would take care of itself. The cellarmaster plastered in November and then would later note the result.

Plastering was abandoned in the 1950s, replaced by systematic pumping over: during fermentation, a wooden board was placed on the thick cap formed by the grape skins that rose to the surface under the pressure of carbon dioxide produced during fermentation. The fermenting juice under the cap was then pumped out and poured back into the vat, allowing the juice to run through the cap of skins. Every 10 minutes, a worker moved the board to ensure that the entire surface was sprayed evenly.

Several vats were old and in a bad state. The wood became encrusted over time and no doubt was impregnated with bacteria. It was difficult to clean, and keeping volatile acidity at an acceptable level during fermentation was an ambitious and difficult task. During the summer, the wood dried out and the staves that made up the vats would separate. As the harvest approached, the vats were often like sieves.

To avoid leaks, two weeks before the harvest, the tanks were filled with water and kept full for a few days to allow the wood to swell. There was no temperature control system. When a vat needed to be cooled at all costs to prevent the fermentation from stopping, the Glacières Bernat, a company that provided ice, was called in from Bordeaux. Ice blocks were thrown into the vat covered by a protective bag; at least in theory. When heat was needed instead, coal-fired braziers were placed in the main aisle, which filled the room with choking fumes, but had almost no effect on the temperature of the fermenting juice.

On the first floor, from which you could access the top of the vats, nothing had changed since the days of the system described in 1842 by the agricultural engineer and botanist Auguste Petit-Lafitte at Château Lanessan – later reproduced by all the managers of the great Médoc estates and their architects Henri Duphot, Louis Garros and Ernest Minvielle.

This level had a slatted floor that allowed the carbon dioxide from the fermentation process, which is heavier than air, to float downwards to the ground floor below. It meant that the staff could work upstairs in complete safety, 24 hours a day. The slatted floor was also studded with numerous trapdoors, through which the stalks and grape skins left over from winemaking could be dropped to the ground floor to be collected in buckets, then removed by horses.

Pierre Skawinski, an agricultural engineer who graduated from the Grignon school and oversaw the Cruse family estates (Châteaux Giscours, Laujac and others), was the most famous architect of this new system that used gravity to gently handle the grapes and the wine. It was a revolutionary technique at the time, eagerly taken up by the most forward-thinking châteaux.

The wooden pails full of grapes were brought to the vat house from the vineyards on a horse-drawn cart. At the vineyard, the cart driver would have conscientiously trampled the grapes so that they took up less space, meaning they would arrive at the cellars already crushed.

The carriage drew up outside, below a large sliding door that opened onto the first floor. The buckets were hoisted up through this door by a crane, at first manually and later with the help of electricity. They were emptied one after the other into a fairly large *conquet* – a low, wooden receptacle, four metres square. Mounted on wheels, it moved along the entire length of the building along rails. One or more destemming tables were installed on it. The grapes were then crushed once more before being shovelled into the vats – for many decades the only way the crushing could take place was by foot.

Once the grapes had been crushed, the *conquet* was moved towards whichever tank was being filled. When in position, thin wooden wedges were slid under the wheels to give the whole vessel a slight tilt. The juice then flowed out through the hole in the side of the conquet while one or two workers in boots, wading through the grape must, unloaded the grapes into the vat with a wooden shovel.

The last bit of the system involved a rope-pulley-hook set and a wooden *baillot* which was used to scrape out the final grape skins that remained in the vat after fermentation and draining.

The whole operation required at least six workers, one of whom was a specialist who would climb down into the vat. This was an honour reserved for only the most experienced and courageous of men. The work was hard and dangerous because of the accumulated carbon dioxide; it was also very hot in the tanks, as there was no side door to allow a draught. The last man to perform

Above: *Xavier Tibur, our master winemaker, who would always tackle the most dangerous cellar tasks himself.*

Below: *The upper level of the vat room, designed and fitted out in 1866 by Pierre Skawinski. Modern vat rooms have taken up its revolutionary innovations: the open floor allows staff to work safely and cleanly. Skawinski ensured that grapes and wine were handled gently by taking advantage of gravity.*

the task was Xavier Tibur, an unrivalled wine grower who spent his entire career at Château Lynch-Bages.

Xavier would descend into the vat carrying two empty buckets of about 50 litres each. He would fill one with a shovel, while the previously filled one was hauled up by a rope that ran around a pulley suspended from a beam in the roof structure. Outside the tank, it took two workers to pull on the rope with all their might to bring up the full tub as it was so heavy by this point. They would catch it on the fly and empty it into a mobile cart, also mounted on rails. Nothing stopped, even for a moment. The fast pace must have been exhausting. A third worker supervised the manoeuvres and packed the load into the cart with his feet. The full carts were then conveyed to the hydraulic pressing station by means of a turntable, after which the press wine was collected on the ground floor.

This is when what we used to call an 'airship' came into play. This was a large, horizontal, steel cylinder with metal teeth inside suspended from the wooden beams. The compact blocks of skins from the first pressing were put into this to 'crumble' or break them up ready for a second pressing to get as much juice out as possible.

Destemming, pressing and crumbling were originally manual operations. Around 1920, a crushing and destemming machine was installed in the conquet itself. When the whole apparatus was in operation, the noise, the creaking, the movement made it seem like the system was inspired by Jules Verne.

WHEN I TOOK OVER the management of the estate, my grandfather had been out of action for a year. He was losing strength and two years earlier had given up paying wages in cash. My father had opened bank accounts for those employees who did not have one (which was almost all of them), and we began to pay salaries by bank transfer.

We had kept official records since 1971. Before that we were governed by the agricultural tax system, which did not require accounting records. The flat-rate tax on agricultural companies was based on a classification of the value of the land that was established by the Pétain government in 1942.

Under this system, investments – if any – were not able to be off-set, which kept things simple but meant that most estates had remained frozen for decades. Now, things were changing, and we were required to operate under what was known as the 'real' tax regime.

Wine was still not subject to VAT but to a flat-rate tax per bottle sold, a system that would only disappear a few years later.

Our staff came from many different places. For decades, the Médoc has been a land of immigration. This was true for my family, who came from Ariège and Creuse at the end of the 19th century. In the 1920s, many Italians, driven by tough living conditions and their rejection of the Fascist regime, arrived, mainly from Piedmont. They were often found in the building trade, where they worked as labourers, bricklayers or painters. A few years later, on the eve of World War II, the Civil War caused many Spanish peasants to flee, and many found agricultural work in France. They were followed by the French Basques who settled in large numbers throughout the region. Finally, at the end of the 1960s, the Portuguese wave from the Douro Valley and Trás-os-Montes arrived, leaving behind the misery and the dictatorship of Salazar.

Many Portuguese arrived without papers, crossing the highly permeable Pyrenees mountains on foot, secretly. They made the '*o salto*' – the rabbit's leap, as the saying goes. They found work quite easily, settled down and then brought the rest of the family. Around the same time, another wave came from Morocco. Formerly wine growers in North Africa, they had begun to settle in the Médoc after Tunisia's independence in 1956. The events in Morocco and then Algeria accelerated the movement. The agricultural worker population therefore embraced many different cultures, but integration generally went smoothly thanks to the state school system, which effectively became a melting pot for the children of the disparate immigrants.

Almost all of our staff were housed free of charge in dilapidated houses in and around the village of Bages. Most of the houses lacked the most basic comfort. Long periods of crisis and economic difficulties had meant almost no maintenance work had been carried out, and there was no sewage system. Even running water had only recently become available.

Until about 1965, only two wells supplied the village with drinking water. It was not advisable to drink the water from the other wells, which could only be used to water the vegetable gardens (or, at a pinch, for washing).

Agricultural pensions were miserable. When a wine grower or a cellar worker reached the retirement age of 65, we kept them on our books for some additional work that justified a small supplementary salary. However, few of them reached the age limit. In general, they started very young and worked hard, and living conditions were harsh. Alcoholism also continued to wreak havoc in the Médoc countryside.

In addition to their wages, workers received a monthly allowance of firewood and wine (28 litres per month for the men, half for the women). We bought the wood from local lumberjacks and the 'everyday' wine was supplied in barrels by a local merchant. Each worker received the allocation in his personal *barricot*. Distribution was handled by Father Perez, a former winemaker who watched over proceedings until he was well over 90 years old and ruled over a small cellar adjoining the stable.

To sum up, from a social point of view, everything needed to be reviewed and modernized. My father introduced monthly salaries in 1972. He decided to abandon the system of '*prix-fait*', that is to say the task-based remuneration in force in most Médoc estates, even the most prestigious ones. It was time to jump resolutely into the 20th century. Throughout the 1970s, to encourage our workers to buy or rent their own homes, we created a housing bonus. Wood and wine allowances were abolished and replaced by allowances of labelled bottles. Less wine, but better…

IN THE VINEYARD, the situation was not good. The size of the Lynch-Bages estate had been slightly increased by my grandfather, who replanted a few hectares that had been torn out after the phylloxera crisis. It grew from 35 hectares of vines in 1939, when he bought it, to about 48 hectares in 1972.

In the aftermath of the war, he focused on modernizing the vineyard. The 1935 *appellation contrôlée* laws defined the grape varieties that could be planted on noble terroirs. However, there was still a long way to go from the rule to the reality on the ground. Cabernet Sauvignon reigned supreme in Pauillac where it was the king grape variety, dominating Merlot, Cabernet Franc and Petit Verdot. But these authorized grape varieties had for a long time lived side by side with Alicante Bouschet and hybrids of all kinds, remnants of a still-fresh past, when they were useful for improving the thin and angular wines made from the noble grape varieties by adding well-coloured grapes with a high alcohol potential.

My decision to return to Pauillac prompted my father to buy two small, quality vineyards next to Lynch-Bages; they were the remains of an old estate, Domaine Averous, which was not classified in 1855 and had not survived the economic crises of the first half of the 20th century.

Lynch-Bages also owned about 20 hectares in the commune of Pauillac where a pine forest had replaced vines torn out after phylloxera. During my childhood, my grandfather and his friends from Pauillac used to reserve this vast area for rabbit hunting. It was, however, an excellent vineyard site, which we planted with Cabernet Sauvignon and Merlot from 1973.

The existing vineyard was in a bad state, with many gaps in the rows of vines. My grandfather, in the last years of his life, was less attentive and didn't go into the vineyard much. The yields were very low. The 1971 harvest produced 15 hectolitres per hectare, to the despair of my father. He began to replant, but even today this is never a quick or easy task.

We had fallen behind some of our neighbours, who had been replanting since the 1960s. There were some innovative and dynamic owners in the Médoc, notably Jean-Eugène Borie of Ducru-Beaucaillou in Saint-Julien-Beychevelle; Alain Ducellier in La Lagune; Lucien Lurton, who was extending his hold on the classified vineyard of Margaux; Jean-Louis Charmolue at Château Montrose in Saint-Estèphe, and Jean Cordier at Talbot and Gruaud-Larose in Saint-Julien.

At Les Ormes de Pez in Saint-Estèphe, the picture was the same as at Lynch-Bages… only worse. The work in the vineyard was overseen by a strange character, Gabriel Alvarez. Some 50 years before, his parents, Spanish workers who came to harvest the grapes, disappeared, leaving behind their newborn child. He was taken in and brought up by my grandfather's sister, Marie, who for a long time, with her daughter Amélie, ran the Ormes de Pez farm on behalf of Jean-Charles.

After Amélie's death, Gabriel stayed, living in a room and the kitchen of the old château, which had been uninhabited for 30 years. He has been married, but I always knew him to be alone. At Les Ormes de Pez, he was supposed to supervise the work in the vineyard, but it seemed that he did only as much as he liked and waited for retirement.

The wine was made under the supervision of Roger Mau in a battery of outdated concrete vats that André Gimenez had built for my grandfather in the 1950s to replace the old wooden ones. The concrete vats were poorly designed and inconvenient to use. You had to crawl through the building's roof structure to reach the upper trap door. The floor of the barrel cellar was still dirt. In order to do the 'bottling at the château', the administration authorized my grandfather to transfer the wine to Château Lynch-Bages, where he was a little better equipped.

The other properties of Pauillac were not much better off. There are 18 *Crus Classés* in 1855 in the appellation. Most of them changed ownership in the years before the war. Only four properties, Châteaux Lafite, Latour, Mouton

Rothschild and Pontet-Canet, had remained in the hands of the same families since the 19th century… For two of them, it wouldn't be for much longer…

Château Latour, tested by the crisis, was split between the heirs of the de Ségur family (descendents of Nicolas-Alexandre, Marquis de Ségur, owner of Lafite, Latour and Mouton Rothschild in the 18th century, known as the 'Prince of Vines'). The last of the family was swept away in 1962. The buyer was the Pearson Group, British owner of the *Financial Times*, among other properties, in association with the Harveys wine house in Bristol. The purchasers installed two locals at the helm: Henri Martin, mayor of Saint-Julien-Beychevelle, and Jean-Paul Gardère, a wine broker from Pauillac, with the mission to modernize the estate.

Martin was one of the great figures of the Médoc, born into a family of wine growers and coopers. He had a strong personality, with great energy, and was a good communicator and an excellent manager. By dint of hard work and tenacity, and with the good advice of my grandfather, as Martin himself told me, he gradually acquired plots of vines in his commune, thus creating the Château Gloria vineyard from scratch. He built his winery and vat house in the heart of the hamlet of Beychevelle, and it wasn't long before Gloria became a highly sought-after name.

Jean-Paul Gardère also came from a modest background. He was born in Margaux into a family of resin workers who tapped the pine trees of the Landes region in southwest France. After returning from Germany where he spent five years in a prison camp, he started a career as a wine broker. He entered the profession by the back door, and through hard work, he competed with the big Bordeaux brokerage firms.

Following the example given by Jean Delmas at Château Haut-Brion a few years earlier, Henri Martin and Jean-Paul Gardère enlisted the help of professors from the Bordeaux Institute of Oenology. As early as 1963, the new vat room at Latour was equipped with stainless-steel tanks, the first in the Médoc. 'It's like a dairy' mocked numerous critics, but the quality of the wines produced in the new installations – starting with the remarkable 1964 vintage – silenced them quickly.

At Lafite, the management of the estate was tightly controlled by its Paris offices, although the director, André Portet, did what he could. When I asked him about the pitiful state of his vines in the hamlet of Milon, he replied: 'I'm tired of having to ask for permission from Paris to buy every single grape vine; I mainly maintain what can be seen from the terrace.'

Fortunately, Baron Eric de Rothschild took over as head of the estate, and with him, Yves Le Canu, who proved to be a sensitive and wise manager. With his new director, Gilbert Rokvam, he called on the technical advice of Emile Peynaud, professor of oenology at the Bordeaux University, from the 1975 harvest. The quality of Lafite's wines quickly returned to form.

In 1973, Mouton seemed to be the best placed of the three Premiers Crus of Pauillac. Since his arrival at the head of the estate in 1923, Baron Philippe de Rothschild had worked tirelessly, and his wine had just been crowned a First Growth by the new classification. It had the wind in its sails.

He was the first in the Médoc to understand the benefits of opening up to the public and to the world of art, and with his wife Pauline created a place where exceptional works, collected over the years by the Rothschild family, were displayed. Even today, the Mouton Museum remains unrivalled.

He also showed initiative and boldness in winemaking. He was the first to start bottling the entire harvest at the château, and entrusted the management of the estate and the commercial companies that revolved around it to a highly efficient triumvirate: Philippe Cottin for the commercial side, Lucien Sionneau for the technical side, and Raphaël Héras for the legal and financial side. The trio was solid and competent and the property was run in an exemplary manner.

Château Pontet-Canet did not change hands in the years before the war. But the Cruse family could not withstand the coming crisis, and they had to part with it in 1975.

9 La Place de Bordeaux

FOR BORDEAUX, THE FIRST YEARS of the 1970s were the 'beginning of the end' of a crisis that had lasted 80 years. We hit rock bottom in the 1930s. The families who owned vineyards in the 19th century had mostly disappeared, swept away by the tornado, like Félix de Vial who had to sell Lynch-Bages in 1939.

Driven by American demand, the selling prices of the 1970, 1971 and 1972 harvests rose to a crescendo. But the market had frozen since the spring of 1973, after a short and frenetic 'Primeur' campaign for the 1972 vintage.

In 1973, the methods of the Bordeaux wine trade hadn't changed much since its golden age in the mid-19th century. The heirs of the founders of the great négociant houses of Chartrons had taken over without changing their way of operating. Their focus for many decades was essentially the British Isles and the major ports of the North Sea and the Baltic. Under the impetus of a few enterprising personalities, most notably Alexis Lichine, the American market began to open up in the early 1970s.

In the first half of the 20th century, these traditional companies were forced to give up a slice of the cake. New operators, often from the Corrèze region of France, moved down the Dordogne to settle throughout the Bordeaux region, starting with Libourne, the natural gateway.

They opened up new trade routes by attacking the Belgian market and northern and western France, and brought in new blood. Some of them, such as Jean-Pierre Moueix, Fernand Ginestet, Eugène Borie and Lorrain Désiré Cordier, showed great talent.

I can hear the story of my own family in this one from Jean-Pierre Moueix: 'I became a négociant the day I had to sell my parents' wines. Like many Corrèziens, driven out of their home by an extremely tough life, they followed the Dordogne River to come to Libourne where they bought Château Fonroque. I saw them work themselves to the bone. During the financial crisis

A Bordeaux broker in the 1930s checks that a delivery of wine conforms to his needs.

of the 1930s, my father swallowed his pride to take out a bank loan. We began selling my uncles' and cousins' wines along with our own. Believe me, in those days, it wasn't an easy sell… Pétrus was far from the most expensive wine in the world. What made it successful, I think, was the experience and the professionalism of those who made it… and undoubtedly helped by the margin that I left to the retailers.'

In order to dominate and control the market, the most important merchants formed a hierarchical arrangement. Two groups emerged. The first included the most prestigious companies, with greater financial clout and more established distribution capacity. This 'Group A' formed around its leader Calvet – the 'Grande Maison' – the merchant aristocracy of La Place; it included Cruse & Fils Frères, A de Luze, Jean-Pierre Moueix, Ginestet, Eschenauer, Delor, Barton & Guestier. The group's relations with the brokers were based on a certain etiquette. The brokers met every week at Calvet, cours du Médoc, for the weekly tasting meeting where they presented their samples and made their offers.

In Group B were those who, although respectable, were considered to be of lesser lineage: Chantecaille, La Bergerie (Philippe de Rothschild's trading company), Mestrezat, Mähler-Besse, Schröder et Schÿler, Joanne… Access to the most sought-after wines was reserved first for members of Group A, who often benefited from more favourable conditions. The system encouraged brokers to form cartels. For example, the three major brokers of La Place: Lawton, Blanchy and Fouquier often agreed to split the famous two percent of business handled by one of them into three.

Alexis Lichine burst onto the scene in the early 1950s. He was a kind of UFO. Born in Moscow, he was educated in Paris, London and New York. His knowledge of languages and his multiculturalism earned him the position of aide-de-camp to General Eisenhower during the war. When peace returned, he began a career as a journalist, travelled around France and became a tireless propagandist for wine in the United States. Skilful and convincing, he launched himself into the trade, and soon became an important player on the Bordeaux scene. He created a prosperous trading house in Bordeaux and acquired two large vineyards in Margaux (Châteaux Lascombes and Le Prieuré, both classified in 1855). He was also very active in the *Commanderie du Bontemps*[1] whose work he immediately understood and supported.

After sharing a bottle of Mouton Rothschild 1870 with a few friends, Alexis told me how he had been subjected to the law of Group A when the 1961 vintage was released. At the beginning of May 1962, he had bought a lot of Château La Lagune 'while still on the vine'. A few days later, a spring frost destroyed a large part of the budding grapes. Once the harvest was done, it was clear that some of the estates – including La Lagune – had harvested less than they had sold. Alexis was summoned by Emmanuel Cruse, who told him that the members of Group A, of which he was not included, had allocated the harvest to themselves. So, he would have no wine! 'What do you think I did?' Alexis asked me… 'I bowed, of course, and threw my purchase slip into the wastepaper basket!'

In 1973, a few historic trading houses remained powerful, but many were no more than a façade. Bernard Ginestet, the young son of the family that owned Château Margaux, who saw himself as the renovator of the wine trade, was trying to shake up a rheumatic system. Four brokers dominated the market. The trio of Daniel Lawton, Georges Fouquier and Alain Blanchy were firmly established at the head of the pack. They had very different personalities, but complemented each other well. Daniel Lawton was straightforward and inspired confidence. Georges Fouquier was sharp, imaginative and clever. Alain Blanchy was friendly, and a good networker and tennis player.

---

[1] One of France's oldest wine institutions, the *Commanderie du Bontemps* is a collaboration of the most prestigious châteaux, estates, brokers and merchants of Bordeaux's Left Bank.

The fourth musketeer was the Balaresque office, recently taken over by André Balaresque's son-in-law, the young Alain Moses, who played the role of d'Artagnan. André Balaresque, who specialized in bottled sales, was not very interested in selling En Primeur, the preserve of the leading trio. Alain Moses was not from Bordeaux. As soon as he arrived in the Gironde, he extended his approach to the En Primeur market. He quickly played a significant role, thanks to his dynamism, his intelligence and his hard work. To the great displeasure of the triumvirate who considered him a bit of an intruder.

The rise in demand since 1970 led many merchants to try to set up multi-year supply contracts with the estates, where they committed to buying a large part or even all of the production over several years. In exchange, they received exclusive distribution rights. This was the case for Château Giscours and our neighbour Château de Pez, which were distributed exclusively by the British International Distillers and Vintners (IDV); for Cantenac-Brown, linked with the Bordeaux house of Luze; for Beychevelle, which had a direct agreement with Dreyfus-Ashby in New York; and for Cos d'Estournel linked with Ginestet, among others. My father, rightly holding on to his independence, did not make any commitment. In fact, he was so preoccupied by his job as mayor that he even missed the short but frenetic marketing of the 1972 harvest, which meant we still had the stock on our hands.

In the summer of 1973, however, we were not yet too worried. Before the September oil shock, the horizon seemed more or less clear and the system still seemed to be fulfilling its role in a more or less satisfactory way. However, the machinery had been working in fits and starts for the previous 20 years and hid a great fragility. The succession of very bad vintages in the 1960s (1963, 1965 and 1968 were disasters in terms of quality) had led to shortcuts being taken in the cellars. The final blow to the edifice was triggered by the oil crisis of September 1973. Many merchant houses, even the most established and prestigious, disappeared in the turmoil. But let's not get ahead of ourselves…

10 First Harvest

AS A CHILD, I HELPED with harvest and often accompanied my grandfather to the vat room or the vineyard. But in 1973, I knew nothing about oenology and was happy to simply observe. There was plenty to learn, because under the impetus of researchers at the University of Bordeaux, in particular Jean Ribéreau-Gayon and Emile Peynaud, scientific oenology was gradually spreading out into the châteaux.

Oenology taught, for example, how to understand the mechanism of malolactic fermentation. Wine growers often observed a slight effervescence in their barrels in May following the harvest, but they had no idea why this was happening. I heard them attribute it more than once to the harmony between wine and the vine, and specifically to their symbiosis in springtime, at the moment when the sap rises in the shoots.

We let it happen naturally, and more often than not all was fine. However, since the 1972 harvest, the price of wine had risen considerably, and with the oil crisis coming straight after, it was no longer okay to get by on a wing and a prayer.

The producer knew that the merchants, for those estates lucky enough to have concluded purchases of the 1972 vintage En Primeur, would be expecting delivery of technically finished wines. And that for future En Primeur sales, tasting samples would need to be of irreproachable quality. It was therefore essential that this damned malolactic process took place, and if possible, to be on the safe side, before the wine was put into barrels.

This was complicated by the fact that, at this point, almost all vats in the châteaux were dilapidated and most cellarmasters, even the most experienced, didn't understand the process.

This was definitely true for Gaston Mau, a small estate owner in Bages. He sold his entire 1972 harvest, and sold it very well indeed. But his buyer refused to take delivery, and refused to pay. The wine was still in barrel and, according to the technical analysis, it had not completed its malolactic fermentation. Gaston

Mau was upset: he gave me a sample to taste: 'What's wrong with my wine? Malo... what? My wine is very good!' He didn't understand what was happening.

At Lynch-Bages, his cousin Roger Mau was doing his best to bring out the 1973 vintage, but the secondary fermentation was proving stubborn. The lactic bacteria, instead of attacking the malic acid as it was supposed to, was focusing its efforts on the alcohol instead; the spectre of everything turning to vinegar grew, day after day... A nightmarish prospect.

In desperation, I called Emile Peynaud, who agreed to come to Bages. We visited the installations together and tasted through the vats. The visit ended with a long conversation in the small office of the cellarmaster. Thanks to his knowledge of practical winemaking and academic rigour, Peynaud gained the confidence of Roger Mau, who declared to me after his departure: 'This man knows what he's talking about.' It was close, but we followed the advice of the scientist and saved the crop. The danger passed.

I have vivid memories of my meetings with Emile Peynaud. In 1946, he joined the faculty of Bordeaux. The oenology department was then headed by Professor Jean Ribéreau-Gayon, a descendant of the illustrious Ulysse Gayon, inventor of Bordeaux mixture (*bouillie bordelaise*) in the 19th century. Despite his doctorate in oenology, Peynaud did not then have the title of 'professor', as some of his colleagues who were jealous of his fame were quick to point out. Jean Ribéreau-Gayon was brilliant but was discreet with his expertise. He was the boss, but did not explain himself as well to those in the field as the self-taught Peynaud, who started working in the cellars of the Maison Calvet at the age of 15 and kept his language simple, intelligible to all.

Peynaud had been in every situation and knew how to deal with difficult cases – and, above all else, he managed to be reassuring. For vinification, he applied a few simple principles. Like the Ten Commandments, they were always authoritative:

1. Grapes must reach a good phenolic maturity. This seems an obvious point, but it requires great care in the management of a vineyard and the choice of harvest date to get this right. It is easier said than done!
2. The fruit must arrive at the winery in good condition.
3. Cleanliness of the premises and the wine vessels is essential. The winemaker must have facilities that are practical and easy to clean.
4. The pumping over must extract the tannins with both suppleness and softness.

Roger Mau in the Lynch-Bages bottle cellar. For 30 years, he produced great wines with my grandfather, but at the beginning of the 1970s, he was overtaken by the technical revolution...

Emile Peynaud from the University of Bordeaux – specialist in Grands Crus and an outstanding taster and blending artist. He advised dozens of estates in France and abroad, and partnered us for 10 years.

5   The quality of the tannins – not the acidity – determines the wine's suitability for ageing.
6   The temperature must always be controlled throughout fermentation.
7   The maceration time should be carefully measured.
8   The maturing process must preserve the fruit of the wine, which must be enjoyable to drink in its early years.
9   If you work effortlessly, you work better – and for this you need the right equipment.
10 The purpose of wine is to be drunk with food. Wine is not made for entering in competitions; its most important quality is to be thirst-quenching.

Emile Peynaud was a great taster and an artist of blending, qualities that he was able to pass on to his successors: Michel Rolland, Jacques and Eric Boissenot, and others. To top it all off, he had a real talent for writing: his book, *Le Goût du vin* (*The Taste of Wine*), published in 1980, has not aged a day.

He began to make a name for himself in the 1950s, helping enterprising wine growers such as Jean Delmas at Haut-Brion and Jean-Eugène Borie at Ducru-Beaucaillou. He quickly became a key figure, advising several dozen estates in France and abroad. After his intervention at Lynch-Bages in October 1973, Emile Peynaud consulted for us for about 10 years. From the beginning of the 1980s until his final retirement, he devoted himself mainly to the development of Château Margaux, for which the new owner, André Mentzelopoulos, had ambitious plans.

This 1973 harvest was for me a sort of baptism of fire, given by Roger Mau, a man who I still miss. Alongside my grandfather Jean-Charles Cazes, Mr Roger produced great wines for many decades, but by the beginning of the 1970s, he found himself overwhelmed by technical developments that he just didn't understand.

At the end of 1973, reassured about the marketability of the vintage, I spent most of my time getting to understand my real new profession – insurance. I was a 'general agent', which meant I covered accidents, theft and fire, various catastrophes, hail, civil liability, and so on. At the same time, it had become clear that I lacked scientific knowledge about winemaking – and that things were advancing fast in this field. I could also tell that it wasn't just me, but our own equipment and technology had fallen behind too. As winter approached, and even though my work as an insurance agent was time-consuming, I signed up

Above: *The arrival of the harvest at the vat house, in around 1965.*

Below: *The Lynch-Bages harvest kitchen in the 1970s.*

for the weekly courses given by Emile Peynaud and his team at the Bordeaux Institute of Oenology.

It was obvious that we needed to modernize our facilities. Our vat house, built in 1866, had remained unchanged for over a century. It was, of course, of great historical and cultural interest, but it was no longer adapted to modern oenology. The 1974 harvest was approaching fast, and we decided to buy half a dozen epoxy-coated steel vats (cheaper than stainless steel), which were easy to clean and could be cooled (a little) by running water down the sides. We had been using them in an old barn and stable for a few years.

There were worries, also, on the commercial side. The market had not absorbed the high prices of the 1972 wines. The oil crisis and its impact on interest rates was beginning to take its toll on the merchants... and on the estates which had no cash reserves – which was definitely the case for us since we had not sold any 1972 Primeurs. The window of opportunity was narrow and it closed very quickly.

In our family life, on the other hand, all was well. We had the joy of welcoming Jean-Charles into our home, born in June 1974 at the maternity ward of the Pellegrin Hospital in Bordeaux. And we hoped for a good harvest in the autumn.

Things were off to a good start... It was hot and dry in July and August. But the bad weather arrived in September and settled over the region. Day after day, the Atlantic sent rain-laden clouds. The grapes refused to ripen and rot threatened. Even when it was time to harvest, bad weather kept interrupting the schedule, and the extra vat room wasn't ready. In short, the 1974 harvest was a difficult one.

The harvest lasted more than three weeks instead of the usual 12 days, and the problems with vinification, without being as acute as in 1973, were there again. Once again, Emile Peynaud guided us through the worst of the pitfalls but, despite all our efforts, we couldn't entirely transform the character of the year. We had no magic wand and the wine was thin and somewhat diluted. To top it all off, we had further difficulties when we began using our first automatic bottling unit, a prehistoric Ducourneau that proved never to be reliable.

It is a tradition in our family, at the birth of each child, to put aside a few bottles of the vintage. For Jean-Charles, born in June, I didn't want to break the rule. However, as the ageing potential of the 1974 seemed to be less than stellar, I took the liberty, a few years later, of labelling the bottles of a few cases of the excellent 1975 vintage '1974', writing the three letters JCC on the label in red ink, so as not to confuse them with others...

*My assessment of the 1974 harvest: a late year with poor maturity…
There were no Excel spreadsheets to help back then! With the red numbers,
I wanted to symbolize the weather of the day: from 1 (good conditions) to
5 (continuous pouring rain).*

11 The Collapse

LET'S GO BACK A FEW MONTHS. In the spring of 1974, the best we could say about the 1973 vintage En Primeur campaign was that it was lacklustre. Interest rates exploded, putting any buyers of the 1972 vintage in an uncomfortable position. Nothing was selling. In an attempt to shake up the market, Jacques Théo, then CEO of the Alexis Lichine trading company, which its founder had sold in 1966 to the English group Bass Charrington (to fund his move to Florida), took a bold initiative: he 'went shopping', as they say.

He set his buying prices at a spectacular 30 percent discount on the previous year's prices. Châteaux were happy to sell to him, and we watched to see if other merchants would follow his example. They didn't. Théo was practically alone in adding to his stocks, the weight of which would lead to the collapse of his company in the near future.

A stampede followed. Deals were made at increasingly low prices. It was at this time that the old practice of the 'cellarmaster's case' disappeared. The usual unit of sale until this point had been the 'Bordeaux barrel'. It had no physical existence; it was simply a unit of measurement equivalent to four 225-litre Bordeaux barrels (300 75-centilitre bottles). That meant, in theory, 1,200 bottles.

In practice, the sales slips for En Primeur purchases drawn up by the brokers specified: 'Delivery at the rate of 1,152.' The difference between the two numbers – four cases of 12 bottles – corresponded to the 'cellarmaster's case', a hangover from a time when the cellarmaster was paid by the job, at the rate of one case of 12 bottles per barrel.

In 1974, the merchants, who had paid a lot of money for their 1972 Primeur wines, demanded to be given all the production from the 1973 barrels, and the estates had no option but to give in. It meant that after 1974, the idea of keeping a little wine back to pay the cellarmaster disappeared – and in any case, by that point the cellarmaster was a salaried employee, and the wine had just been retained by the estate.

Similarly, the 'ancillary costs' disappeared. Until 1973, racking, fining and bottling were invoiced separately by the properties. From the 1974 vintage onwards, prices were given per bottle and invoices were written in terms of number of cases.

In the autumn of 1974, we began to worry. My father organized a lunch at his house to which he invited our three main brokers to discuss the situation: Daniel Lawton, Georges Fouquier and Alain Blanchy. It was my first real encounter with the Bordeaux wine trade. I was struck by the lack of initiative and the feeling of powerlessness that emerged from these prestigious representatives of the brokerage trade. I thought they were the driving force behind the marketing of our wines, but I began to see that they were only a passive transmission belt. And I understood that négociants had plenty of worries of their own that rated higher than keeping the heads of the properties in difficulty above water.

We were beginning to suffer. Our cash flow had been depleted by the acquisition of my uncles' company shares, by the renovation of the ageing vineyard, the 1972 vineyard purchases, the refurbishment of the insurance agency's premises and the meagre investments made in the spring of 1974 to improve our winemaking facilities. We were in debt to the Crédit Lyonnais and above all the Crédit Agricole and our current operations were being financed by warrants (short-term loans guaranteed by unsold stock).

I found a handwritten note from my father to his brother, dating from the end of 1974, which give the measure of our situation. 'Half of our 1972 harvest and more than half of that of 1973 could not be sold. Commerce no longer buys, except for the vintages for which it has compulsory purchase contracts, which it has since denounced. All merchants have large stocks at high prices and are currently hampered by credit restrictions and interest rates,' before explaining that it was imperative to sell wines, which seemed possible for the 1974 vintage, provided that very low prices were offered. He continued: 'The trial that is taking place in Bordeaux at the moment, which has a worldwide impact, is not helping us.'

My father was talking here about what is known as the 'Cruse Affair', named after its most famous protagonist. In fact, a good 20 merchants had been engaging in fraudulent behaviour by bottling wines under incorrect appellation labels.

The affair broke out like a thunderclap in the summer of 1973. Following denunciations, an investigation ordered by the Ministry of Finance targeted a certain number of companies which, taking advantage of a loophole in the administrative procedure for monitoring wine movements, marketed so-called 'everyday consumption' wines, most of which were bought in the Languedoc, under the Bordeaux appellation.

These companies stood to make a good profit, of course. Consequently, tax agents were sent to check the stocks in the wineries. At Cruse, the management were offended at not having been warned about the visit and kicked the investigators out. Obviously, this gesture did not calm things down – quite the contrary. The public prosecutor's office immediately opened a judicial investigation. Names appeared in the press and were thrown around, first and foremost that of the Cruse family, which had been a fixture on the Place de Bordeaux for over a century.

It turned into a considerable scandal and the image of Bordeaux wine took a terrible blow. The gossip reached London, New York and even Tokyo. In France, acres of newsprint were expended, with every new article keeping wine lovers, the wine trade and wine growers on their toes. Some used the opportunity to satisfy old grudges against the merchants, and everyone tried to defend themselves as best they could. Most of the merchants pleaded good faith, all of them saying they were deceived by a crooked broker called Pierre Bert.

What was certain was that heads had to roll. 'Fraud among wine appellations is commonplace. But not when the culprits are part of the oldest families of Bordeaux,' wrote Hervé Chabalier in *Le Nouvel Observateur* (a man who would go on to champion the Evin law, which controlled the advertising of alcohol). He continued: 'The Chartrons families, these great wine merchants who came from Great Britain, Germany or Holland in the 18th century, are called Barton, Lawton, Schÿler, Cruse, de Luze… They marry among themselves, frequent the "club" for bridge, the Villa Primrose for tennis, the Saint-Nicholas Church for worship, willingly retain, even today, an Anglo-Saxon accent, and mix as little as possible with the other Bordelais. In short, the clan…' His article summed up the general hostility. Moreover, the investigation took place during the months preceding the 1974 presidential election. The political confrontation between the mayor of Bordeaux, Jacques Chaban-Delmas, and his competitor, Valéry Giscard d'Estaing, added fuel to the fire.

The drama reached its peak with a tragedy. When the scandal broke, Hermann Cruse, who ran the family business with his two brothers Lionel and Yvan, suddenly left his office on the Quai des Chartrons at the stroke of noon, walked to the Pont d'Aquitaine and threw himself into the Garonne.

The trial took place in the autumn of 1974. *Le Nouvel Observateur*, again, published a photo of Lionel Cruse, with the caption: '*La main dans le sac!*' (the hand in the till). In court, Bordeaux wines and Bordeaux society were on trial. In the box, 20 or so defendants crowded together.

During the verbal jousting between lawyers and witnesses, there were endless debates on the relationship between the taste of wine and regulations. The main defendant was, of course, the broker Pierre Bert, the mastermind of the scheme. In his later book *In Vino Veritas* (1975), which had his name on the cover but which was written by the excellent writer Florence Mothe, he explained himself: the idea, the escalation, how it all began in a makeshift cellar in the village of Saint-Germain-des Grave, the arrests, the threats… 'As with Stavisky,[1] will death come to me in some mountain chalet?' he wrote… He described the situation not without humour: 'Of course, we may also be forgers. But didn't Han van Meegeren or Elmyr de Hory give as much pure joy as Vermeer de Delft or Modigliani?' Above all, he never missed an opportunity to point out that the fraud he devised had many followers.

For Bordeaux, it was an earthquake. The trial ended with a series of convictions. The Cruse brothers, in particular, were sentenced to a heavy fine. To pay off the fine, they sold one of the family's historic properties, Château Pontet-Canet in Pauillac, to their brother-in-law Guy Tesseron, a Cognac owner. But this was not enough. The trading house carried vast stocks, which were unsaleable at the current prices.

To study the conditions of sale, the management called upon Alain Moses, the young and enterprising broker who ran the company of Balaresque. He suggested slashing the posted prices by three as the only way to sell. After hesitating in the face of the magnitude of the sacrifice, Lionel and Yvan Cruse, left with no other options, finally agreed. Together, they put together what the Bordeaux milieu would call the 'Cruse list', on which everyone had to align themselves in the following weeks. In all the cellars of Bordeaux, the stocks of wine had suddenly lost 65 percent of their value.

This tidal wave triggered a series of bankruptcies and led to the resignation of the elected members of the *Conseil Interprofessionnel des Vins de Bordeaux* (CIVB) and its president, Henri Martin. They were held responsible

---

[1] Alexandre Stavisky (1886–1934) was a French financier and embezzler whose fraudulent dealings led to political scandal. He fled to the Alps to escape dishonour but died mysteriously in Chamonix with bullet wounds to the head.

for the downturn and widely pilloried. The end of 1974 and all of 1975 were marked by bankruptcy filings.

The historic Bordeaux trade was engulfed by the crisis. Among the resounding bankruptcies were those of Cruse, of course, but also of Delor, a powerful English firm, Calvet (the ex-Grande Maison), de Luze, and many others. Ginestet, led by Bernard, the family's flamboyant son, couldn't avoid the fallout, and the collapse of his business led to the sale of Château Margaux, which his father had agreed to put up as collateral, against the advice of the house's executives who had begged him not to do anything with it.

Bernard Ginestet, the *enfant terrible* of the wine trade, retired to a pretty house, the former Château Durfort, at the entrance to Margaux, where he lived with his family, his shell collection and his works of art. He was always friendly and relaxed, and took advantage of his forced retirement to write a tell-all book which appeared in 1977 under the title *La Bouillie Bordelaise*, in which he described – with great penmanship – the Bordeaux world. He hit the nail on the head… Globalization, speculation, productivism, the Rothschilds, the Cruse affair, it's all there… I highly recommend reading it.

FOR OUR FAMILY, the year 1975 began with a catastrophe. On February 7th, Thereza and I returned by train from Paris, where we had spent a few days. Claudine, my mother, was to pick us up at the Saint-Jean station in Bordeaux. Unfortunately, we delayed our departure at the last moment. We only arrived in the afternoon, at about 5pm, instead of noon as planned. Surprised not to see her on the platform, we left the station, to find my father coming towards us. He fell into our arms. Claudine had taken advantage of our delay to visit one of our employees in Vertheuil. She was killed at an unguarded level crossing on the Bordeaux-Le Verdon railway line.

A few days after the funeral, attended by an impressive crowd of Pauillac residents, I dragged my father to the local sports stadium. To take his mind off things, we played a game of tennis. It was absurd; neither he nor I were in the mood for it. I'll always remember it.

This tragedy marked a change of direction for me. When, at the beginning of the 1970s, I was talking to my father about my future in Pauillac, I could see myself working for the local municipality, as my father had done. He worked hard, needed a rest and had hoped to retire soon, at least as mayor of Pauillac. He had dreamed of finally taking a few holidays with his wife, getting away from the daily grind, seeing the country, travelling… We had talked about my possible candidacy in the municipal elections.

Given his popularity, I had a good chance, especially as my job as an insurance agent brought me into constant contact with my fellow citizens. I liked the thought of having a civic duty and being close to the local community. But faced with my father's boundless grief, I encouraged him to take solace by staying busy. The misfortune that struck our family put an end to my plans, and he remained as mayor.

Thanks to its oil port on the Gironde and the Shell oil refinery, Pauillac was a prosperous town. There were plenty of shops, active associations and a lively social life. But the local economy did not survive the closure of the refinery in 1992. The Shell company, which had excess production capacity, condemned its Pauillac site, located far from the industrial centres, leading to the forced departure or unemployment of several hundred employees.

At the same time, several large retailers were attacking small businesses with formidable efficiency. Shops closed one after the other; soon, there were no more butchers or greengrocers… only a baker resisted. The town lost nearly a thousand inhabitants. In the new housing lots that had been built in the 1960s, the Shell employees were replaced by an impoverished population. The newfound prosperity of the wine industry slowed this descent into hell, but the gains did not compensate for the losses and, as in many small provincial towns, the social fabric frayed.

12 Making it Through

IN 1975, OUR FINANCIAL SITUATION became increasingly tense. Our usual Bordeaux customers had given up. Disregarding all the usual principles of Bordeaux, I tried to find direct buyers in France and abroad.

In Paris, the sympathetic Laplace brothers, from Charenton-le-Pont, accepted a few cases of our Saint-Estèphe wine in the association of producers which they had created under the name 'Race et Fidelité'.

For Lynch-Bages, I hoped to repeat the feat of our friend Aymar Achille-Fould, owner of Château Beychevelle, popular deputy of the Médoc, then secretary of state for the national postal services. He had succeeded in signing a regular supply contract of 100 *tonneaux* per year with the Dreyfus-Ashby company in New York, and kindly put me in touch with his American contacts, who showed no interest in repeating the operation with us.

We received several Englishmen from merchants who hadn't bought for a while: Lay & Wheeler, Friarwood and a few others. They were all ready to buy direct, without going through the Bordeaux wine merchants, but were only interested in very small volumes. Bill Sokolin, a colourful New York importer, travelled all over the Médoc to wrap up smart purchases, but we didn't attract his attention either.

My approaches to Anthony Sargeant, who lived at Le Moulin, in the heart of the Margaux vineyards, and who acted in France on behalf of another leading New York importer, weren't successful. The only victory I had was with the London-based Berry Brothers & Rudd, which had opened an office in Bordeaux to bypass the négociants and buy directly from the estates. It had only one requirement: we must change our label and add a hand-cranked coffee grinder, the emblem of their company. Things weren't that desperate yet, and we said no.

I tried everything I could think of. La Providence's sales network was spread throughout the country, and the insurance company's general agents were in contact with thousands of potential customers. I promised my colleagues an additional source of income if they helped me sell wine to their customers – with mixed success. At least we sold a few bottles.

My uncle Gilbert Cazes, a retired banker, told me about a transaction to buy a sizeable stock of Armagnac that was being carried out by the 'special operations' department of Crédit Lyonnais, a section that offered original investment ideas to the bank's wealthy clients. Gilbert suggested introducing me to Michel Lévignac, who headed up the department.

I headed up to Boulevard des Italiens in Paris, where I met this warm and flamboyant man who exuded success and self-confidence. He had indeed had private clients of the bank buy lots of Armagnac belonging to the Damblatt house in Castelnau d'Auzan in the Gers, which was struggling. He invited me to meet the man responsible for structuring the investment products so that together we could study the feasibility of offering 'a great Bordeaux wine'. This is how I met Jacques Abeillé, with whom I spent many productive hours over several years.

My new contact was constructive. Very quickly, I managed to convince him. Wine prices were low, the time was right. Together, we put together a proposal for a batch of wines from various vintages of Lynch-Bages and Ormes de Pez. There were 1974s En Primeur, 1973s and 1970s. About 30,000 bottles in total, which we divided into lots of 100 or 200 bottles.

But Jacques Abeillé's support was not enough. I also needed to convince Elie Baronchelli, who managed the management advisers in charge of contacting the customers. Selling En Primeur to individuals who had not been able to taste the wine was an entirely new thing. Baronchelli demanded quality assurance for the 1974s that were still in vats or barrels. I called on Emile Peynaud, who kindly drew up a tasting certificate for the occasion. According to his judgement, if 1974 was not the vintage of the century, it was not far off! Thank you, Professor…

After several months of discussions, we were ready to go with our first offer to potential investors. They were spread all over France and even beyond. Some had accounts in Luxembourg, Monaco, Switzerland or the Gulf Emirates. The management of the central database of clients was entrusted to Jean-Paul Planchou, a representative for a large French trade union called the French Democratic Confederation of Labour (CFDT) and a militant in Michel Rocard's Unified Socialist Party who would be elected as a socialist deputy for Paris a few years later. Not the most obvious of men to head up a private client business for

An advertisement for the insurance firm of A and J-M Cazes (1973–2001). 'Never sell this company,' my father told me: 'With the firm, you will always be sure of being able to survive.'

an elite bank, but Planchou never let his political opinions get in the way of the need for discretion that was so essential for his professional activity.

The offer was very successful, and sold out in record time. I played a sort of amateur broker's role, without being paid – the satisfaction of selling some of our wine was more than enough.

A few weeks later, my contacts at Crédit Lyonnais told me that they wanted to do it again, but that given the demand, they wished to extend it to wines beyond those of the Cazes stable. I immediately contacted several friends from the region: Jean-Eugène Borie of Château Ducru-Beaucaillou, Michel Delon of Léoville Las Cases, Henri Martin of Gloria, Aymar Achille-Fould of Beychevelle, Jean-Louis Charmolue of Montrose, Bertrand Bouteiller of Pichon-Longueville, Bruno Prats of Cos d'Estournel… all of them were experiencing difficulties and happily agreed to participate. A fine bunch!

Later, on the proposal of the local branch of the Crédit Lyonnais, which had heard of the initiative, the group was joined by Rauzan-Ségla and La Tour Carnet, which I knew less about, but they too had wine to sell. We repeated the same thing several times over the next three years, always with success: in total, eleven offers were made, each for between 150,000 and 200,000 bottles

Making it Through 95

of Grands Crus. The last one took place in 1978. In the spring of 1979, the rise in prices observed when the 1978 vintage was put on the market made me nervous to do it again, because the rise in prices, even if it remained modest, made me fear that I would later have to deal with disappointed investors.

An implied part of wine investment is that resale will be possible – even though neither Jacques Abeillé nor Elie Baronchelli, and even less Michel Lévignac, had ever asked about this specifically. It was simply assumed that when the buyer wanted to realize his investment, he would be able to. Basically, they trusted me. For my part, for fear of seeing the project fail, I had been careful not to mention the question of resale and the legal and fiscal uncertainty that accompanies it. One day at a time…

Things became more complicated: the stocks were still kept at the original dozen properties, but now belonged to several hundred clients in France and abroad. In addition, in 1977, some clients began to put their lots up for sale, even though there was no official avenue for doing so. Of course, they could go to the auction houses, but wine auctions were still new entities at this point – and in any case they would not have been able to cope with the amount of wine.

Crédit Lyonnais was not a wine trading company and had no intention of becoming one. My contacts instead turned to me and said: 'All you have to do is create a trading company!'

First thing to do: locate the wines and identify their scattered owners. For this task, I acquired an IBM Model 32 computer, whose programming language I still had a rough grasp of. I wrote my lines of code between six and eight in the morning, before the insurance agency opened. Within a few weeks I had developed an inventory management and billing application, which thrilled me.

At the same time, I created a trading company of which I was the manager and sole employee, without salary, of course. I gave it a fancy name: '*Société Médocaine des Grands Crus*.' Jacques Abeillé advised me to use the term '*Compagnie*', which 'sounds more traditional! It reminds me of the *Compagnie des Indes*…' No sooner said than done: this is how the *Compagnie Médocaine des Grands Crus* (CMGC) was born.

I considered closing the company in the early 1980s, but instead developed it further with my friend Pierre Montagnac, formerly of the British group IDV, and then sold it to the AXA Group in 2001. Since then, the company has been managed by Georges Haushalter, who is also President of the Bordeaux Merchants' Association, which is now one of the biggest négociant companies on the market.

Now equipped with this indispensable tool, I waited with bated breath for the orders transmitted by Crédit Lyonnais. When a client decided to resell his lot of a few dozen or a few hundred bottles, I proposed it by telephone to a broker, generally the very reactive Alain Moses. As the price of wine rose slightly from 1977 onwards, he had no difficulty in finding a buyer on the market at a good price, and most sales proved profitable.

Overall, these private client operations at Crédit Lyonnais were not a magic wand, but they helped us to survive between 1975 and 1978, when we really hit rock bottom.

Our relations with the other traditional financial institution of the sector, the Crédit Agricole, had been steady for a long time, since the investments made by my father in 1971 and the acquisition of his brothers' shares were financed by this bank. But the economic downturn was brutal. At the end of 1975, when the collaboration with Crédit Lyonnais was still in its infancy, we were living more or less hand to mouth. Our cash flow had dried up. The traditional bankers were absent. At the end of December 1975, we would not be able to pay our salaries. To meet the most pressing needs, I dug into my savings, which essentially meant proceeds from the sale of the Paris flat I had acquired during a good period, when IBM was paying a reasonable salary and I was receiving commissions on sales. But that wasn't enough.

It was at this point that the general manager of the Crédit Agricole Regional Bank of Bordeaux summoned us to Bordeaux, to the headquarters on Boulevard President Wilson. My father and I turned up, a little embarrassed. After giving us a lesson in management that we could have done without, he informed us that the bank had refused our loan application. Crédit Agricole had decided to turn off the tap. Moreover, they demanded the immediate repayment of the 'short-term' loan that had been granted to us two years earlier. We had been promised that it would be renewed every year – but not in writing. Dumbfounded, we took our leave and found ourselves on the pavement in front of the bank, totally distraught.

We spent the next few days in the same state. We tried several other banks, with no luck. I headed up to Paris to try the CIC, the Société Générale, the BNP, the European Union Bank, whose president I had known well during my time at Schneider. I got a bad reception everywhere. 'When trading is sick, property dies,' said one banker in a detached tone as he led me back to the lift.

The government's decision to regulate credit was unyielding, and there was no solution in sight. It was then that I received a phone call from the director of the Pauillac branch of Crédit Lyonnais. He knew our situation, was unsure if he could help, but announced the forthcoming visit of his regional director, André Durousseau. 'Do you want to receive him?' I answered in the affirmative, without much hope. A few days later, my father and I met with the two bankers around the round table in my office. We explained our catastrophic situation. At the end of the presentation, André Durousseau asked a simple question: 'How much do you need?' I pinched myself to make sure I was awake… After so many rejections, these words sounded like sweet music. 'We will not let you down.' I'll never forget those words. Crédit Lyonnais released the amount we needed to get through the end of the year *in extremis*.

13 Tourism and Gastronomy

AT THIS POINT, only a few rare visitors made it up to Bages. A few Bordeaux brokers, sometimes a merchant from La Place, a stray foreigner or, occasionally, a British journalist. Never a simple touris… until one afternoon in the summer of 1975, when I was parking in the courtyard of Lynch-Bages. I saw somebody that I didn't know standing by the old manure pit. There was nothing Médocain about his appearance. Out of curiosity, I approached him and introduced myself. He answered me in English and introduced himself in turn. His name was Sherwood Deutsch, an American wine merchant from Rochester, New York, and he said he was interested in what we were doing.

In these lean times, I welcomed the traveller with open arms. I took him around our cellars and organized an impromptu tasting. He asked lots of questions and we formed a friendship that would last for decades.

This meeting was the first of many. Over the following months, the Médoc saw the arrival of increasing numbers of wine professionals from America, eager to get to know more about the places where these wines, which were beginning to gain a reputation in the United States, were produced.

The American merchants took things seriously, but several groups of non-professional travellers also arrived around this time, and I began to understand that these visits reflected a rising public interest in our property. I also realized that every visitor was a potential customer. The fact that they had made it this far showed their interest – it was up to us to then convert them. I pooled my resources with a few friends, in particular Jean-Eugène Borie from Ducru-Beaucaillou and Jean-Louis Charmolue from Montrose, and set about 'making friends'.

In our eyes, this simple principle was a key part of our job from that moment on. We were helped in our efforts by the open-mindedness of many owners, notably Philippe de Rothschild, who had a head start over most of us in terms of hospitality and put his resources and his team at our disposal.

After Sherwood Deutsch, they came from all over. Mainly Americans, often young, serious and attentive. My friends from the Médoc and I put on a big show. At the time, there were no hotels or restaurants worthy of the name in the area, so we hosted visitors in our homes and organized lunches or dinners at each others' châteaux. Meals at Ducru-Beaucaillou or Montrose, where Monique Borie and Anne-Marie Charmolue lived, were always exceptional moments. Thereza and I were unable to entertain at Lynch-Bages, where the main house had been empty since my grandmother's death in August 1975, and needed a full overhaul, but we often ate in the dining room of my father's house – he, at this point, lived alone on the quays of Pauillac, and was very welcoming. His dining room also offered a panoramic view of the Gironde, as well as his cellar, well stocked with Christmas gifts given to the mayor of Pauillac by the owners of the Grands Crus of the appellation.

Frank Johnson, from New York, would later describe his first visit in September 1975: 'While I was staying with the Cazes', Jean-Michel burst into my room one morning at 8 o'clock and said: "Frank, get up! Forget that you only had seven hours of sleep after drinking Armagnac last night with Thereza and me at the Saint-James. Jean-Eugène Borie is welcoming his new head of culture. He's organizing a breakfast and we're already late…!"

'"Do I have time for a shower?"

'"Make it quick. No breakfast. We won't need it."

'We quickly got ready and jumped into his car. Then I couldn't believe my eyes… At Château Ducru-Beaucaillou, all the Ducru staff were outside in the morning sun, with huge steaks being grilled on the vine shoots. Next, they land on our plate, surrounded by *pommes frites* and *cèpes* – the wild mushrooms from the forests of the Médoc – all accompanied by Ducru-Beaucaillou 1971. It was the first time I've had Bordeaux for breakfast! Maybe also the last…

'Jean-Eugène was known as the gentleman of the Médoc. […] A few days later, I had a modest lunch at his house, which started around noon and lasted until 5pm, with samples of Ducru dating back to the 1860s. Even Edmund Penning-Rowsell, the famous British claret specialist, told me he had never had such an experience…'

We strived to give our guests a very personal experience. And in doing so, we built strong relationships with both professionals and ordinary wine lovers.

Plenty of other people were following suit. In Bordeaux, in 1975, the CIVB had a new team, under the leadership of Jean-Paul Jauffret, a brand-new president. He was the head of an important trading house, the *Consortium*

A father and son portrait: André and Jean-Michel Cazes.

Vinicole de Bordeaux et de la Gironde (CVBG). Another key figure was André Gausset, active director of the *Comité Départemental du Tourisme*, an offshoot of the *Conseil Général de la Gironde*. Since 1973, Gausset has organized the *Rencontres Gourmandes de Bordeaux*.

Both of them used the services of an ebullient Parisian communication officer, Jean-Pierre Tuil, who had contacts with journalists from the national food and wine press. Every year, the *Rencontres Gourmandes* brought together a number of famous chefs in Bordeaux for three days – names such as Paul Bocuse, Pierre Troisgros, Alain Chapel, Michel Guérard, Jacques Maximin and Alain Dutournier. Celebrity wine lovers also frequently turned up, such as Margaux Hemingway, who landed at our place in Pauillac for a memorable evening, or singers Mort Schumann and Michel Berger, and many others. These stars met a local band of young chefs – Jean-Pierre Xiradakis from La Tupina, Christian Clément, Jean Ramet from Le Chapon Fin, Francis Garcia… all forming a group around a leader, Jean-Marie Amat, who had a shop called Le Saint-James at the corner of Cours de l'Intendance and rue Sainte-Catherine. The halo effect of this spotlight helped them all.

In addition to a good exposure in the national press, Jean-Pierre Tuil succeeded in getting a one-page article in *Time* magazine entitled 'Le Réveil de Bordeaux' (Bordeaux Wakes Up). It was a landmark and fired up Tuil's imagination even further. His next plan was a gastronomic match at the summit, Bordeaux-Lyon.

Chef Paul Bocuse caused a scandal by summing up Bordeaux's cuisine with a can opener, which he showed off when he arrived in town. In Paris, Jean-Pierre Tuil organized Michel Guérard's birthday party at the Paradis Latin. It was a wild evening for which I gave the wines, and decanted them myself backstage at the cabaret. A few years later, he celebrated the '1,000 years of Brussels'. Rémi Krug from Champagne was in charge. In the Salle de la Madeleine, on loan from the Brussels City Council, 12 top Belgian chefs each prepared 80 covers. To accompany the champagne, I provided magnums of Lynch-Bages, which were extremely well received.

These were my first trips to promote my wine to an audience I didn't know. It was all new.

Another feat of Jean-Pierre Tuil came in the middle of a wine crisis. He disguised himself as the personal secretary of a certain Mohamed Zaker, a fictional emir from the Middle East – the role of whom was played by the Franco-Lebanese journalist André Bercoff – who had come to study the investment opportunities in the Bordeaux economy. Both of them settled in the Pullman hotel in Mériadeck. Jean-Pierre Tuil made the contacts and organized the meetings. André Bercoff, who spoke Arabic and expressed himself in French with a thick accent, made a rather credible emir. For several days, the duettists received all the region's bankrupt traders, wine growers in difficulty, inventors eager to place their finds… I remember a special bidet for ritual ablutions that its designer wanted to place in the hotels of Mecca.

The masquerade concluded with a press conference at the Chamber of Commerce, where the behaviour of the pseudo-Arab investors kept the audience intrigued, then, a lunch at Jean-Marie Amat's Saint-James, where the impostors finally aroused suspicion among the guests with their bizarre remarks. The false emir and his sidekick owed their salvation to a hasty retreat.

As you might imagine, this incredible hoax somewhat dented the popularity of Jean-Pierre Tuil among the good society of Bordeaux, but it didn't stop him. Shortly afterwards, he brought together a group of wine growers: Henriette Fournier, Alexandre de Lur Saluces, Thierry Manoncourt, Alexis Lichine, Anthony Barton, myself and some others. The photographer chosen to immortalize the gathering was Francis Giacometti, who was then the lens behind the Pirelli calendar.

The photo was taken in the salons of the Chamber of Commerce. A few weeks later, the result was published as a double-page spread in issue 147 of *Lui* magazine, framed by images of lightly clad ladies. 'Where has the nobility of wine gone?' grumbled the self-righteous Tout-Bordeaux. It was a first for me, in any case, and an insight into the power of the media.

I increasingly realized the importance of communication and relations with the press. Thanks to Jean-Pierre Tuil, I meet the cream of gastronomic journalism, led by Robert Courtine (the influential La Reynière, of *Le Monde*), Philippe Couderc, Henri Viard, Michel Piot, Nicolas de Rabaudy, Claude Jolly dit Lebey (*L'Express*), Noël Mamère (TV news presenter), Chantal Lecouty, Jean-Pierre Le Brun, Michel Dovaz… Henri Gault and Christian Millau stood out from the rest and began their crusade for the 'Nouvelle Cuisine'.

I became friends with Pierre-Marie Doutrelant, who brought a new sensitivity and a modern vision to wine, and did not hesitate to break taboos. A journalist with a sparkling talent, he was independent and incorruptible. In his book *Les Bons Vins et les Autres* (Seuil, 1978), he gave his readers a ferocious assessment of the situation, but sadly he all too soon died of a heart attack while out jogging.

The movers and shakers in Bordeaux wine, photographed in 1976 for the magazine Lui.
Front row (l–r): Helyette Dubois-Chalon (Château Ausone), Alexandre de Lur Saluces (Château d'Yquem), Thierry Manoncourt (Château Figeac), Joseph Fourcaud-Lussac (Château Cheval Blanc), Madame Fournier (Château Canon), Alexis Lichine (Château Prieuré and Château Lascombes).
Back row (l–r): Antoine Merlaut (Château Grand-Puy Ducasse), Anothony Barton (Château Léoville-Barton), Léo de Malert Roquefort (Château La Gaffelière), Elysée Forner (Château Camensac), Pierre Tari (Château Giscours), Antony Perrin (Château Carbonnieux), Bruno Prats (Cos d'Estournel), Jean-Michel Cazes (Château Lynch-Bages), Claude Ricard (Domaine de Chevalier).

Through my Médoc friends, I also met the great British wine writers, who were at the top of the wine world at the time. In the front row, Edmund Penning-Rowsell, world-famous author of an authoritative history of Bordeaux wine, who had the reputation – I don't know why – of being a communist. People weren't quite sure what to make of him. He lived with a notebook in his hand, in which he wrote his comments on the wines that were offered up for his wisdom. He was a font of scientific knowledge and liked to display it all rather pompously.

I met Hugh Johnson, author of *The World Atlas of Wine*, a huge international success that has since reached its eighth edition... I also met Harry Waugh, a great propagandist; Nicholas Faith of the *Financial Times*; the sharp-witted beginner Jancis Robinson; and, above all, Michael Broadbent, the omniscient director of the wine department at the London auction house

Christie's, an expert who was respected throughout the world, and the author of a collection of thousands of tasting notes published in a 'bible' to enlighten wine lovers. These, to name but a few…

In the United States, Alexis Lichine broke new ground with Frank Schoonmaker, also a journalist and wine dealer. Others took up the message in the 1970s. The most influential were Robert Finigan, editor of a newsletter to wine lovers, and *Los Angeles Times* critic Nathan Chroman. The most challenging was Frank Prial, *The New York Times* wine columnist whose prose carried a lot of weight. Frank was the Paris bureau chief for his paper and knew France well. He didn't just write tasting notes, but clearly outlined the evolution of taste, describing the style of the wines and explaining the winemaking techniques.

He discovered the Médoc while reporting on Bordeaux for the *NYT Magazine*, and became friends with Henri Martin. Seduced by the personality of the mayor of Saint-Julien-Beychevelle, he put Château Gloria on the map, and thanks to him it became a huge success in the United States.

In addition to these representatives of the Anglo-Saxon press, there were cohorts of Belgians, Flemish as well as Walloons, Dutch, Danes, Germans and Swiss… A tidal wave of journalists sweeping through Bordeaux and carrying the reputation of our wines far and wide.

At Château Latour, the British beachhead in the Médoc, Michael Broadbent was a regular, as was Harry Waugh, buyer for Harvey's, who sat on the company's board. In 1974, the visit of Prince Philip caused a stir. The whole of the Médoc came to Pauillac to welcome him to Latour.

I was lucky enough to greet him and to admire the best polished pair of shoes I have ever seen. The royal family was at home in the region: a little later Her Majesty Queen Elizabeth The Queen Mother came to the town hall of Pauillac and spent a few days of relaxation at Mouton, the home of her friend Philippe de Rothschild. Prince Andrew and his then wife, Sarah Ferguson, stayed at Beychevelle on a separate occasion, while Prince Edward stayed at Château Marbuzet.

At Château Latour, I got to know René Pijassou – a regular visitor with his own napkin ring. This academic was as friendly and good-natured as he was competent and hard-working. Following the example of the geographer Henri Enjalbert who, through his research a decade earlier, had shed light on the history of the Bordeaux vineyards, René Pijassou's doctoral thesis was devoted to the Médoc. It focused on the birth of the Grands Crus at the end of the 18th century and their role in what he called the 'birth of quality' and the advent of 'the new French claret'.

His research relied on documents kept by the Médoc châteaux, particularly the Latour archives which proved to be an exceptional treasure trove, a collection that is probably unique in the French wine industry. René Pijassou devoted 14 years of his life to this monumental work. In 1980, thanks to the support of the *Commanderie du Bontemps de Médoc et des Graves*, the 'Pijassou thesis' was published by Tallandier under the title *Un Grand Vignoble de Qualité, le Médoc*. Two volumes, 1,500 pages in total, based on a documentation whose description, given in the appendix of the book, makes one dizzy and allows one to measure the dimension of the work, which will remain a monument forever.

14 Loudenne, a British Enclave

AS SOON AS WE ARRIVED in the Médoc, thanks to Jean-Eugène and Monique Borie and a few friends such as Pierre Tari (from Château Giscours) and Robert Dousson (from Château de Pez), Thereza and I were welcomed into a group that almost invariably gathered at Château Loudenne, near Saint-Yzans, in the northern part of the Médoc.

Château Loudenne, then the Bordeaux headquarters of the highly important International Distillers and Vintners (IDV), successor to Gilbeys Ltd (a very traditional house in Oxford Street, London), was a haven of peace. For a century, it was a British bridgehead in the Médoc. On a table in the library, the 'visitor's diary' detailed the stay of Gilbeys' English clients who, from here, went to visit the surrounding Grands Crus by horse-drawn carriage, then by car.

Château Loudenne was run in the 1970s by Martin Bamford. Small, pudgy, with big glasses, Martin was single, refused to drive and only ventured out with a chauffeur. He had a large cat that he adored and called 'Cat'. He had inherited a genuine Estonian noble title from his father – Baron von Sederholm – but never boasted about it. He was an extremely civilized character, who brought infinite taste to everything he did.

Master of Wine and marketing expert, he joined Gilbeys, and therefore IDV, after having worked at Harveys of Bristol, and having earned his stripes by happily integrating Piat Beaujolais into the catalogue of this former English wine merchant, which was no mean feat.

Appointed director of Château Loudenne and responsible for supplying Gilbeys with Bordeaux wines, Martin made the estate he was in charge of into a special place – a 100 percent British land set on the Médoc shore of the estuary, with a view of the open sea. A cosmopolitan place where the most unexpected encounters were possible.

In the early 1970s, Martin set up exclusive distribution contracts for IDV with a few large châteaux. But when the bubble burst in 1974, the owners, pressured by their bankers, demanded that the agreements be adhered to: a commercial nightmare, and one that IDV then had difficulty honouring.

The signed contracts had to be terminated, and Martin found himself in the firing line. The years 1976–80 were undoubtedly a period of extreme professional trauma for him, and it seems likely they may have contributed to his premature death.

Martin Bamford came to an abrupt end. After a dinner party with some friends, he went up to his room, put on his pyjamas and went to bed… and died suddenly of a heart attack. He was 42 years old. It was a Friday in September, the day before the *Ban des Vendanges* festival, which we celebrated – without him, unfortunately – at Château Giscours where the Commanderie du Bontemps, a few days before the magnificent 1982 harvest, welcomed Henri Gault and Christian Millau, then at the height of their glory as food writers.

Martin was the soul of Loudenne and the original and refined symbol of a wine civilization rooted in the links forged over centuries between Bordeaux and the British Isles by generations of winemakers and merchants. He is now buried in the cemetery of Saint-Yzans. He was one of a kind.

At Loudenne, we of course met a few Bordelais, and first of all the owners of the *crus* with which IDV had concluded exclusive distribution contracts in the good years: Nicolas and Marie-Antoinette Tari, owners of Château Giscours in Margaux, accompanied by their son Pierre (president since 1975 of the *Union des Grands Crus de Bordeaux*) and their daughter Nicole; the placid and competent Robert Dousson, from Saint-Estèphe, an inveterate gourmet, who was then managing Château de Pez on behalf of his aunt, the self-effacing but determined Mademoiselle Bernard; Pierre Lillet, distinguished head of the family that created the eponymous Bordeaux aperitif, a great dancer, and his ravishing daughter Pompon; or Christian and Marie-Laure Moueix who, coming from Libourne, did not hesitate to abandon their Château Pétrus, cross the river and travel more than a hundred kilometres for an evening.

We often met Michel Guillard, a Parisian dentist and talented photographer who was preparing a book on the Médoc with various authors, including Emile Peynaud and Hugh Johnson: *Médoc, Presqu'île du Vin*, was published in 1982. Magnificently illustrated, it was the first French coffee table book devoted to the region.

The English colony of Bordeaux was well represented: we met Peter Allan Sichel, an important wine merchant of La Place, who later took over from Pierre Tari as president of the *Union des Grands Crus de Bordeaux*, and his wife

Martin Bamford and 'Cat' on the terrace at Château Loudenne: Martin was the finest of hosts.

Diana, who was very involved in charity work; William Bolter, also a wine merchant, a scholar and a fine gourmet, a former collaborator of Alexis Lichine for his *Encyclopaedia of Wines*, and his wife Trudi, an American with an artistic, cultured temperament; the lively Sue Johnson-Hill and her husband Alan who, after a Hong Kong career in finance, bought the vineyard of Château Méaume, in the Hauts de Gironde.

Martin Bamford was helped in organizing these receptions by his assistant, the very British Pamela Prior. The 'hostess', Priscilla, was an athletic New Zealander with whom I played furious tennis in Pauillac. Michael Longhurst, IDV's sales director, and his French wife Catherine were often with us. John Davies, a small, round Welshman with a golden voice (that he didn't hesitate to demonstrate), would often join from his home at Château Lascombes, where he managed the estate on behalf of the London group Bass Charrington. He was usually accompanied by John Salvi, who also represented an English firm in Bordeaux and looked a bit like him, with an abundant beard. As they were about the same size, he, John and Martin mischievously gave themselves a nickname: 'The Three Little Pigs'!

Also regulars were Peter Vinding-Diers, originally from Denmark, but he and his British wife Susie fitted snugly into the Loudenne scene as they arrived from their vineyard in the Graves, Château Rahoul. There, Peter had built up a reputation as a white Bordeaux specialist. Economic difficulties in Bordeaux would later lead him to emigrate to Italy and then to Hungary, near Tokaj, where he put his skill and reputation to good use. I mustn't forget, either, the couple formed by Jacqueline and Thurloe Conolly: she French, he a son of Albion. Both architects and decorators, inseparable, they were entrusted by Martin to refurbish and furnish the château. They turned it into a special place that resembled a Sussex country estate. In the 1980s, Thurloe and his wife were involved in the redevelopment of Lynch-Bages.

A few more 'exotic' characters were also part of Martin Bamford's inner circle, notably New Yorkers Mo and Loretta Leibovitz. Mo was a small, wiry man, an excellent musician, and an art printer who ran a shop on Long Island called the Antique Press. He redesigned all the catalogue labels for IDV, and I later asked him to design the first label of our Michel Lynch range.

'Sandy' Irvine Robertson was another prominent figure. Originally from Edinburgh, he was the head of distribution for the J & B whisky company. A solid guest, Sandy was given a specific mission by Martin: when it was time for dinner, wearing his kilt and wool socks, he grabbed his bagpipes and provided a musical accompaniment to guide the guests to dinner.

Finally, there was the cohort of the British specialist press. The British columnists were all at home in Loudenne and I met Hugh Johnson, Nicholas Faith, Margaret Rand, Jancis Robinson, David Peppercorn – always accompanied by his wife Serena Sutcliffe, the ebullient head of Sotheby's wine department – and many others…

The kitchen and service, including the wine, were kindly taken care of by Josette and Sylvain, discreet employees who did everything. All the regulars held them in high esteem.

Thereza and I first discovered Chinese cuisine at Loudenne. The Brazilian musician Sérgio Mendes and his wife Gracinha, with whom we became good friends, introduced us to many international dishes. They told us about the talent of Wai Lin (William) Poon, who ran a famous London restaurant, Poon's of Covent Garden. I invited him to come and show his skills in Bordeaux, and Martin Bamford put Loudenne at his disposal. A dozen or so regulars were invited to a demonstration dinner. Jean-Marie Amat and Jean-Pierre Xiradakis, who at the time were carrying the torch for the renaissance of Bordeaux cuisine, were present. I welcomed Wai Lin Poon at Bordeaux airport. He arrived loaded with food… Fearing, with good reason, that he would not find the equipment he needed, he had brought his wok. In order to use it, a gas burner had to be cobbled together in the château's kitchen. We made a diversion to Bordeaux via the Capucins market to complete his supply. Two hours later, assisted by Josette and Sylvain, Wai Lin took to the stove to prepare what I believe to be the first authentic Chinese meal served in a Bordeaux château. On the menu:

Watercress soup with shrimp ravioli
Braised abalone with Chinese mushrooms on a bed of spinach
Pork sausages, duck sausages
Sliced chicken in a 'stir-fry' with chrysanthemum petals
Seared fillet of beef with salted black beans
Stuffed peppers with shrimp purée
Shrimp Cantonese style
Whole sea bass simmered Chinese style

And, by way of dessert…
Egg noodle stew with crab meat!

It was an unforgettable evening. For the wines, the red and white Loudenne were followed by a 1962 Ormes de Pez and a Canon of the same vintage. We finished with a Léoville-Las Cases 1959. Our solid group of friends were able to verify that the great wines of Bordeaux matched well with the cuisine of the Middle Kingdom. Towards midnight, we realized that we couldn't go home without paying tribute to the musicians who had made this experience possible… Gracinha was willing to sing, but only if accompanied by her husband and we had to find a piano for Sérgio… I suggested that we go to my father's house, in Pauillac, where we arrived in force in the middle of the night. Woken up with a start, André gave us a warm welcome…

Our move to the Médoc also enabled us to meet up with a friend from Paris. Indeed, Jean-Pierre Engrand, whom I had succeeded at IBM in 1968, had been appointed director of the agency for southwest France and had settled in Bordeaux. His taste for good wine and good food remained undimmed, and it didn't take him long to become a friend of young Bordeaux chefs, notably Jean-Marie Amat. As he had done in Paris, Jean-Pierre Engrand introduced us to his entourage, which soon became ours.

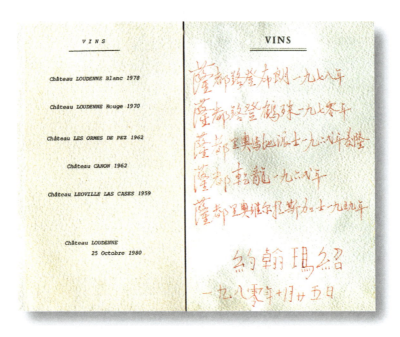

My first Chinese menu, prepared in Loudenne by Wai Lin Poon.

Another important memory was the visit of the prestigious Club des Cent, a gastronomic association of prominent businessmen and industrialists. The lunch was at Jean-Marie Amat's house. For the wines, he called on some friends, and on Emile Peynaud to coordinate the service. I gave Lynch-Bages 1962, which tasted magnificent.

I decided to decant the bottles in Pauillac, in the cellar where they were kept, and then to re-cork them before taking them to Bordeaux. When I timidly handed over my bottles at the restaurant door, Peynaud glared at me: 'You've ruined them!' I learned my lesson. To keep the fruit and freshness, so fragile in an old wine, I now always decant my bottles just before drinking them.

Throughout France, in the 1970s, good food became an important subject. This was the era of Nouvelle Cuisine, a school that advocated light sauces and pure flavours. Under the impetus of Henri Gault and Christian Millau, the great national chefs such as Paul Bocuse, Alain Chapel and Michel Guérard became media stars in their own right. At the same time, some wine growers, myself included, began advocating the idea of food and wine matching. Not just because it was the right moment to do so, but because we were discovering ourselves how much fun it could be.

15 Daniel LLose

IT TOOK ME ALMOST A YEAR AND A HALF of living in the Médoc to really become aware of the technical backwardness of our properties in Pauillac and Saint-Estèphe. The few courses I took at the Institute of Oenology were not going to save us. They simply allowed me to see how far behind we were.

A few estates in the Médoc had begun to hire professional oenologists by this point. Among the best was Georges Pauli, an agricultural engineer and graduate oenologist who had been hired by Jean Cordier to head up the technical department of his trading company and estates. Pauli, whose accent left no doubt as to his Catalan origins, was a hard worker, who travelled the Gironde by car, criss-crossing between Bordeaux, Saint-Emilion and the Médoc. He was also active in the Commanderie du Bontemps, where I had the opportunity to meet him – and quickly realized I needed somebody similar for Lynch-Bages and Ormes de Pez.

We had to act quickly, because Roger Mau, although in good health, was well past retirement age. Once again, my years in the Air Force helped. As a reserve officer, I was from time to time called up for a military 'period'. This was actually a simple meeting, where I had to spend a day at the 106 Air Base in Mérignac, in the suburbs of Bordeaux. In general, it consisted of a lunch, followed by a tour of the base, which allowed me to admire the war machines of the French military aviation.

In the spring of 1976, I put on my handsome airman's uniform (which I could still button up at the time) decorated with my reserve captain's stripes and presented myself at the guard post in Mérignac. After the tour of the place, I had lunch – as was the tradition – with Lieutenant Colonel Rolland, commander of the air base.

He was interested in wine, and as we talked, I explained to him our situation, telling him about our difficulties and my desire to recruit a technical manager. I described the ideal candidate: young, with a degree in agriculture and oenology. Among the young people doing their military service at the base, the officer suggested that there were two who might meet the definition and were available for release at short notice.

When we entered the clothing shop where the two soldiers were assigned, only one was present, sorting shirts that had just returned from cleaning. He stood up, greeted us and introduced himself: Daniel LLose – he pronounces it '*Liose*', Catalan style, and spells his name with two capital 'L's at the start (which has meant a lifetime of people spelling it incorrectly!). As we had agreed, the lieutenant colonel pretended he had a phone call to make and slipped out of the room.

Without saying who I was, I asked the young conscript about his background. Like Georges Pauli, he came from French Catalonia, from Argelès-sur-Mer to be precise, where his parents own a small vineyard. He had graduated from the *Ecole Nationale des Industries et Techniques Agricoles* (ENITA), an excellent engineering school in Bordeaux, and was around three months away from his release from the Air Force.

When I asked him about his future plans, he replied: 'My dream would be to take charge of a wine growing business. But – he added – there are few opportunities and I'll probably end up in selling products to control vine disease, like my friends...' At this point I introduced myself.

We met again soon afterwards when he was conducting a survey for ENITA on phytosanitary treatments in the Bordeaux region, for which he interviewed Roger Mau and our vineyard manager Gabriel Bérard. He later told me that this survey highlighted our technical backwardness – the information he collected from Lynch-Bages was not used in the survey results because of 'insufficient data'!

A few days after the survey he came up to Pauillac, and I was more or less convinced that he was the person we needed. Over the next few days, André Moga, a former member of the French rugby team, also recommended Daniel to me as someone who had shone in the local Bègles team as scrum-half. Added to this was the friendly pressure of my childhood friend Jim Martin, a butcher in Pauillac, who looked after the local rugby team and dreamed of being able to recruit a talented scrum-half.

Daniel LLose and I quickly reached an agreement. Daniel asked for an early release from the air force, two months before the regulation date, so he could join in with the harvest, and settled in Pauillac with his young wife in August 1976.

Contrary to 1975, when the weather was balanced and favourable, the summer of 1976 was marked by a severe drought. A disaster that led President Valéry Giscard d'Estaing – never short of ideas in the tax field – to invent the 'drought tax': a 10 percent increase on the income tax of all French people in support of the agricultural industry. The initiative was very unpopular and led to the resignation of Prime Minister Jacques Chirac, even though he had previously been Minister for Agriculture.

In the first days of September, the grapes were ripening well ahead of time, but they were very small. Suddenly, around September 10th, rain set in. The grapes began to swell, but too quickly, and burst, paving the way for widespread rot. It was time to harvest, and fast!

At Lynch-Bages, we did the best we could. For the fermentations, we had abandoned our old wooden tanks and were using the metal vats installed in the barn the previous year. We had added five more, bringing the total to 12, meaning that technically, we had no problem: even if we had to shorten the vatting time to ensure the vessels could cope with the entire harvest coming in so quickly, we had plenty of space.

The summer heat had concentrated the berries; the sugar level was high but the rot had affected the skin of the grapes and the quality of the tannins left something to be desired. Daniel and I decided to select the best vats and blend them together. This 'first wine' was to be bottled under the Lynch-Bages label. The wines that followed provided the basis for a second label.

This was the first time that we created a 'second wine'. This practice, unusual at the time, was intended to improve the quality of the first label and to produce a wine that would undoubtedly age less well, but would be enjoyable to drink more quickly while remaining representative of the style of the estate.

In this spirit, a few years earlier, Château Latour had created Les Forts de Latour, joining Château Margaux and its Pavillon Rouge. However, the decision had to be approved by my father. My father listened without much enthusiasm, mainly because the second wine could only be sold for a fraction of the price of the first label, and we were not rolling in money… However, he finally agreed.

The share for the second wine set aside in 1976 represented only a little more than 10 percent of the harvest. For the label, my idea was to use the name of the small Pauillac property I had bought a few years earlier: Château Haut-Bages Averous. This complied with the legislation, but I can see now that it was a little misleading, as the estate no longer existed under that name.

Cellarmaster and right-hand man: Daniel LLose in the harvest kitchen.

Later, to avoid confusion, we decided to drop the notion of 'château' for our second wine and renamed it Echo de Lynch-Bages.

From the 1976 harvest onwards, we made an increasingly rigorous selection every year. The second wine quickly rose to 20 then 25 percent of the harvest, and it can now be up to 40 percent, even more in some years. The policy has been adopted by almost all the Grands Crus of Bordeaux, who see it as a way of maximizing the quality of a harvest and producing a second wine that is more affordable, but true to the character of the terroir in which it was born.

AT LES ORMES DE PEZ, things were not going well. The fermentation, which had started smoothly, ran out of steam after a few days. In many vats, there was still a lot of sugar, which was slowing down the activity of the yeasts. Every evening, Daniel and I would observe the musts in the concrete tanks built by André Gimenez for my grandfather. This involved climbing a ladder and then slipping between the beams to access the inspection hatches. There was no lighting up there, so we took a torch to examine the inside of the tanks, watching bubbles burst on the surface and wondering if they were a good sign of the fermentation getting back underway.

Things were not entirely blocked, but a slow fermentation runs the risk of lactic bacteria turning the wine to vinegar. The local Pauillac oenology department wasn't much help – until the director of the laboratory said: 'We could try thiamine…' Neither Daniel nor I knew anything about this miracle product. We were told that it is a high dose of vitamin B1, used in humans to reinforce energy and improve skin and hair growth! A sort of yeast doping, in a way. But the substance has one major flaw: it was not entirely legal for use in wine and was therefore difficult to obtain. Nevertheless, we could be provided with a pinch of it…

The next day, an envelope arrived containing a few grams of the mysterious white powder. Daniel LLose and I went to Les Ormes de Pez at nightfall. We chose a vat where fermentation seemed to have stopped and took out 400 litres of must, moving it into a small mobile vat. We poured the contents of the envelope into it and stirred it with a wooden shovel. Before our horrified eyes, the liquid turned blue. A deep blue, quite beautiful, but far from the natural colour of grape juice. We looked at each other, unsure what to do next, before deciding to take the risk of sacrificing a tank. We pumped the contents back into the main vat, and held our breath. Victory! The samples taken a few minutes later had a beautiful ruby colour. The blue, presumably due to the high concentration of product in a small volume, had disappeared.

Fermentation started again and proceeded normally over the following days. We injected must from the restarted tank into the others, and finally finished our fermentation.

I will never forget those anxious evenings spent with Daniel. We realized our powerlessness and the extent of our ignorance.

At Les Ormes de Pez, in 1976, we had not been far from disaster, and we were determined to do something about it. At Lynch-Bages, where we had decisively abandoned wood for metal vats, we didn't experience any difficulties at all.

During the long evenings spent anxiously studying our vats in Saint-Estèphe, I came to appreciate Daniel's personality more and more. One of his challenges was to get along with Roger Mau, who had learned the trade on the job. It was the young graduate versus the old hand. Daniel was good: he knew how to get things done without looking like a know-it-all, and he had the old man in his pocket within a few weeks. Roger Mau faded from the cellars in 1977 without any clash or revolution, subsequently maintaining a dignified relationship with a successor who he clearly respected.

IN THE YEAR BEFORE HIS RETIREMENT, Roger Mau did us another great service. As in many traditional wineries, our cellarmaster had 'his' cat, which lived on the premises. A good way to get rid of rats and mice. Every day, including weekends of course, Mr Roger fed it a little milk from a plate under one of the wooden vats. One Saturday morning, as he came to look after his cat, he smelled smoke. When he climbed the steps to see where the smell was coming from, he discovered flames escaping from a vat that had caught fire. The evening before, a cellar worker had burned a wick of sulphur in the vat – a classic procedure designed to prevent the development of lactic bacteria. The ribbon, badly positioned, was not suspended over the vat as it should have been, but left in contact with the wall. The wood had smouldered during the night and fire broke out in the morning, shortly before the cellarmaster's visit. Within minutes, the tank and probably the whole building would have gone up in smoke.

After the departure of Roger Mau, Daniel LLose was firmly in place. He was an unfailingly reliable man who quickly became a good friend. As head of the technical team, he was a rigorous leader, attentive to everyone's needs.

Daniel LLose enjoying the process of blending in Mendoza, Argentina.

No effort was too much for him and he knew how to find solutions to the most complicated problems. Together, we launched a programme of work at Lynch-Bages and Ormes de Pez, which was to last for 25 years. He has been of great importance to me on a daily basis and has accompanied me in all my undertakings, whether on my own account or for the insurance company, AXA. Together, we have experienced some failures, but also many successes and satisfactions. On top of that, all my family love him.

    I owe him a lot.

16 The Conquest of the West

IN 1978, I RECEIVED a phone call shortly after the harvest. On the other end of the line was Philippe Cottin, general manager of what we in Pauillac call 'La Baronnie' – in other words all the companies that Philippe de Rothschild created around his Mouton estate since he took office in 1922.

For several years, the First Growths of the 1855 Classification, Lafite, Latour, Margaux and Haut-Brion, joined by Mouton in 1973, had made a habit of organizing a presentation of the new vintage in the United States, where the market was booming. It was a continent-wide promotional operation, punctuated by tastings, lunches and dinners in a dozen American cities, all supported by local distributors who advertised the events to their customers.

Each year, a different representative of the owner families would take part in the trip to spread the word. For 1979, the First Growths had a problem: the planned member was unable to attend and had to be replaced at short notice. No one was available. Philippe Cottin, who knew that Thereza and I spoke good English and had spent time in America, thought of us. The First Growths asked him to invite me to take over as interim manager. Of course, he said, we will add Lynch-Bages to the tasting programme… How could we resist?

For Thereza and me, this was our first major excursion in 10 years of marriage, and the first time I would return to the United States since 1967.

The coordinator of the trip was a man called Miklos Sandor Dora, whom everyone called Miki, based in Santa Barbara on the California coast. After a commercial career in the wine business, he was more or less retired and working for Philippe de Rothschild as a representative in the United States.

Miki Dora was an unusual character. Born in Budapest, he was 20 years old in the 1930s when he seduced a beautiful American woman in Vienna, tore her away from her partner and ran away with her to live in Argentina. He threw himself into all sorts of jobs, from restaurant owner to trader and shrimp farmer, and changed countries several times. In the United States, he worked

1979. At the request of those whom, in Pauillac, we call 'La Baronnie', Thereza and I went to the United States to represent the First Growths of the 1855 Classification. Of course, we were permitted to add Lynch-Bages to the tasting programme. Here we are in New York.

for the importer of Philippe de Rothschild's wines, and helped him launch the Mouton-Cadet brand.

Their considerable success earned him the esteem of the Baron and they became friends. In 1974, Miki introduced Robert Mondavi to Philippe de Rothschild. 'Bob' was the visionary winemaker of the Napa Valley; Philippe had the temperament of a conquistador… The two men liked each other and decided to produce a Californian Premier Cru together: it would be called Opus One. The news of this alliance was a bombshell in the traditional – and somewhat stuffy – world of Bordeaux Grands Crus.

Our American visit began on April 22nd 1979, a Sunday, with a dinner organized by Dennis Overstreet (proprietor of The Wine Merchant, Beverly Hills) at the restaurant Ma Maison, run by Patrick Terrail, whose uncle owned the Tour d'Argent in Paris. Wolfgang Puck, a young Austrian chef who highlighted local Californian products with impeccable culinary techniques, had just invented the 'California Nouvelle' along with Terrail, and the restaurant was the toast of LA businessmen and Hollywood stars. The dinner took place in the fog of our jet lag, which the Lafite 1928, served at the end of the meal, did nothing to dispel…

Our first dinner in Los Angeles at Eddy Kerkhofs and Michel Yhuelo's restaurant 'The Dôme' on Sunset Boulevard: Miklos Dora (centre) gives instructions to Thereza.

The next day, Miki invited the leading wine distributors in Los Angeles to The Dome on Sunset Boulevard. The restaurant was owned by two partners: Michel Yhuelo from Brittany and Eddy Kerkhofs from Belgium. Both had emigrated to America at a very young age via Canada and worked in a variety of jobs, from steward to barber. They made The Dome the place to be for Hollywood artists, especially musicians.

Soon after our arrival, I had lunch with Nathan Chroman, the dreaded *Los Angeles Times* columnist. Miki had warned me: at restaurants, he had the habit of ordering the wine himself – ensuring his choices were at the finer end of the list – and leaving the bill for his guest to pay.

Nathan Chroman was true to his reputation: as soon as he was seated, he grabbed the menu and ordered a bottle of Mouton Rothschild… He asked me about Bordeaux, Pauillac, my job… Miki, who mistook me for my father, announced everywhere that I was the mayor of Pauillac!

We kept meeting new people and forming friendships that turned out to be lifelong. Bipin Desai, a professor of quantum mechanics at the University of Los Angeles, originally from Mumbai, India, and a wine collector, invited us to dinner at Michael's, a fashionable restaurant in Santa Monica. The meal was accompanied by a dozen vintages of the famous Californian wine, Martha's Vineyard… I had only drunk American wine once in my life, during a visit to New Orleans some 20 years earlier, and I had no memory of it… but this time I was happy to discover that there were extremely good wines made in Napa Valley.

The year before, I had met the Brazilian musician Sérgio Mendes at Lynch-Bages. Sérgio's band, 'Brasil 66', was a worldwide success. He suggested I call him if I came to Los Angeles, so I asked him to join me and my wife at the Beverly Wilshire for the Society of Bacchus dinner.

His wife Gracinha and Thereza had a wonderful rapport… in Portuguese of course. The Mendes' invited us to their home in Encino, in the heart of the San Fernando Valley. Sérgio arrived in a sumptuous Rolls-Royce Corniche convertible. Their home was the old ranch that Clark Gable gave to his wife Carole Lombard before the war. It was a sort of long Mexican hacienda, absolutely charming, that stretched out under the branches of a colossal oak tree (*encino*, in Spanish) which was several hundred years old. At the bottom of the garden, a small wooden building hid a recording studio built by a carpenter who would one day make his way in the cinema: Harrison Ford!

In Encino, Sérgio and Gracinha introduced us to Japanese cuisine and we spoke about wines and vintages. We felt far, very far from Pauillac. For years, our paths would cross in Paris, Montreux, Singapore, Las Vegas, Amsterdam, Tel Aviv, San Francisco… In Bordeaux, we liked to meet up around in the restaurants of Amat and Xiradakis… and we would often go on expeditions together to the Gers, to my friend André Daguin, or to the home of Michel Guérard in Eugénie-les-Bains.

The highlight of our 1979 stay in Los Angeles was an invitation to a reception at City Hall, organized by the Bordeaux-Los Angeles Sister City Program, an association whose role is to promote the twinning of the two cities. In the presence of a hundred or so people invited for the occasion, we were received by the Mayor of Los Angeles, Tom Bradley, and his wife.

I had been warned that I would have to say a few words to the public. I discovered at the last moment that Miki Dora had once again failed in his preparations: the programme announced this time the presence of the Mayor of Bordeaux no less… As it was too late to correct the mistake, Miki simply concluded: 'You'll have to be the mayor tonight!' He assured me that most of the guests had no idea who Jacques Chaban-Delmas was – the real mayor – and would probably have difficulties placing Bordeaux on a map!

When it was my turn to go up to the podium, I kept things brief. I delivered my little speech on Bordeaux and its wines, expecting at any moment to be cut off by a listener, pointing an accusing finger at me and exclaiming: 'This is not the mayor of Bordeaux!' But it didn't happen.

After meeting Dennis Overstreet on our first outing, we spent a short time with Steve Wallace, the 'other' wine merchant, based at Wally's near Century City, before leaving town. A small man with glasses and a soft voice, Steve had something of Woody Allen about him. He showed us around his shop, which had an incredible array of products – it seemed as if the competition from all over the world had gathered here. I was happy to see that Bordeaux had a prominent place on the shelves, and that our wines were highly regarded by the high-end customers.

We left Los Angeles for San Francisco – still California, but different, less culturally distant from Europe. I was expected at the Vintners Club for a tasting, where I met about 40 enthusiasts, including a few wine growers from the Napa Valley. In the lower part of the city, near the port, I visited the Draper & Esquin shop. As at Wally's, the welcome couldn't have been warmer, but here the presentation of the wines was more down to earth. No more shelves or racks, instead, the wines were in their original boxes placed randomly on the floor.

During one memorable tasting, we compared three bottles of Lynch-Bages 1953 bottled in three different places: a château bottling, an English Wine Society bottling and an American bottling from Ridge Vineyards near Cupertino. The 1953 vintage was one of my grandfather's great successes, and with an unobstructed view of San Francisco Bay, we enjoyed the great pleasure of tasting these superb wines, made over 25 years ago thousands of miles away.

We couldn't leave California without a trip to the vineyards. Miki Dora took us to the Napa Valley where our first visit was to John and Janet Trefethen, who received us with their family. They managed a beautiful vineyard created in the centre of the valley a decade before. The land was not very hilly, but the vines were very well kept and the farm buildings impeccable. The Trefethens were an engaging couple. John was the founding president of the Napa Valley Grapegrowers Association, which brought together the region's leading winemakers. In 1979, they won the title of 'Best Chardonnay in the World' at a tasting competition in Paris, and were rightly proud of their success.

A little further north, following Highway 29, just before arriving in Oakville, we met Robert Mondavi. He was the same age as my father and looked a bit like him physically. Like him, too, he had a great sense of family. Also present were his wife Margrit and their two sons: Michael, who was very close to him at the time as the winery's director, and Tim, an oenologist. Their daughter Marcia was also involved in wine, but she lived in New York. In the early 2000s, after the winery was sold to the Constellation Group, she joined Tim to develop Continuum Vineyards, an adventure in which the brother and sister maintained the spirit of their family.

Bob Mondavi invited us to taste his legendary Cabernet Sauvignon Reserve. He then took us on a tour of the mythical winery that bore his name, created in the 1960s. It was a revelation to me. Everything was designed to showcase the wine in an intelligent way and to take advantage of the many tourists who visited Napa Valley.

Bob Mondavi had done in Napa what I was trying to do in the Médoc – even if we were not in exactly the same situation. In Pauillac, we didn't have a population centre of more than five million inhabitants within an hour's drive.

With Anthony Barton of Château Léoville-Barton (left) and Robert Mondavi (centre), the visionary American winemaker who contributed so much to the international reputation of the Napa Valley.

The Conquest of the West   125

Ab Simon, President of Seagram's Château & Estate Wine Co, a leading importer in the US, in his New York office.

Tourists do not crowd the roads of the Médoc as they do Highway 29. His attention to detail was impressive – while listening to Bob, I looked for a sign to the toilets, before finally deciding to ask our host. 'This is my house,' he replied. I receive visitors in my house. In your house, would you put a sign on the door of the toilet? It was clear what he meant: he wanted to treat visitors personally. It was also a way of making me understand the requirements of 'wine tourism', to use a word that had not yet been invented in 1979.

Robert Mondavi was a visionary and undoubtedly a pioneer of hospitality. In the 1980s, once our first renovation work was completed, we would try to open Lynch-Bages to visitors. My daughter Kinou did a three-month internship in the reception department in Napa at the Mondavi Winery. When she returned to Pauillac, she gave us the benefit of her experience in organizing our reception service.

The tour culminated in a dinner at the Four Seasons Hotel on Park Avenue in New York, hosted by Ab Simon, owner of Seagram's Château & Estate Wines Co, the leading importer in the United States. Around 100 wine lovers gathered in the restaurant, which was located on the ground floor of the Seagram building that belonged to two partners – originally from Hungary, Paul Kovi and Tom Margittai had turned this into the meeting place for New York society and a temple of local gastronomy.

Ab (Abdallah) was born in Baghdad, Iraq, where his father, a textile merchant, traded with England. He attended the American University of Beirut where he learned his perfect French. In 1944, he emigrated to the United States and discovered wine for the first time during his crossing on the liner *Queen Elizabeth*. He decided to make it his profession, and started at the bottom before working his way up to create the Château & Estate Wine Company for the Bronfman family (Seagram's), who dominated the spirits market.

His company became by far the largest importer of Bordeaux wine in the United States, and, for 25 years, Ab was a wonderful supporter of ours in the American market. He often invited me to attend meetings of Château & Estate's regional representatives in the idyllic setting of a grand hotel in Florida or California, where friendships were made and deals done.

On a human level, Ab Simon was cultured, perfectly educated, softly spoken and even-tempered. He knew the market perfectly and was a smart and trustworthy buyer, held in high regard by the Bordeaux producers. He explained the secret of his success: 'Great wine improves with age and becomes more valuable, while with time there is less and less of it… Which pushes its price up.' It sounds simple, but you needed sound judgement.

This first trip to the United States, in 1979, had been a great success, to the satisfaction of the First Growths, and was followed by two more – until the sponsors decided to change their policy and abandoned this type of collective promotion altogether.

Miki Dora, who had become a friend, wanted to continue the concept; so, I gathered together a few other owners in four different appellations: Bruno Prats (Château Cos d'Estournel, Saint-Estèphe), Michel Delon (Léoville-Las Cases, Saint-Julien-Beychevelle), Claude Ricard (Domaine de Chevalier, Pessac-Léognan) and Thierry Manoncourt (Figeac, Saint-Emilion). We represented the main terroirs of Bordeaux, and for more than 20 years, we travelled together to the United States every year, even if the makeup of the group underwent a few changes – Anthony Barton, from Léoville-Barton, replaced Michel Delon, who didn't like to travel. Olivier Bernard, whose family acquired Domaine de Chevalier in the 1980s, succeeded Claude Ricard. Miki himself retired, but the torch was taken up by Nancy Rugus, who I met while working in New York at Seagram's Châteaux & Estate.

Our 'Bordeaux Festival' – the name given to the operation by Miki Dora – consisted of visiting about 12 cities in a fortnight, in a punishing programme that left little time for tourism. We arrived by plane in the morning and immediately had lunch with the local wine distributors. The afternoon was devoted to shop visits and meetings with selected wine lovers. The dinner, attended by sometimes 50, sometimes 200 people, would feature a tasting of the most recent vintage and the serving of two 'older' wines from each member of the delegation. In total, 15 different wines.

Each of us made a short speech and presented his property and his production. Thierry Manoncourt didn't speak much English, so I acted as an interpreter for him: I sometimes had fun deviating in English from his original script. We criss-crossed the country from Seattle to Miami, from Boston to San Diego, from Houston to Saint Louis, from Las Vegas to Nashville… often with the support of the local chapters of the Commanderies de Bordeaux.

We also benefited from the support of the French expatriates we met on our way. In Texas, François Chandou, son of the president of the *Caves Coopératives de la Gironde,* was an energetic preacher of wine. In the seventies, he created La Cave Warehouse and Restaurant in Dallas. Jean-Louis Palladin from Gers, after abandoning his restaurant in Condom, La Table des Cordeliers, moved to Washington into the Watergate building. Feted by the media, he became the standard bearer of French cuisine in the United States. And there was Daniel Boulud, from Lyon, whose restaurant Daniel in New York was a runaway success in the 1990s.

We met many other talented chefs who were ardent defenders of good wine: Eric Ripert at Le Bernardin in New York; Luc Meyer at Left Bank in Vail, Colorado; Jean-Louis Dumonet at Trois Jean in New York; Laurent Manrique at Aqua, then Café de la Presse in San Francisco; Michel Richard at Citronnelle in Los Angeles and Washington… The list goes on.

Among the French ex-pats in America, Ariane Daguin was the star of the show. The daughter of my old friend André Daguin had left Auch, aged 20, to study in the United States. To earn some money, she worked as a saleswoman at the Trois Petits Cochons, a modest deli in New York, which she left after a few years to create the D'Artagnan company. Just like her father, she radiated an infectious energy, and was a worthy ambassador of the Gascon art of living; Ariane took on the mission of popularizing foie gras and duck breast in the 50 states of the Union, and to reinforce the message I sometimes accompanied her, as a private sommelier, on her trips to New York, Washington and as far as Puerto Rico.

My friends and I criss-crossed the United States and Canada for over 25 years. We were lucky: in the 1980s, the fluctuating dollar helped our business.

Above: *I travelled the world for 25 years with most of them: Michel Delon (Léoville-Las Cases), Bruno Prats (Cos d'Estournel), Claude Ricard and Olivier Bernard (Domaine de Chevalier), Thierry Manoncourt (Figeac); on my right Emile Peynaud, Jean-François Moueix and the chef Jean-Marie Amat at Hauterive.*

Below: *New York tasting sessions are sometimes massive...*

The Conquest of the West 129

With Ariane Daguin, from Auch in Gascony: a fine ambassadress for Gascon living, she popularized the cuisine of the region across the US.

More importantly, we were usually accompanied by our wives, who were always very popular with our audience. Thanks to Miki Dora and his knowledge of the market, and then to Nancy Rugus, we met the best distributors all over the country, strengthened the action of the Bordeaux trade and established contact with thousands of consumers. In a word, we put into practice a phrase that I like to use to describe my profession: 'Making wine is about making friends.'

When, in 2020, Miki celebrated his 107th birthday, to our great regret Thereza and I could not, because of Covid-19 travel restrictions, go and congratulate him in person, as we had often done in previous years. I uncorked a bottle of Opus One in his honour, a 2013 that is perhaps still a little young, but seductive. Everything was there. The power and sunshine of California, the finesse of the great Cabernet Sauvignon grape, and the winemaker's touch of magic…

17 The Oenological Revolution

BACK TO 1976. We had to urgently take care of Lynch-Bages. With the help of the engineer Paul-Jacques Larrégieu, Daniel LLose and I studied the most appropriate work to be done to meet the needs of the coming decades. We drew up a set of specifications corresponding to the vinification of the harvest of a vineyard of about 80 hectares, which seemed ambitious to us at the time, but time would one day prove that we were thinking too small. Taking as a starting point the metal vats installed in the old cowshed in 1975, we drew up a programme to extend the equipment and renovate the buildings.

In 1976, we added five vats, giving us 12 for the 1977 harvest. Each one could contain 209 hectolitres of wine. The harvest went off without a hitch, but the summer leading up to it had been mediocre and the ripening of the grapes difficult, giving a forgettable vintage with a slightly vegetal character.

In 1978, we acquired six additional stand-alone vats of 180 hectolitres, so slightly smaller. Working in the cellar became more comfortable and the harvest, which was late that year, was good quality. The rainy summer was saved by six weeks of good weather in September lasting until mid-October, and the resulting wine was balanced, delicious, well-structured without being hard: the equal of the 1975, but less tannic and more supple. At Haut-Brion, the day after the harvest, I had the opportunity to taste a preview. I was struck by the quality, the finesse and the 'modernity' of the wine.

IN THE COMMERCIAL LANDSCAPE, we finally saw a patch of blue sky. In the spring of 1979, the market was buzzing. It seemed that, for the first time since 1972, the En Primeur sales campaign could be successful.

Knowing what was at stake, tension rose as we waited for the wines to be released. Brokers scoured the vineyards, the owners watched each other and hesitated… Suddenly, at the beginning of spring, Henri Martin came out of the woodwork; offering his Château Gloria at 24 francs a bottle, an increase of 75 percent on the year before.

There was an outcry. The négociants, unanimous, accused him of 'sawing off the branch on which we are all sitting'. Jean-Yves Parde, boss of the English company Delor (which had not yet completely disappeared), wrote an open letter to the profession along the same lines. Jean-Paul Jauffret and Philippe Cottin, whose wisdom I always appreciated, shared this opinion. Both of them advised me to try to calm things down, to set an example by 'getting out' as quickly as possible at a 'reasonable' price. My father wasn't sure. If Martin was right, taking into account the hierarchy of the vintages, we should offer Lynch-Bages at around 32 francs. But we were frightened to make such a jump. For his part, Henri Martin, when I visited him, claimed he had sold out entirely – but was it just bravado? I had no way of checking.

We needed to sell and were not in a position to fail, so finally I listened to our friends' advice of moderation. My father agreed with me and we set the price at 28 francs. Our price was well received, brokers and merchants congratulated us and we were relieved to see the sales pouring in.

We waited for our wisdom to be imitated by our peers. Nothing happened for a fortnight… until one fine morning, when I learned of the release of Château X… at 32 francs! In the same breath, Y, Z and the other Second Growths or 'Super Seconds', as they called them, also announced… all at 32 francs. A little sheepishly, I went to tell my father the news, who replied placidly and indulgently: 'Well, we've lost money.'

The reality was that this successful campaign allowed us to begin our modernization programme. Cautiously, because the payment of the sales during En Primeur doesn't all come immediately – we received some at the end of 1979 and the balance in the middle of 1980. But as soon as we could, we created a modern harvest entrance and fitted out underground vats to allow pumping over during vinification and blending. The 1980 harvest, of average quality, was, for the first time, carried out in real technical comfort.

However, in 1981 we had a potentially serious incident. At the end of the harvest, with all our vats full, and a third almost finished with fermentation, we found that in a dozen vats, fermentation slowed down, then stopped completely. We had no idea why.

After a more or less normal start to the process, the yeasts seemed to give up the fight, leaving a sugar level in the must of around 10 to 12 grams per litre – the perfect breeding ground for bacteria, which would soon produce acetic

André, Sylvie and Jean-Michel Cazes in the bottle cellar at Lynch-Bages.

The Oenological Revolution

Daniel Llose and Guy Bergey (cellarmaster at Lynch-Bages from 1976 to 2004) study the blending options...

acid. The spectre of vinegar was looming, just like in 1973, but this time more serious and inexplicable. We tried the classic '*pied de cuve*' technique, which consisted of inoculating the recalcitrant vat with a little fermenting juice. It was a complete failure.

The prospect of losing two-thirds of the harvest kept me awake at night. Of course, we called on our mentor, Emile Peynaud, but he didn't have an explanation either, although he did reassure us that he had seen this before, and advised us to add sulphur to protect the must and let the cold of the winter take hold, and then wait: 'It will start up again in May.' It wasn't an encouraging prospect, but I agreed with him. What else could we do?

Daniel LLose, however, refused to give up. He noticed that fermentation had finished, or stopped, in all the vats, except for the one with the number 12. That one continued to work, but very slowly. After having proceeded, for safety, to a light sulphiting of all the vats, he observed and waited for the end of the fermentation of this vat 12, which happened about 10 days later.

He then withdrew a few hectolitres, with which he sowed other vats. Another failure. Finally, he decided to empty the vat entirely but reserved a little of the liquid at the bottom that was loaded with active yeast. He then refilled the tank with the contents of one of the tanks that had stopped fermenting, and waited. The '12' began to ferment again, slowly, and managed to transform all of its sugar into alcohol. Daniel started the operation again, still in the same vat 12, and repeated the process until all the must had been transformed into wine. In the end, two-thirds of the harvest went into the magic vat and we celebrated the end of fermentation on January 1st 1982, two months late. But what a relief that it was finished!

We regularly spoke with Emile Peynaud and the specialists at the Bordeaux Institute of Oenology about our 1981 adventure. We would later learn that the same phenomenon affected many properties. In 1981, and especially in 1982, the Pauillac laboratory was overwhelmed with samples until Christmas. No one has a precise explanation. It simply seemed that the yeasts, which are after all living beings, failed for some reason. In 1983, the Institute's team, led by Pascal Ribéreau-Gayon, was able to find the solution by demonstrating that the addition of 'yeast hulls' was enough to stimulate and activate alcoholic fermentation by counteracting certain inhibitors. It was the last time such an issue occurred.

Meanwhile, the 1982 harvest was looking good. The weather was fine and hot during the summer with just the right amount of rain, and the grapes ripened early. The harvest started ahead of schedule and took place under a radiant sun – with the exception of a heavy storm which did the vines some good.

We introduced a change, a revolution in fact. Abandoning the hand-drawn colour curves and the handwritten tables dear to the hearts of oenologists in the 1970s, and at the time indispensable for monitoring the vat room, we bought an Apple II, the first portable personal computer in the young history of computing. With this magical device, I installed the VisiCalc software, the ancestor of Excel tables.

Impressed by its possibilities, I entrusted its use to my father-in-law João-Maria Carregal Ferreira. A retired airline pilot, he had been flying for African airlines for years and was fascinated by new technologies. In 1981, he fled his native Mozambique, where civil war had broken out after the 1975 declaration of independence, and now spent his time between France and Portugal.

He threw himself into learning about the fledgling computer. In the early hours of the morning, as we approached harvest, he settled down at the keyboard of the Apple II. Thanks to VisiCalc, we now recorded all the information necessary for traceability in an organized manner, noting for each barrel of grapes arriving from the vineyard which plot it came from, its analytical characteristics, its destination vat, as well as all the data covering the progress of fermentation. We archived everything on disc drives that are now prehistoric, and set up the very beginning of computerized wine management.

There can't have been many of us in Bordeaux in 1982 to bring a computer into the cellar, and we may even have been the first. Of course, ever since the lightning progress of technology has seen new advances every year, and will continue to do so...

The year 1982 was also when, for the first time – and I don't think I've seen it since – the grape pickers took advantage of the weather to go to the beach as soon as their day's work was over. The Atlantic coast, at Hourtin, was only 35 minutes away.

After so much good weather, the harvest was abundant, and we were still a little short of space. While managing the vats, we sometimes needed to store extra wine in a tanker lorry lent to us by a cousin who worked as a transporter. It stayed parked in front of our vat house for a month. I have also heard – although I have no proof – that some wine growers used their swimming pools for extra storage.

The wines, once finished, seemed good, really good, almost too good. They had an unusual character. The alcohol level was quite high, the tannins were very supple and there was a lot of flavour. The style was clearly different from previous years. The vintage was a kind of UFO, and we weren't quite sure what to make of it.

Around December, Emile Peynaud suggested to the small group we were forming for promotional operations in France and abroad that we should organize a tasting of the vintage. Bruno Prats from Cos d'Estournel, Michel Delon from Léoville-Las Cases, Claude Ricard from Domaine de Chevalier, Thierry Manoncourt from Château Figeac and I met Peynaud in Bordeaux, at Francis Garcia's restaurant, Chapon Fin.

The lunch was kicked off by a comparative tasting of our newborn vintage. A little anxious, I set off for Bordeaux with my sample. We all tasted it in silence. I immediately felt a great relief: all the Lynch-Bages wines showed a distinctive character – and what's more they fitted in perfectly among this distinguished company. When the tasting was over, I rushed to a phone to congratulate Daniel LLose: 'Bravo! Our 1982 is magnificent!'

In the weeks that followed, merchants, brokers and journalists came from all over to get to know the new wine. As we ourselves had perceived at the beginning, some found it too good, too supple, and criticized its supposed lack of ageing capacity. This was particularly true of the old-guard English critics, who were fairly unanimous in reproaching it for a lack of tannic structure. In reality, there was no lack of it, but the tannins had a different profile that year.

A piano was brought to the vineyard for Sérgio and Gracinha, so the grape pickers could enjoy bossa nova...

They were more savoury, more supple, more ripe. Some people also criticized the wine for being too low in acidity, which, according to them, would not allow it to age well.

In reality, this was exactly the type of wine that Emile Peynaud had been advocating for the past 20 years. I can still hear him telling us: 'A good wine is a wine with low acidity, without harshness. It is not the acidity, but the quality of the tannin that allows the wine to age harmoniously.'

Despite the disagreements at the beginning, consumers loved it, and therefore so did the trade. A wine that could be drunk early; what could be better for merchants? The Primeur campaign was successful in the spring of 1983.

The subsequent harvest confirmed the recovery. The month of September, hot and very dry, made up for the summer's distinctly average weather. In terms of quality, without reaching the level of its predecessor, the 1983 vintage was good. Commercially, it was somewhat overshadowed by the extreme media coverage of the previous vintage, and sales were lacklustre, but went ahead without a hitch. We were, by this point, more or less out of the rut of the 1970s, and could finally look forward to the future with more peace of mind.

At Lynch-Bages, the following years were marked by many improvements. We repaired the roofs and enlarged the vat house, which by now bore no resemblance to the old stables and cowshed. We installed seven new tanks and for the first time chose stainless steel, which was stronger, easier to maintain and held the temperature more evenly – something that had previously been prohibitively expensive to achieve.

This meant no more wet hessian cloths wrapped around the tanks to cool them down. Each new tank was equipped with a heat and cold exchanger that allowed precise control of the fermentation temperature. We built a new reception building and moved into new, better laid-out offices.

The harvest kitchen, where meals had been prepared in the large wood-burning fireplace since 1870, was equipped with modern equipment, and the building itself renovated. A large refectory was built for the vineyard and cellar workers, replacing an uninhabited wine grower's house, which was falling apart, and the *'bûchère'* where the vine shoots were stored. The old garage, where the grape pickers ate, was demolished at the same time, taking with it a century of memories. The new building doubled as a reception room. On the first floor, the old attic was transformed into comfortable rooms for our visitors.

Harvests follow one another and are rarely alike. The 1984 harvest, carried out in rainy weather, gave us wines that were a little diluted, but nevertheless pleasant. The Cabernets resisted better than the Merlots but it was an average harvest in terms of volume and quality. Fortunately, the technical means we now had at our disposal allowed us to work comfortably. The 1984 was soon eclipsed by the 1985 vintage. During the winter, it was bitterly cold and three beautiful hundred-year-old trees in the Lynch-Bages garden were destroyed by the freezing temperatures. I had climbed them so often as a child that I was sad to see them disappear. In terms of quality, the year was excellent. The summer was superb, the grapes were picked in perfect conditions of maturity. The wines were balanced, the concentration good, the tannins supple and melting…

Later, well after the spring En Primeur sales (which were a success, with the dollar peaking at nearly 11 francs in 1986), I received a visit from James Suckling, then columnist for the New York *Wine Spectator*. Charged by Marvin Shanken to cover the wines of Bordeaux, he came in the autumn of 1988 to taste the latest vintages. We received him at Lynch-Bages. He seemed to appreciate what we offered him. As he left me, he said in a mysterious tone: 'You will have good news tomorrow.' I asked what he meant, but he did not say anything more and went on his way. The next day, I received a phone call from a New York importer who congratulated me: the *Wine Spectator* had published, for the first time, its list of 'Top 100 Wines of the Year'. Lynch-Bages was at the top with its 1985. I was filled with joy.

One day later, another phone call. It was Ab Simon, the head of Seagram's Château & Estate Wines Co. He told me that he had recently reviewed his wine stocks. He found himself a bit light on a few vintages. Which ones? Finally, he said: '1985! I need a bit more 1985 Lynch-Bages!' I burst out laughing and asked him if he had read the *Wine Spectator*...

YOU NEVER KNOW where wine will take you.

Autumn 1984. It was 7pm and I was still at my desk in the insurance agency. The telephone rang. On the other end of the line, a man with a pronounced French regional accent from the Béarn department introduced himself, rolling his 'r's: it was the fashion designer André Courrèges. He immediately asked me a question that was unexpected, to say the least: 'Do you want to send your wine to the moon?' Like everyone else, I had heard of Courrèges. At first, I thought it was a joke... but it was really him.

Courrèges explained that he was in contact with the astronaut Patrick Baudry, who in a few months' time was due to become the first Frenchman to fly on board the American space shuttle *Challenger*. Originally from Bordeaux, he was a wine lover, and wanted to honour his home region by taking a sample of the local production with him into space.

He had tried to interest several of the regional Bordeaux associations in the operation, without success. Busy training in the (then) USSR's Star City, he was unable to come to the region to look for the ideal partner. Courrèges told this story to a friend of mine, Christian Morin, who was then hosting a programme on Europe 1 radio, who gave him my telephone number and assured him that I would be more receptive.

The whole thing seemed crazy, but I was immediately hooked. I arranged for Patrick Baudry to visit Lynch-Bages. The astronaut could only spare a short time, so I sent a helicopter to fetch him. He spent a day with us and explained that he didn't yet know how he would be able to take wine with him in the space shuttle, but he needed a partner who was willing to supply it in the appropriate form, which had yet to be defined. He was also extremely clear: it was not to be about advertizing a brand, but about honouring Bordeaux and its wine.

The space shuttle *Challenger* was due to take off from Cape Kennedy in March 1985, and finally Baudry obtained the necessary authorization to put a half bottle of wine and some vine leaves in his luggage. He invited me to attend the launch in Florida with my family. In the end, Baudry was not on *Challenger*,

Right: *A first visit to Lynch-Bages for astronaut Patrick Baudry – originally from Bordeaux, he appreciated good wine and wanted to take some into space!*

The Médoc as seen from space by the space shuttle Discovery.

which had technical problems, but on *Discovery*, which left on June 17th 1985, and we were there to watch the deafening, emotional spectacle of the take-off.

While Thereza and the children returned to France, I flew to California for the landing at Edwards Air Force Base, near Los Angeles, almost a week later. The atmosphere was radically different, and I could feel the anxiety of the ground crew as we waited. All eyes were on the sky. *Discovery* suddenly appeared, high in the sun, and landed in a glide, almost stealthily, in a strange and unexpected silence. It was nothing like the take-off, but it was still an emotional experience.

As *Discovery* orbited the planet, the 'Fête de la Fleur', organized by the *Commanderie du Bontemps de Médoc et des Graves*, took place at Château Cantemerle on June 22nd 1985. I was told that Grand Master Henri Martin, surrounded by the Order's dignitaries, concluded his welcome speech by proudly pointing his finger to the sky: 'The first wine from space is passing over our heads tonight. And it is a Bordeaux wine!' Mission accomplished.

The little bottle of Lynch-Bages that has circumnavigated the world 110 times is now on display in our reception room. We didn't drink it. I doubt that its journey of less than a week in weightlessness has had any qualitative impact. It is the 1975 vintage.

EACH VINTAGE WAS NOW APPROACHED with fewer and fewer technical difficulties, and both the 1986 and 1987 harvests went smoothly. The 1986 is a classic vintage, which stood out for its tannic power. Blend tastings took time, as it was difficult to taste more than a dozen samples in the same session. The 1987, lighter in style due to the rains at the end of September, benefited from the improvements in our working methods.

In 1988, we launched a vast project to renovate and extend our farm buildings. Our architects, the British Rigby Lee, who had lived in the Médoc for some years, and Lionel Haïrabedian from Bordeaux, set to work. Lee refined our reception areas and enlarged the vat room, where we installed a new row of stainless-steel vats, doubled by a battery of additional underground vats. The work added a special room for our two hydraulic presses. Haïrabedian rebuilt our entire barrel cellar and added a large bottle storage room. Yves Jugla, a childhood friend from the Pauillac football team and now a masonry contractor in Saint-Estèphe, was enthusiastically and skilfully in charge of construction. We were a long way from the rusticity of André Gimenez, my grandfather's favourite mason.

We also improved the technical nature of the installation. We added a temperature exchanger coil in each tank and installed hot and cold water networks controlled by thermal probes connected to an illuminated panel that showed a stylized, coloured plan of the vat room floor. The temperature of the tanks could be read in real time. New independent circuits supplied compressed gas (which replaced the old bellows for racking) and nitrogen, whose chemical inertia made it possible to handle the wines safely, in particular during racking or storage in vats.

At the same time, we worked on Ormes de Pez. The work here was less extensive, but we renovated and enlarged the barrel cellars and installed a brand-new vat room in 1981.

In November 1989, with the harvest and vinification finished, I set off for the Hôtel Le Gray d'Albion in Cannes, where I had been invited to present our wines by the three-starred chef Jacques Chibois, who reigned over this high palace of French gastronomy. I was in the middle of my presentation when, at the back of the room, somebody began signalling that I was wanted on the phone. It seemed urgent. I made an excuse, left my audience and rushed out to take the call. Our secretary Annie Ayestaran then told me that a fire had broken out at Les Ormes de Pez. I ask her if it was serious. She simply replied: 'I see smoke!' 'Where are you?' I asked. 'At my office in Bages.' If Annie could see the smoke from nine kilometres away, then the fire was serious. She assured me that the fire brigade was at work…

Back in Pauillac the next day, I realized the extent of the disaster. Fortunately, the wall that separated the brand-new vat room from the room where the fire developed acted as a firebreak. The 1989 harvest, still entirely in the vats, was safe. But the main barrel cellar was destroyed, and with it two-thirds of the 1988 harvest.

Once the fire was out, we turned to our insurers. It was a delicate matter. A large proportion of our 1988 wines had been sold En Primeur, as usual. They had not yet been paid for; the first instalment being due at the end of 1989. As an insurer myself, I knew how important it was to be well covered in the event of a claim and our contract was up to date. That said, the insurance company raised a problem: we were no longer the owners of the wines sold.

According to their interpretation, the wines belonged to about 30 buyers, many of whom had already sold them on to foreign importers. The expert, dealing with this kind of problem for the first time, therefore decided it was necessary to check that each buyer was properly insured. It would then be up

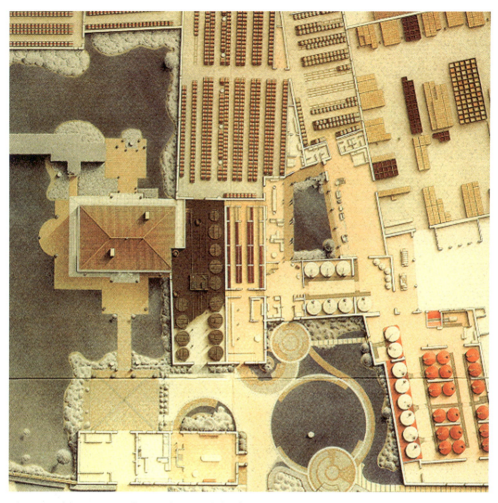

Above: Lynch-Bages 1988 – this was the general plan for renovating and extending our winery buildings.

Below: The fire at Château Les Ormes de Pez – smoke could be seen from nine kilometres away...

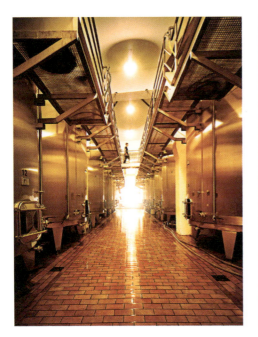 

Above: The new winery at Lynch-Bages in 1989, and Jean-Paul Polaert, technical director, at the controls.

Below: The renovated exterior of Lynch-Bages in 1989.

to the owner of the wine to make the claim, which would be paid to them, if they were well covered, by their insurer. In other words, mission impossible, because it would be incredibly difficult to find owners scattered all over the world. The settlement would take years.

My father and I contested this. We wanted to show that the action of selling En Primeur did not lead to a change of ownership, and maintained that this only occurred at the time of delivery. We were therefore still the legal owners of the wines in our cellar. It was obviously essential for us – and for our customers – to deal with a single insurer.

For once, wine taxation came to our rescue: it had recently been ruled that VAT on wine sales was due at the time of physical delivery of the goods, not at the time of the commercial act, whether it took place En Primeur or not. Physical delivery is defined by the date on which the batches of wine were 'individualized'. This meant, in practice, at the time of bottling, which is generally carried out between 18 months and two years after the harvest. If payments are made before this 'theoretical delivery', they are considered to be mere advance payments. Partial or even total payment did not therefore lead to a transfer of ownership. The producer was still responsible. As we had not yet received any payment, we were unquestionably the owners of the wine. The insurance company accepted our arguments, and, from the beginning of 1990, we were able to offer our customers either partial delivery (the third of the harvest saved made it possible to make a few deliveries) or compensation.

The only issue was that the amount of the indemnity was equal to the value of the property on the day of the loss. Between the Primeur campaign and the month of November, Ormes de Pez 1988 had gained 20 percent in value. For many, the choice was quickly made: they preferred to receive the indemnity and gain 20 percent on a purchase commitment for which they had not yet paid anything. This case has remained a textbook example for the profession, which finally established clear rules for the settlement of claims concerning wines that have been the subject of a *'Vente En Primeur'*.

After 15 years of effort and work, and despite an often difficult economic situation, we had by this point established a solid operation at our two properties. For my father and I, the time had come to celebrate this by showing our friends and the wine world the work we had accomplished. A Fête de la Fleur celebration would be the ideal occasion at which to do this. In 1988, we applied to the Commanderie du Bontemps authorities to host the event. Our request was granted for the spring of 1989; the date set for June 23rd!

FETE DE LA FLEUR had become an important event in the life of the Médoc, an opportunity to receive wine friends from all over the world at a time in June when the Médoc is always at its most beautiful. I was determined that the Lynch-Bages festival would make an impression.

Interested in the history of the town of Pauillac, I did some research in the archives of the commune. I found the minutes of the municipal councils held during the French Revolution – a mine of anecdotes that bring back to life characters whose names can be found in the contemporary Médoc: Pichon-Longueville, Castéja, Lynch, and so on. The idea came to me to bring some of these figures back to life. I imagined a stage in which they would participate in the evening and transport our guests to the Pauillac of the Revolution...

Having no notion of how to actually achieve this, I invited the new director of the National Theatre of Bordeaux to lunch. I had been to several performances, and knew he was an artist and an intellectual who put on ambitious plays. I asked if he would like to help, and he replied that he found the idea 'interesting', and would think about it. I didn't hear from him again.

Shortly afterwards, I received a telephone call from Michel Le Collen, a helicopter pilot in Bordeaux who had previously brought a few particularly distinguished visitors to Lynch-Bages. His son Eric, he told me, was a 'director of large-scale shows'. He was the kingpin of the *Battle of Castillon*, an open-air show that attracted many spectators every summer.

Eric had been contacted by the Bordeaux city council to organize a large wine festival, based on the model of those that were popular in the city at the beginning of the 20th century. He was enthusiastic but he knew nothing about wine or its history in Bordeaux. His father therefore asked me to help by providing him with some historical elements: a 'crash course', as it were.

I received Eric Le Collen in Lynch-Bages, where we had a long conversation. The longer we spoke, the more interested I became in him. He was a director, an actor, a musician, sometimes a dancer, and had experience of directing. While talking about wine, I mentioned my project and asked him if he would like to think about it.

Two weeks later, he visited me again. The French Revolution in Pauillac, he explained, 'is a good idea... today, in 1988'. But the Lynch-Bages festival would be taking place the following year, in 1989, when the whole country would be celebrating the bicentenary of the national event. All the newspapers, radios and television channels would be full of it, and the subject would be saturated. In his opinion, a different theme had to be found, and he had a suggestion...

The barrel cellar at Les Ormes de Pez, reconstructed after the devastating fire of 1989. The complicated insurance situation that followed this event led to the establishment of clearer rules for wine trade cover.

Having learned that in 1985 our wine went around the world on board the space shuttle *Discovery*, he devised a scenario: 'Bordeaux wine is widely distributed on all continents of the globe. All that remains is making it known in the cosmos… It so happens that Captain Desquet, commander of a spacecraft, is a distant descendant of Jean-Odule Paulin d'Esquet, mythical founder of the Commanderie du Bontemps in the 12th century. The Grand Master of Bontemps observes that the wines of the Médoc are suffering from a distribution deficit in the stars, where they are not yet sufficiently well known, and he then asks d'Esquet to set off on a new mission, with the aim of opening up new markets…'

Eric le Collen envisaged a musical that would take place during dinner. He imagined transforming the room into a spaceship whose passengers would be our guests, designing costumes, writing an original text and music, and hiring actors. He didn't want a 'high-tech' aesthetic and instead suggested we recreate a Jules Verne-style universe, inspired by the novel *From the Earth to the Moon* (1865).

Eric set to work on the texts, to which, as a faithful reader of Jules Verne in my youth, I contributed. Dominique Pichou started working on the sets and costumes. Our whole team got involved. For almost a year, everyone worked hard towards the preparation of this evening, which we wanted to be original, memorable and successful.

JUNE 23RD 1989. The rehearsal, which took place the day before, was not a success. Coordinating the serving of food and the scenes of *The Amazing Adventure of the Esquet Mission* was no small task, and by the time our guests arrived, we were all on edge.

The cocktail party began on the lawn, and the evening got underway. In our new storage room, transformed into a spaceship thanks to the magic wand of Dominique Pichou, we installed 1,200 guests with their boarding passes. Alongside the wine personalities, we received many friends of wine, and in particular the astronaut Patrick Baudry to whom Lynch-Bages owed the honour of being the first wine in space.

He was accompanied by three of his colleagues, including Joseph Allen, NASA astronaut, and the first American to have performed a spacewalk. The compere for the evening was my friend Christian Morin, radio and television personality and clarinet player, acting as master of ceremonies.

The Commanderie's Grand Master, Henri Martin, made a welcoming speech. His health was not good at this point and he had been waiting for the meal to begin in his car. At the last moment, he put on his robe and grabbed his sceptre before going on stage. His duty done, too weak to attend the evening, he returned to Beychevelle. It was his last public appearance, and I know the effort it required of him. He wanted to take part in our Festival and I will always be grateful to him for being there.

The Grand Chancellor – that is, my father – followed him to announce the theme of the evening. I recently found the few words he had scribbled on a piece of paper: 'I met the captain several months ago and told him of our desire to make our wines known everywhere… "The earth is too small," he replied, "for the glory of the Médoc and Graves. If you accept my offer, I will set up an interplanetary mission that will make our wines known throughout the entire universe." He convinced me. He patiently selected his crew and mapped out his itinerary. Present every day on the construction site of this vessel in which you are now sitting, he has prepared the F89-LB mission with precision and skill. This is an extraordinary journey that you are going to be part of tonight. Let's go to the galaxy! I welcome here Captain Jean-Odule Paulin d'Esquet!'

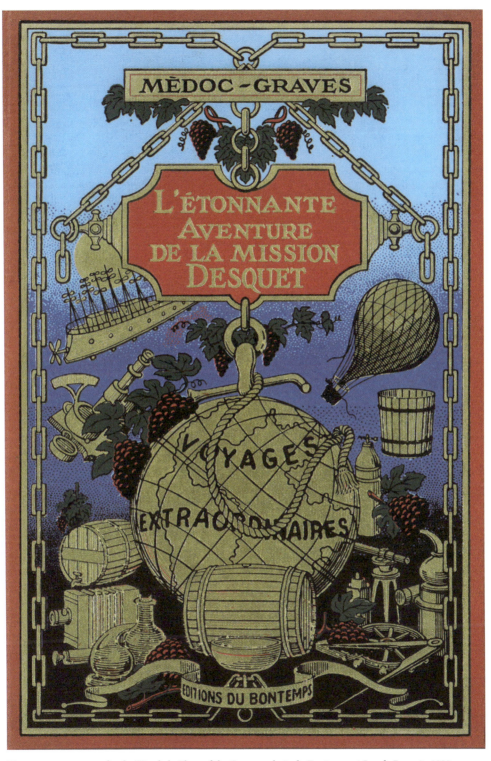

The menu-programme for the Fête de la Fleur of the Commanderie du Bontemps at Lynch-Bages in 1989.

The Oenological Revolution

The lift-off began. In contrast to the previous day's rehearsal, everything went without a hitch. During dinner, which was perfectly coordinated with the show, the captain and his crew visited one planet after another, experiencing the most surprising adventures. The show was a complete success and the audience was captivated. Marvin Shanken, owner of the *Wine Spectator* in New York, grabbed me by the shoulder and said in my ear: 'This is major league!' Coming from such a champion of marketing and publicity, this was indeeed no small endorsement.

The dinner ended with the return to earth of the captain, received, with deserved congratulations, by the Grand Chancellor. The Chancellor asked him to leave immediately, as there were still some remote corners of the universe where action was needed. He suggested that he should go without delay to the space rocket which was waiting for him in the garden of the estate. It was almost midnight. Our 1,200 guests followed and applauded the crew as they entered the small raised kiosk at the back of the park, illuminated by spotlights.

No sooner had they disappeared than the rocket rose into the night, shooting jets of fire towards the ground. At the controls of his helicopter, hidden behind the wall, Michel Le Collen took off vertically. The illusion was perfect and the audience was amazed. Only the prefect of Aquitaine seemed to sulk at the show. I would learn a few days later that he was angry with the pilot for having taken risks by flying over the crowd.

For our family, this 1989 Fête de la Fleur marked the culmination of 15 years of study, reflection, investment and work, an important stage in the life of our family company. It was one of many rich celebrations held by the Commanderie de Bontemps, and set the bar high for future events. I went on to be involved in the organization of three other Fêtes de la Fleur, always working with Eric Le Collen: they were at Pichon-Longueville in 1992, Cantenac-Brown in 1997 and Ormes de Pez in 2002, plus a Ban des Vendanges harvest festival at Cantenac-Brown. On each occasion, we tried to do as well as we had done in 1989 and sometimes came close, but none of them gave me as much joy as the Lynch-Bages festival.

18 The Beginnings of AXA-Millésimes

I THINK I MET Claude Bébéar at high school in Bordeaux, but I'm not sure. What I am sure of is that I met him up in Paris, in the Latin Quarter, where we were both boarders, he on boulevard Saint-Michel at the Lycée Saint-Louis, and I, 200 metres further on, on rue Saint-Jacques at the Lycée Louis-le-Grand.

We were the same age, and met on the rugby fields and on the train from Bordeaux every holiday. A good sportsman and good student, he was brilliantly admitted to the Ecole Polytechnique, unlike me, to the great disappointment of my grandmother, as I have already recounted. We continued to see each other from time to time on the sports fields during our student years, and then later, every summer, at Cap Ferret where he had acquired a holiday home next to my family's. He married a little earlier than I did, but our children were about the same age and shared their summers on the shores of the Arcachon bay.

Claude Bébéar had an unusual professional background. On leaving school, he chose to study actuarial science, which led him to insurance. From his start at a modest mutual insurance company based in Rouen, he showed a spirit of innovation and, within 20 years, built up a global giant in the sector: Anciennes Mutuelles, the company that became AXA.

My father and I were insurance agents at the time. In a way, we were in the same business. When we met Claude in Cap Ferret, we liked to listen to him talk about his progress. He would ask us about the reactions of the 'base' that we represented in his eyes. As his company grew, and bought up others, he united them under one banner, choosing the name AXA because it was simple and short and, thanks to its spelling, had every chance of appearing at the top of any alphabetical lists.

Claude Bébéar was also – and still is – a well-informed gastronome and wine expert. We would sometimes go together to visit a good restaurant or a famous vineyard. All in all, we had a lot in common: rugby, cooking and wine and, each to his own scale, our profession.

The Fête de la Fleur at Pichon-Longueville in 1992: Claude Bébéar (left) and Thereza with jazz pianist and wine lover Ronnie Kole from New Orleans (standing) and Frank Prial, the New York Times *wine columnist.*

At the beginning of the 1980s, almost all of the Médoc Grands Crus were still owned by families or family-owned companies, both French and foreign. The first notable arrival of the *'zinzins'* (institutional investors) occurred in 1982, when the *Garantie Mutuelle des Fonctionnaires* (GMF) bought Château Beychevelle in Saint-Julien from the Fould family, who had owned it for over 100 years.

I have often been asked the question: why would an insurance company invest in agriculture, an area so far removed from its core business? The answer is that they collect large sums of money every year in the form of contributions, which do not really belong to them and which they must keep in reserve to meet any future obligations. These are the counterpart of the indemnities they will have to pay in the future against claims.

Some risks (fire, accidents and so on) are insured against for the short or medium term, while others, such as life insurance, tend to be medium- or long-term policies, and it makes sense that the reserves kept by the insurance company should similarly reflect the structure of the commitments.

Part of the funds held by the insurance companies must, therefore, be used for long-term investments. The acquisition of a quality property, such as an 1855 Cru Classé, is comparable in nature to a well-placed building in the heart of Paris, and is therefore an excellent example of a long-term investment. Located on a well-defined, quality terroir, its production remains limited and follows precise rules. These properties are a relatively safe asset. It was this reasoning that led GMF to acquire Château Beychevelle, and it would also be the reasoning of Claude Bébéar and his staff.

In 1985, AXA had owned a Saint-Emilion Cru Classé, Château Franc-Mayne, for several years, as it had been part of the investments of one of the companies acquired by the group over the years. Claude personally oversaw the renovation of the property's residence, which became an elegant house, surrounded by a vineyard. He was also interested in Burgundy, where AXA acquired the modest Domaine de l'Arlot in the Côte de Nuits in 1987.

At the end of 1986, Claude Bébéar contacted me: his team in charge of investments was studying an important acquisition in Bordeaux, but they had little knowledge of the Bordeaux region and lacked wine experience. Would I agree to give them my opinion?

The property in question was Château Cantenac-Brown, in Margaux, owned by a family allied to Marquis Bertrand du Vivier, head of the House of Luze, which had exclusive distribution rights for the wines. Its reputation, despite being a Cru Classé, had slipped over recent decades. The vineyard had been neglected, the quality of the wine was considered mediocre, and its commercial strategy consisted of presenting it as one of the cheapest of the Médoc *Crus Classés*, using it as a loss leader.

That said, the estate had good potential: about 50 hectares fairly well located in the Margaux appellation, and the status given by its Third Growth 1855 ranking. Its vines surrounded a magnificent park and an imposing château, built in around 1865, in the English manor style, by Bordeaux merchant Armand Lalande. Like the vineyard, the immense château was poorly maintained. Some of its rooms were rented out or lent to occupants in need of accommodation who had nothing to do with the running of the estate. The cellars and vats needed modernizing.

Claude Bébéar entrusted the negotiation to a loyal member of his team, Bernard Robin. A talented financier, he was part of the old guard and managed AXA's investments. He had already had several conversations with the sellers. The main decision-maker was not the Marquis du Vivier, but a certain Ortmans, a Dutch citizen of poor reputation, linked to the Deutsch de la Meurthe family and the founder of the Royal Dutch Shell company.

I made a few remarks to Bernard Robin who met the seller's representative the following Friday to finalize the details of the transaction. The two parties agreed on the various points and decided to meet again on Monday, for signature. I was to attend the final meeting. But on Monday morning, Bernard Robin told me that the seller had concluded the deal during the weekend, behind our backs, with someone else.

To explain this sudden turn of events, we had to go back a few months. The previous year, the AXA group took control of a small bank in Bordeaux and integrated it into the group, removing its manager. This man harboured a grudge towards AXA and Claude Bébéar, and when he learned that Cantenac-Brown was up for sale, he did his best to find the person or entity capable of buying it, in order to exact revenge on Claude Bébéar.

The Bordeaux financial centre was aware of the rivalry between Claude Bébéar and Bernard Pagézy, president of the *Compagnie du Midi*, for control of the Présence insurance group (the company I represented in Pauillac, by the way). AXA, which was still only a French insurer, had recently won the battle, and apparently Pégazy was only too happy to give the green light for the purchase when presented with an opportunity to beat his rival on this deal at least. Apparently, he had never visited Cantenac-Brown, but signed a memorandum of understanding the day before the meeting between Ortmans and Robin.

I returned to Pauillac, disappointed.

A few months passed, perhaps a year. Towards the end of 1986, Claude Bébéar told me about a new opportunity, and that negotiations were well underway. It was Château Pichon-Longueville in Pauillac, known as Pichon-Baron to differentiate it from its neighbour Pichon-Longueville Comtesse de Lalande (Pichon-Lalande), and one of the leading growths in the 1855 Classification.

The château had been built in 1850 by Baron Raoul de Pichon-Longueville. An emblem of Médoc architecture, it is framed by fine turrets that stand out in the landscape like a fairy-tale castle. The Pichon-Longueville heirs had not survived the great economic crisis of the pre-war period, and in 1933, they had been forced to sell their exhausted and shrunken estate to Jean Bouteiller. He was an excellent wine grower, a skilful and innovative winemaker, and a respected personality who managed the estate as best he could for about 30 years, and had produced high-quality vintages until his death in the early 1960s.

His son Bertrand succeeded him, acting on behalf of his mother and three brothers. He also managed Château Palmer, in Margaux, of which the Bouteiller family was a major shareholder. Hubert Bouteiller, who was very involved in trade union activities, had run Château Lanessan in Cussac, the family's centre of gravity, since the 18th century; Jacques, an engineer, lived in Paris; Serge was an insurance agent and I knew him well because he worked at our Pauillac agency.

On paper, the deal didn't seem so great. The sellers were reluctant to discuss price, and Bernard Robin was unwilling to raise his offer. The château was undoubtedly impressive but the vineyard much less so, because, since the phylloxera crisis at the beginning of the century, the estate had been reduced to 27 hectares of vines. I tried to play the 'fair intermediary' between the AXA managers, who I knew fairly well, and the Bouteiller family, who had been close to mine for many years.

I knew that the estate owned, in its westerly section, around 15 hectares of bare land that fell within the boundary of the Pauillac appellation. The vines once grown there had been uprooted in the first half of the century and never replanted. If it was possible to replant on this classified land, the price of the property could suddenly become more attractive… but we needed to get plantation rights first, and Pichon-Baron didn't have any.

In those days, it was possible to buy a 'rights exchange', and although my friends at AXA understood the interest of these 15 hectares, they were unwilling to commit without having first secured those rights – particularly since the whole question of planting was extremely political, and there was talk at the time of tightening the rules and potentially even forbidding any new plantings.

Louis Deroye and Bernard Robin, both great wine lovers, were appointed by Claude Bébéar to monitor AXA's wine business. Here, in San Francisco.

The Beginnings of AXA   155

To get over the issue, I decided to buy the necessary rights myself, on behalf of Lynch-Bages, so that I could count on their availability when needed. Bernard Robin now felt confident that he could almost double the size of the vineyard upon purchase, and the negotiations were wrapped up by the beginning of 1987.

Until that point, I had acted as an external advisor, out of friendship for Claude Bébéar and his team. We had become closer during the Cantenac-Brown affair the previous year, and especially during the weeks of discussions with the Bouteiller family. I knew that the new owner would have to organize the management of his purchase, but I was busy with my insurance agency and my estates at Lynch-Bages and Les Ormes de Pez. I was simply happy to have been useful. However, when Claude Bébéar unexpectedly offered me the responsibility of managing his new estate in Pauillac, I was excited. There was a lot to do in the vineyard and cellar, and the distribution system needed an overhaul. Bernard Bouteiller had begun selling direct during the tough years, bypassing the Bordeaux wine trade, which I thought was an error. It was an intriguing challenge.

Bernard Robin suggested that I think about a profit-sharing contract. As I had no experience in this, I consulted my friend Georges Pauli, director of the Cordier properties. The Cordier trading house, which Jean had split up a few years earlier, continued to market the wine of the separate properties. Jean Cordier, who had been around the block, signed water-tight contracts with his distributors, and I used this as a basis for writing my own, which I submitted to Bernard Robin.

Two years later, with business having gone well, it became clear that if my contract was applied to the letter, I would be owed a significant sum. I didn't mention it, and concentrated on work, trusting the company to do whatever was necessary. Bernard Robin avoided the subject for some time, then one day Claude Bébéar asked me to come and see him in his beautiful office on Avenue Matignon in Paris: 'I looked at your contract,' he said. 'It's impossible to apply it as it stands: you'd earn more than me!' I readily agreed that the mechanics of our relationship had to be revised.

This is how AXA Millésimes, owner of the land, and Châteaux et Associés, the company that runs the business and owns the stock, came into being. I was the operational manager. AXA Millésimes was 100 percent owned by AXA. I owned 25 percent of Châteaux et Associés. The structure was open and could, if necessary, accommodate future investments by AXA in the wine sector. This new organization, now on a firm footing, would work successfully for us both for a number of years.

19 Pichon-Longueville

SPRING 1987. I took over Château Pichon-Longueville. Both Daniel LLose and myself were excited by what lay ahead.

Pichon was – and remains – one of the Médoc's most emblematic *crus*. The vineyard, on the southern plateau of Pauillac, was created in the second half of the 18th century by Pierre de Rauzan, a well-known Bordeaux wine merchant, who gave it to his daughter in 1694 as a dowry for her marriage to Jacques de Pichon, Baron de Longueville. It remained in the same family for almost 250 years, until the great crisis of the 20th century and the sale to the Bouteiller family in 1933.

In 1850, however, it was divided for reasons of inheritance and gave birth to a second estate attributed to an heiress of Baron de Pichon, the Countess de Lalande. Hence its name: Pichon-Longueville Comtesse de Lalande. This new château followed a path parallel to that of its parent until its sale in 1925 to Edouard and Louis Miailhe, who were wine brokers.

Edouard died in 1959, followed by a long family dispute during which the estate remained undivided. The family then entrusted its management to Michel Delon from Château Léoville-Las Cases, who did a good job, particularly in recruiting Jean-Jacques Godin in 1978, who proved to be an effective technical manager. With Michel Delon's guidance, Godin produced, vintage after vintage, wines whose quality was quickly recognized.

The year 1978 was also when Edouard's daughter, May-Eliane de Lencquesaing, took over the estate and immediately decided to replace Michel Delon with her young nephew, Dominique Hessel. Torn between Jean-Jacques Godin, who did as he pleased, and May-Eliane, his aunt, who wanted to decide everything herself, he didn't stay at Pichon-Longueville for more than six months, instead devoting himself to his personal property, Château Moulin à Vent in Moulis-en-Médoc, and to the *Syndicat des Crus Bourgeois*, of which he was president.

Apart from a period during World War II, the Baron's huge building had remained uninhabited since the sale in 1933. May-Eliane de Lencquesaing, who lived on the other side of the road in Pichon-Lalande, told me how sad she was to have to contemplate the lifeless façades of the château opposite her. All the windows were blacked out by shutters that were never opened. In 1987, my first decision was to open the 56 shutters on the façade. We had to make this house live! Claude Bébéar entrusted the renovation to the Parisian architect-decorator and antique dealer Didier Aaron. The mission was to make the château a reception area for AXA's distinguished guests… and for greeting our future clients.

I then took care of the name of the property. All my life I had heard my fellow Pauillac residents refer to the château by its full name, 'Pichon-Longueville', and call its neighbour 'Pichon-Lalande'. However, brokers and merchants were used to using the term 'Pichon-Baron' when they talked about the estate's wine… Bertrand Bouteiller had a letterhead printed two or three years earlier with the name 'Pichon-Baron' and posted this name on the farm buildings in large, inelegant letters.

The official name of the estate remained Pichon-Longueville, the full name of the family who created the estate in the 18th century; and I didn't think that we should change the official name for the sake of convenience. As soon as I took office, I had a letterhead reprinted as 'Château Pichon-Longueville' and had the Pichon-Baron sign taken down from the façade – a move that caused a stir, with the neighbour across the street, relayed by several English journalists, accusing me of wanting to change the identity of the property. I was motivated by the simple desire to return to the historical truth, and defended myself… The debate raged in the British specialist press. Much ado about nothing.

After I left in 2001, my successors went back and adopted the name 'Pichon-Baron' once and for all, which was shorter and easier to pronounce. The salesmen won… They were probably right.

I also had to tackle more mundane issues: reorganizing the team, improving and expanding the vineyard, and reorienting the commercial policy. The technical staff was good, but there were two managers who were doing the same job and often stepping on each other's toes. Daniel LLose and I decided to simplify things, and had the tough job of deciding between them. Both were competent, but we agreed to appoint Jean-René Matignon, who had the advantage of living locally. Jean-René announced his retirement in 2022, after a long career producing fine wine for many decades.

The majestic façade of Château Pichon-Longueville – acquired by AXA Millésimes in 1987, and with which Claude Bébéar entrusted me the management.

Château Pichon-Longueville: the circular wine cellar designed by architects Patrick Dillon and Jean de Gastines.

Pichon-Longueville 159

Above: Daniel Llose (left) with the technical director of Pichon-Longueville, Jean-René Matignon (centre), and consultant oenologist Eric Boissenot (right).

Below: Malou le Sommer, who joined Pichon-Longueville in 1987, became commercial manager for all our vineyards. La Place de Bordeaux holds no secrets for her.

For the management, Alain Martung, financial manager of Lynch-Bages, took charge, but we also needed to recruit new staff. I had heard about the young wife of the new director of Château Latour, who had just moved to the village of Saint-Lambert, near Pichon. Marie-Louise ('Malou') Troadec, wife of Christian Le Sommer, was a graduate of the National School of Agriculture. Before joining Latour, her husband was in charge of the Henri Maire vineyards in the Jura region and she sold vineyard treatments in eastern France.

In Pauillac, I could only offer her a job as an assistant to start with, despite her technical background. Malou accepted my offer. She became our first secretary and quickly took on all sorts of tasks. She was quick, sensitive, stubborn (120 percent Breton) and had a keen sense of human relations. She soon became indispensable in the commercial management of all the properties for which I was responsible.

In 1987, the vineyard in production at Pichon-Longueville was just 27 hectares, but it was well kept. We immediately began the plantation project that we had talked about during the negotiations with the Bouteillers. First of all, we had to clear some 15 hectares that had been invaded for 50 years by stunted coppice trees and all sorts of undergrowth, which we piled up before setting fire to it. It took time, but the following year, in 1988, the new vines were in place.

Just two months after the purchase of Pichon-Longueville, I received a visit at my insurance agent's office from Pierre Gauthier of Château Pibran. Owned by his mother-in-law, Madame Billa, it was a pretty vineyard of 10 hectares in one piece, very well placed near Pontet-Canet and Mouton d'Armailhacq.

The family had decided to sell and asked if I was interested. Of course – 10 hectares of good vines, well situated in the communal appellation, don't come up every day! It was too big a piece for Lynch-Bages, but it would be a nice addition to Pichon-Longueville, and I was sure that AXA would agree. The deal was concluded within 24 hours.

These 10 hectares were in fact half of the former Pibran estate. The other half, under the name Château Tour Pibran, belonged to Jean-Jacques Gounel, an agricultural contractor, who preferred to look after his machinery and had leased his property to a neighbouring wine grower. We wanted to be able to reunite these two sections to recreate the original 20-hectare vineyard. I knew Jean-Jacques Gounel well, so I approached him, as I knew the lease had expired.

Gounel would not be opposed to a transfer, but by law, the farmer had a right of first refusal in the event of a sale, a right that would hold for 10 years even after the lease had been terminated. To avoid problems with this, I made an agreement with Gounel: initially, he terminated the lease and became the official operator, and Pichon-Longueville provided him with the necessary means to look after the vineyard and agreed to buy the harvest each year. For his part, he made a verbal commitment to transfer the property to us at the end of the 10-year period. He kept his word.

Over the following years, we bought various small plots of land near the village of Saint-Lambert, within a few hundred metres of the château. From 27 hectares in 1986, its surface area grew to almost 80 hectares of excellent terroir in 10 years. There were some within the corridors of AXA's head office who had questioned the decision to buy Pichon-Longueville, but the results we achieved silenced the critics.

The LLose-Matignon pairing was quick to demonstrate the quality potential of the vineyard. As Emile Peynaud was no longer available, we asked his student Jacques Boissenot to accompany us. Like his master, he was an artist of blending. The 1987 vintage, an average year, was very successful; the 1988 remarkable; the 1989 and 1990 both sumptuous. The rediscovered quality was widely celebrated. The highly respected *Wine Spectator*, which had distinguished the 1985 Lynch-Bages by awarding it first place in its annual ranking of the 100 best wines of the year in 1988, did the same with the 1989 Pichon-Longueville, which it put at the top of its list in 1992. A particular point of pride for Daniel LLose and me – I think we are the only ones to have been so distinguished on two separate occasions.

At the same time, the technical facilities were showing their age. Rebuilding a Médoc Grand Cru is not an opportunity that comes along every day... I wanted to design an ambitious project, both technically and aesthetically, as did Claude Bébéar.

Ten years earlier at Lafite, Eric de Rothschild had shown the way by entrusting Catalan architect Ricardo Bofill with the construction of his new, much-admired, circular barrel cellar. I felt that the quality of the premises in which a wine is made should equal the excellence one expects to find in a bottle from a great terroir. Pichon-Longueville offered the opportunity to show just that.

To achieve this, we enlisted Michel Guillard, a photographer who had travelled the Médoc in all directions. He knew all the wine châteaux, which earned him recognition as an expert in the field, and together with Jean Dethier, consultant architect at the *Centre de Création Industrielle du Centre Pompidou*, he had designed an exhibition project in 1988 devoted to Bordeaux's wine architecture, called Châteaux Bordeaux.

The designers of the exhibition observed the architectural flowering that accompanied the economic expansion of the vineyards in the 18th and 19th centuries, when the current image of a château was effectively invented. They also noted the absence, with a few exceptions, of any significant architectural creations since the beginning of the 20th century, due to the almost uninterrupted economic crisis.

To accompany the images and models of the buildings featured in the exhibition, they asked volunteer châteaux to take part in an exercise to design installations that met today's needs. For Pichon-Longueville, it was too good an opportunity to miss.

Jean Dethier and his team selected three renowned architectural firms for us: the Franco-American couple Jean de Gastines and Patrick Dillon, the Chilean Fernando Montes and the Spaniards from Pamplona, Ustarroz and Iñiguez. I added the Bordeaux firm of Lionel Haïrabedian, with whom we had collaborated at Lynch-Bages. For several months, we worked hard with the four teams who, of course, knew little or nothing about the constraints of winemaking and needed technical support. Mock-ups were used to judge how the proposed buildings would sit within the landscape.

It was time to choose. A jury chaired by Claude Bébéar met in Pauillac to see the four candidates. They decided in favour of the study presented by Patrick Dillon and Jean de Gastines that not only met the technical constraints, but also worked within the surrounding landscape. The new buildings were low-rise with nothing higher than the ground floor of the château. Seen from Saint-Julien, only the château emerges from a sea of vines. The designers had subtly taken into account the relief and the landscape.

As for the architectural style, it was… different. We didn't give any guidelines. Patrick Dillon (who took part in the work on Lafite with Bofill) asked me: 'What is the style of the region?' I replied that the 19th century had sprinkled the Médoc with a number of buildings that were as spectacular as they were disparate: medieval houses of dubious authenticity, copies of ancient temples, ersatz Loire castles and fake English colleges. 'The regional style is precisely that there is none. That's what makes it original and charming. Let your imagination run wild!' He and his accomplice Jean de Gastines had taken me at my word. Their project was unusual, to say the least, but it showed their talent and the jury was unanimous.

Construction work got underway immediately. There were numerous innovations: the vats were installed in a circle, for example – we were only the second château in the Médoc to do this, after Château d'Arcins, where wine merchant Pierre Castel's sister lived. That had only come about because during the build of a new cellar at Arcins, she had refused the suggested long, rectangular building which threatened her small pond and her goldfish, leading the architect to revise his plans and to draw a circular building. When I visited it with the cellarmaster, we were happy. He decided that it would be practical to use, and that the even spacing of the vats around the centre, far from complicating operations, would simplify them.

Everything had to be ready for the 1991 harvest.

Located in the heart of the estate, the circular vat house of Pichon-Longueville was (and remains) semi-buried, hidden behind a long, low façade animated by large stone volutes. The interior was spectacular. A cone-shaped skylight illuminated the centre of the building, and, in turn, added a hint of light to the surrounding vineyard landscape at night. The roof was supported by eight solid columns placed in a circle and inclined at 65 degrees. We housed 30 tanks of two different capacities on two concentric circles, the smaller ones in the middle, the larger ones on the outside. All were equipped with heat exchangers to control the temperature.

Everything was controlled from a glassed-in office that resembled the cockpit of an airliner, located next to a modern (for the time) grape intake system that led directly into the vat room. A network of stainless-steel pipes ran through the room, and a sort of switching station placed in a corner of the room allowed the vats to link with each other, thus reducing the **necessity for swarms of fragile hosepipes. A d**edicated bottling facility was set up nearby.

Next to this main building, a first-year barrel cellar was built, as well as a neoclassical building to house tractors and agricultural equipment. On the other side of a central basin, in which the façade of the château was reflected, was a vast reception centre.

As at Lynch-Bages, I wanted a professional, enthusiastic team in place to receive visitors, and for the new Pichon-Longueville to have an open and welcoming face. This is why I refused to close off the entrance to the main road or to put up a wall or gate. I was convinced that the new complex would become a key tourist destination in the Médoc.

Budget overrun, I have to admit, was significant. This is often the case for a large project, but my partners were unhappy that I had been too ambitious and too conciliatory with the architects and companies... They were probably right – so we put off the planned construction of the second barrel cellar, and

Thereza and I with our four children at the Fête de la Fleur of the Commanderie du Bontemps at Château Pichon-Longueville in June 1992.

it would take 15 years before the project was picked up again. In 2007, the new cellar was built between the vat room and the reception building, under the esplanade in front of the château, to complete the ensemble.

But the results were unquestionable. As of 1991, the new building provided the technology necessary to make the best possible wines. Architecturally, it was the first comprehensive reconstruction at the estate since the 19th century. It was a symbol of its revival and welcomed tens of thousands of visitors in the following years.

There was still much to do. The reputation of Pichon-Longueville had suffered somewhat since the death of Jean Bouteiller at the beginning of the 1960s, and the brand was, as the saying goes, 'not much in demand' on the market. My ambition was to put Pichon-Longueville back at the top of the 1855-classified Second Growths. We had our neighbour Pichon-Lalande in our sights, which had been leading the way for the last 12 years since the arrival of Michel Delon. Since the new team had taken over, the quality was there, but it was not immediately reflected in the enthusiasm of the buyers. That takes time and consistency.

I was determined to improve distribution and to encourage the Bordeaux trade to once again take an interest. Faced with the difficulties of the 1970s, the managers of Pichon-Longueville had tried to develop direct relations with the operators of the French and overseas consumer markets, but I believed we could do better. In the summer of 1987, I took up my pilgrim's staff, accompanied by my daughter Marina, and embarked on a European tour that took us from Brussels and Amsterdam to Hamburg, Copenhagen and Oslo. At each stop, I announced to my local distributors that we were ending the direct relationship that had been established by the previous owner. Most of them understood our decision, and I was politely received (almost) everywhere.

Little by little, Pichon-Longueville regained a foothold in the Bordeaux market. In fact, the return to the forefront was faster than expected. That's the magic of the 1855 Classification: with Pichon being classified as a Second Growth, it was enough to demonstrate over a few vintages that the quality was at the expected level. The brand quickly regained its place. What a contrast with Lynch-Bages, classified Fifth Growth in 1855, which, in order to obtain the same recognition, had to prove year after year that the quality of its wine deserved a higher ranking.

20 Robert Parker

I MET ROBERT PARKER by chance in 1983, in Saint-Julien, in the cellars of Château Branaire-Ducru where he was tasting the 1982 vintage. We learned that his love of wine was born during a trip to France where he joined his future wife Patricia, a student at the University of Strasbourg. He discovered the joy of food and drink in France, and fell in love with our wines, so different from those flavoured beverages he was used to drinking in America.

From this first visit, Parker returned to the United States as a Francophile and a fervent supporter of French gastronomy. A lawyer, he worked for a Baltimore financial institution. While selecting, collecting and tasting the good bottles he found in Maryland and Washington, he plunged passionately into reading the good writers: the Englishmen Hugh Johnson, Michael Broadbent and Harry Waugh, and his fellow American Alexis Lichine. Then he began writing about wine himself and in 1978 published the first issue of a newsletter for wine insiders, *The Wine Advocate*, in a nod to his profession.

When I crossed paths with him in 1982, *The Wine Advocate* was still relatively small, and Robert Parker himself little known. A follower of Ralph Nader, a fellow lawyer and a personality in the environmental movement, he saw himself as a consumer defender and an eloquent advocate for the cause of wine. His language was direct, sometimes blunt, but easy to understand, and he had a way with words. He modernized the approach to tasting and sought out wines that he wanted to share with a wider public.

He started a revolution: abandoning the 20-point rating used by many critics, the British in particular, and rating wines out of 100. Curiously, he only used part of the scale, from 50 to 100. At 100 points, it was the perfect wine. At 80, not very good… Below 70, really bad. At 50, the wine was undrinkable, even dangerous, so better not to talk about it.

Personally, I found it hard to accept that two wines could be distinguished by one point, sometimes even by half a point. For us French, this rating structure seemed strange, but it was similar to the system used in schools in the United States, and therefore spoke to all Americans, contributing to the popularity and influence of its creator.

At the time, in the early 1980s, the influential American critic was Robert Finigan, who had also been publishing a newsletter for longer. His opinions were important and he was a regular visitor to the Médoc. His opinion on the 1982 vintage was aligned with that of the English critics: 'The wine is good to taste now, supple, easy to drink, but it won't go the distance.'

Parker went against the general opinion, and did so with talent, eloquently arguing that the wines had ageability. Arguments followed swiftly.

Parker's judgement was similar to those of Emile Peynaud and Michel Bettane, a literary scholar turned wine critic. The debate raged between supporters and opponents of the vintage, which the natural evolution of the wine quickly settled. Within a few months, the debate was over. When the wines were delivered, the truth was clear to everyone: Parker's ideas had triumphed. As for Finigan, who stuck stubbornly to his initial opinion, I did not see him again in Bordeaux and his influence faded. In the United States, as in Rome, it is not far from the Tarpeian Rock to the Capitol…

This victory marked the debut of Robert Parker, who in a few years would become the most influential wine critic in history and would be placed on a veritable pedestal by wine lovers. For Michel Bettane, it was the dawn of a great career as a taster.

TEN YEARS AFTER THE CREATION of *The Wine Advocate*, Bob Parker gave up his job as a lawyer to devote himself to his passion. He received bottles from all over the world and transformed his house in Monkton into a tasting room. He visited the vineyards of the world and came to Bordeaux at least once a year to taste the wines En Primeur. As he was keen to remain independent of both the estates and the wine trade, he stayed in a modest hotel in Bordeaux-Lac, at the gateway to the Médoc and close to the Bordeaux ring-road, which gave him easy access to all the appellations. These, he visited in a chauffeur-driven limousine. He usually refused the invitations he was bombarded with.

He first visited the properties in person, then reduced his forays into the field and tasted hundreds of samples in his hotel room. He was a tasting athlete, tasting up to 200 wines a day (I often wondered whether the human palate could be exposed to these marathons without damage!).

On a visit to Château Lynch-Bages, Robert Parker (centre) is well looked after! I first met him early on in his career when he was tasting the 1982 vintage – his eloquent opinions on which drew him to world attention.

A few 'scouts' guided him in his choices. The best known was a pupil of Emile Peynaud, Michel Rolland, a famous oenologist from Pomerol. Bob appreciated the style that Rolland gave to the wines he consulted for. Parker also relied on the American Jeffrey Davies, a modest Bordeaux wine merchant, who travelled the vineyards year-round in search of the rare bird.

Many owners saw these advisors as a key to access Robert Parker and a springboard to successfully penetrate the American market. For a few years, Bob was assisted in Bordeaux by Hanna Agostini, wife of Professor Eric Agostini, a renowned specialist in wine law. She organized his tasting programmes, made his appointments and accepted or refused invitations on his behalf, until he judged that she was doing too much and put an end to their collaboration.

Robert Parker came regularly to Lynch-Bages. Each time, it was an opportunity for me to have interesting discussions. We would talk at length about the vinification process and its philosophy. Bob was not in favour of clarifying the wines by fining and he was totally opposed to filtration. We had more or less the same views on filtration, but not on fining. I thought that clarification with egg whites before bottling was necessary to prevent the wine from becoming cloudy over time and to keep its 'brilliance'. 'You are too gullible,' I often told him, 'there are winemakers who fine their wine and others who do not... but there is a third school: those who do and tell you the opposite!' Which made him smile, because Bob, as a good American, was the epitome of honesty. He couldn't imagine anyone lying to him.

His success aroused the jealousy of many of his colleagues, some of whom were not sparing in their criticism. He was sometimes accused, wrongly in my opinion, of standardizing the taste of wine and of pushing it towards tannic over-extraction. It is true that he appreciated rich, well-structured wines, but in this, he was close to the opinion of Emile Peynaud. However, he sometimes went a little too far: tasting one day with Robert Mondavi a vintage of his beautiful Cabernet Sauvignon Reserve, he gave it an average mark, while Mondavi praised the finesse of his wine… 'For you, it's finesse; for me, it's dilution!' he said.

He was criticized for tasting provisional samples and making final judgements before the official blends were made – particularly because, when presented En Primeur, winemakers can easily show whatever sample they wish. Parker sometimes revised his judgements, but for the market and particularly for En Primeur sales, it was his first note that counted. The danger of early scoring is that the tasting takes too much account of the stoutness of the young wine, scored more on its concentration and power than on its finesse and distinction. The strongest, richest wines almost always fare better, to the detriment of the more delicate, aromatic wines that go on to express themselves with age.

Many also criticized his support for the so-called 'garage wines', which emerged, especially on the Right Bank of Bordeaux (from Saint-Emilion and Pomerol), in the 1990s, when a number of small vineyards began to position themselves as luxury products. Robert Parker's scouts would find them, and a high score from the guru would see them reach new heights of fame. As a result, the wines became a means of affirming social status, and were also a potentially rewarding financial investment – a level of speculation that saw some unknown labels almost disconnected from the world of drinks. One day, Jean-François Moueix, from Pétrus, met me at the airport in Mérignac and asked: 'Have you seen the latest issue of *The Wine Advocate*? I can't believe it, I've never heard of most of the wines!'

It must be said that the garage wines, sometimes imitated by some of the more established estates, tended to be body-builders that did well in comparative tastings but were not easy to drink... One critic – English of course – said that 'drinking them is a feat and that punishment is part of the fun!' In order to achieve 'the Parker grade', winemakers began to reduce yields, accentuate selection and reduce the volumes on the market, thus making the wine more concentrated, rarer and more expensive.

Enologix, a company created by Leo McCloskey, a specialist in environmental chemistry at the University of California, went so far as to invent a mathematical model in the 1990s that could predict, and therefore construct, the Parker performance. Its premise: 'Predictive analytics: for luxury wine-growing and market performance'!

NEVERTHELESS, BOB WAS A TRUE WINE LOVER. Genuine, direct, sometimes enthusiastic, he wanted wine to reflect its place of origin and to be as natural as possible. He readily admitted that he liked the richest, most opulent wines, which were destined to age well. Contrary to his reputation, he believed that too much oak masked the fruit and took exception to the criticism that he was attracted to highly oaked bottles.

To highlight the contribution of his work to French viticulture, François Mitterrand made him a Knight of the Order of Merit. His successor, Jacques Chirac, not wanting to be outdone, awarded him the Knight's Cross of the Legion of Honour in 1995.

A few months later, I myself had the honour of receiving this decoration, on the initiative of the Mayor of Bordeaux, Alain Juppé, whom I often meet at events organized by the Commanderie du Bontemps, of which I am a Grand Master. It was given to me by my old friend, the musketeer of the Gers, André Daguin. I am proud of this distinction, but, like many Frenchmen, no doubt out of modesty, I did not wear the ribbon.

I hosted Bob Parker some time after I received the award. When he left me, he congratulated me on my decoration, which he had heard about, and added discreetly: 'You're not wearing it?' I guess he didn't understand my attitude. It is clear that he attached great importance to this mark of recognition from our country. He was obviously proud of it, and rightly so. Ashamed, I immediately had the little red ribbon, whose absence had shocked him, sewn into the lapel of all my jackets.

OVER TIME, IN PARALLEL WITH HIS WORK as a critical journalist, Bob created RobertParker.com, which became a very popular website. He gave lectures here and there and sometimes ventured into the commercial organization of events and tasting, working and travelling constantly, but as the years have gone by, his health has deteriorated and he finds it increasingly difficult to walk. In 2015, Bob sold the 40-year-old *Wine Advocate* to a group of investors from Singapore. It is now owned by *The Michelin Guide* in France.

Robert Parker has not really been replaced. No other critic has been able to express their analyses with such simplicity and talent or to impose their views with such authority and clarity. For some 30 years, he was the most effective promoter of wine consumption in the United States. He usually steered his admirers in the right direction, and his influence extended far beyond the borders of his country. I, for one, have infinite respect for him and the work he has done.

21 Cordeillan-Bages

A STONE'S THROW FROM the village of Bages, an old wine estate was surrounded by a few houses in the hamlet of Cordeillan. It used to produce wine under the name of Château Bellevue-Cordeillan-Bages, but did not survive the economic crisis of the 1930s, and its small vineyard had been absorbed by neighbours.

The cellars and the château itself, an elegant chartreuse from the 19th century, were still standing. I knew the place during the war, when it was rented to a Monsieur de Peufeilhoux, director of the Shell refinery in Pauillac. His sons, Philippe and François, were around my age and we played together in the small park and the old farm buildings. In the 1960s, the property was sold to Pierre Lardat, owner of a tent factory in Avensan, near Margaux.

In the mid-1980s, hotels worthy of the name were rare in the Médoc: on the quays of Pauillac, the France et Angleterre had aged considerably, and the only modern establishment was the Relais de Margaux, created in 1981 by Alexis Lichine with the support of a Texan financier.

There were barely any good restaurants in the Médoc either. Only Jean-Paul Barbier, a hunting enthusiast, had been able to attract customers to Arcins with his regional and seasonal cuisine, and with his exceptional wit. People came from all over the world to have lunch or dinner at the Lion d'Or and to hear him talk passionately about the Médoc. Jean-Paul had the clever idea of surrounding the room of his restaurant with refrigerated glass racks, a sort of small wine cellar where each producer could store a few bottles. In spring, he served them with Gironde shad with sorrel grilled with vine shoots or roast pigeon, in autumn with hare *à la royale* or harvest thrushes, in winter with Pauillac lamb. A great way to please his wine grower clients and limit his wine list to what was strictly necessary.

One day, in 1986, I set off for Bordeaux, accompanied by a colleague. As we passed through Cordeillan, he said to me in a detached tone: 'It seems that

Father Lardat wants to sell… You should turn it into a hotel or a restaurant…' At the time, we had no reception facilities in Bages, and the hamlet of Cordeillan, surrounded by our vines on all sides, was less than 200 metres away. Not such a crazy idea…

I had never met my neighbour, who kept to himself, but I went to his house a few days later. The park, of more than one hectare, with a tennis court and a swimming pool, was half abandoned and studded with rabbit holes. Pierre Lardat explained that he trained his dogs there to pursue game. He also confirmed his decision to sell, as a result of a serious illness. At the age of 60, he had exhausted the joys of tent-making and wanted to devote the time he had left to his lifelong passion: travelling and hunting in Africa. But the figure he asked for his estate was extremely high, and I was not enthusiastic. He encouraged me to make an offer. Without much thought, I halved his figure. Not surprisingly, he didn't like my proposal, and our conversation ended there.

The next day, I got a phone call: 'I've thought about it… I accept,' said Pierre Lardat. All I had to do was to agree. In July 1986, once all the documents had been signed, I found myself the owner of a pretty chartreuse and a few buildings in a poor state of repair, with the rather vague idea of turning it into a reception annex for Lynch-Bages. I was not sure how to begin. I had good friends who were chefs and I had been lucky enough to stay at several excellent hotels, but I was not in the business.

In the meantime, one Friday afternoon, I received a call from the new owner of Château Phélan Ségur in Saint-Estèphe, Xavier Gardinier, president of Pommery champagne. He explained that he intended to stay in the Médoc often: 'Françoise and I would be happy to meet you and your wife. We have to leave for Reims tomorrow. I know it's short notice and it's not done, but if you're free for dinner tonight, come and meet us both at the Relais de Margaux.' Like me, Thereza was curious to meet the newcomers, and we accepted their invitation.

Xavier and Françoise Gardinier and their three sons were all extremely welcoming. The couple expressed their desire to participate fully in Médoc life, and over supper we talked about our shared desire to open up our properties to the public. Xavier described his work at Pommery where he received thousands of visitors each year. He told us how he created the restaurant Les Crayères, where he entrusted the cooking to Gérard Boyer who won three stars in the Michelin Guide.

His experience in Champagne seemed too good to miss, and between a rock and a hard place, I proposed that he join the company. Xavier Gardinier wished to become part of the Médoc landscape and I needed someone who immediately understood the mechanics of the operation. He said: 'I am leaving tomorrow, Saturday, for Reims with my personal plane. I will take you… Take your children, they will meet ours at the Château de Louvois.'

I'm not a fan of small planes. In fact, I hate them. But Xavier insisted and Thereza, daughter of an airline pilot, was equally enthusiastic. In the end, we all boarded the Beechcraft the following morning… Once we'd landed safely, Xavier Gardinier showed us the spectacular cellars of Pommery dug into the chalk, and our new friendship deepened over the course of the weekend. Together, we began to study the Cordeillan project. Xavier advised me to contact Pierre-Yves Rochon for the interior design, a specialist architect who worked on the Les Crayères hotel in Reims. He also put me in touch with Joseph Olivereau, president of Relais & Châteaux.

Gradually, the plans for the new hotel were drawn up. A hotel has to far exceed the standards of a house. Everything had to be done: transforming the old vat house into a dining room, creating a professional kitchen, designing and decorating the reception areas, transforming the old barrel cellar into rooms, and finally planting vines.

Xavier and I wanted to give our project an educational dimension. The hunting ground of Mr Lardat's dogs would become, after planting, the site of an open-air ampelography site where guests would be able to observe all the red Bordeaux grape varieties: Merlot, Cabernet Sauvignon, Cabernet Franc, Petit Verdot and Malbec.

Having witnessed the success of the Académie du Vin, created in Paris by the British Steven Spurrier in the 1970s, and fascinated by the work of Kevin Zraly at the Windows on the World Wine School in New York, I was convinced that we, in France, the country of wine, had progress to make. Not only would the future head of Cordeillan need to have a good knowledge of wine, but he or she would also have to be motivated by the desire to share it.

I called on an authority in the profession, Georges Lepré, who had worked at the Ritz in the Place Vendôme, after having been the elite sommelier at Raymond Oliver's landmark restaurant, Le Grand Véfour (both in Paris). That's where I'd met him 20 years earlier. Georges Lepré pointed out two possible candidates: the experienced Philippe Faure-Brac and Pierre Paillardon, winner of the title of 'best young sommelier' in France at the age of 30, who was responsible for the wine list for Gérard Vié, the two-starred chef of the restaurant Les Trois Marches in Versailles.

The first, who had just set up his own business, was not interested. So I travelled to Paris to meet Pierre Paillardon. His wife Danielle, who used to be in charge of the reception of a Relais & Châteaux establishment on the outskirts of Paris, also had some interesting experience. They both liked my project. They accepted my proposal and soon moved to Pauillac where they prepared to open Cordeillan.

First, they had to find an official name for the establishment. Pierre suggested adding Bages to Cordeillan to emphasize the proximity of the two hamlets, and Château Cordeillan-Bages was born. The small demonstration vineyard would produce its own wine, under an original label.

The new director entrusted the kitchen to Jean-François Thillier, a young chef who trained in Roanne with the (three-starred) Troisgros brothers. At the same time, Pierre Paillardon set up the Bordeaux School programme. Its objective was to offer amateurs and professionals alike the opportunity to improve their knowledge of wine.

We obtained recognition from the Prefecture of the Gironde as an establishment with professional training status. To support our initiative, I brought together a dozen Médoc wine growers in an association we called 'Les Amis de l'Ecole du Bordeaux'. Its members supported our initiative by providing wines for the tastings or by offering a generous welcome to their properties, each one finding its own benefit in this common action.

We opened Cordeillan-Bages in June 1989, on the occasion of the Vinexpo exhibition. Pierre and Danielle Paillardon spared no effort and the restaurant quickly took its place in the Médoc gastronomic landscape, alongside the Relais de Margaux, which it soon rivalled. For the Paillardon couple, the first years were trying and their very young children did not leave them much time to relax. Pierre then wanted to change career direction in order to find a more peaceful family life. I offered him the position of négociant left vacant by Pierre Montagnac, who had embarked on a personal adventure after having participated in the growth of our trading company, the *Compagnie Médocaine des Grands Crus*.

I therefore had to find a replacement for him at Cordeillan-Bages. I was advised to speak to one of the historic members of Relais & Châteaux, Alain Rabier, who ran Château d'Artigny near Tours, as he might be able to help. I described to him the profile of the professional I thought was necessary: a young man, 30 to 35 years old, competent in the hotel and restaurant business and passionate about wine, capable of accompanying us in an original project.

Above: Château Cordeillan-Bages, where our Relais & Châteaux restaurant received two Michelin stars under chef Thierry Marx, then Jean-Luc Rocha.

Below: Arnaud le Saux in charge of the Cordeillan cellar, renowned for the richness and variety of its wines.

'I think I know your candidate,' exclaimed Alain Rabier. 'Me!' I was far from expecting his reaction and I didn't feel that he corresponded to my expectations. Caught off guard, I thought quickly: I absolutely must find someone and I have no alternative. Why not give it a try? In a year or two, the person I'm talking to will have reached retirement age. If things go wrong, they won't last.

We quickly reached an agreement. In 1995, Alain Rabier moved into a flat next to Cordeillan. His extensive experience in the hotel business proved invaluable. He reorganized Cordeillan-Bages and put the establishment on the right track for a new start. Alain had never used a computer, but his sense of hospitality and a job well done made up for his lack of computer skills. In order to affirm the excellence of the table, he recruited a chef in Nîmes, Thierry Marx, who was unknown at the time. An inventive cook and excellent communicator, Thierry quickly took charge of the kitchen. He praised 'unstructured' cuisine and embraced the emerging fashion for molecular techniques that combined aesthetics, chemical processes and flavours. As good at speaking as he was behind the stove, he soon made a name for himself in the small world of gastronomic criticism and was awarded his first Michelin star in 1996, followed by a second in 2000. In just a few years, Thierry Marx succeeded in establishing Cordeillan as one of France's top restaurants and a leader in the region.

LESS THAN 200 METRES from the Relais & Châteaux, the village of Bages, once built by wine growers, had remained untouched by the revival of the 1980s, except for the Lynch-Bages cellars, which had been completely renovated, and the house where I have lived since 1983.

Our technical installations were satisfactory, except for one thing: for the storage of our bottles, we still used old cellars scattered around the village, or converted garages. Our storage capacity was not big enough. In 2002, I asked our architect, Arnaud Boulain, to think about adding a functional room to house our production in good conditions.

He came back to us a few weeks later with a plan of Bages showing the outline of a new building: 'Here is the 2,000 square metres you need.' I noticed dotted lines inside the rectangle. 'These are houses,' the architect explained, 'they are unoccupied, but I checked with the town hall, they belong to Lynch-Bages.'

It's true. For 50 years, the endemic wine crisis had led the inhabitants of Bages to leave the village, one after the other. Most often, the departures were accompanied by an offer made to my grandfather, my father, and then to me to buy a few rows of vines, a farmyard or a vegetable garden: 'You'll have to take the house with it…' they'd say. Or what was left of it, namely a hovel in poor condition. By the year 2000, Bages was a ghost town: its houses in ruins, the streets deserted.

We certainly needed a new warehouse, but I couldn't bring myself to see more than half of the village where I spent my childhood disappear. We had to build it somewhere else. Our site in Macao, where we have now set up our négociant company, answered the problem. We just had to accept the idea that our bottles would be stored 20 kilometres away after bottling. On reflection, it was obvious that wine growing and logistics were two activities that have little in common. Of course, we had to continue bottling in Bages, but it was enough to keep the 'property stock' and our personal cellar on site. On the other hand, I could only see advantages in dedicating a specific location to the management and logistics of the commercial stock. In addition, Macao, conveniently located halfway between Pauillac and Bordeaux, was directly accessible by the main road, which facilitated handling and the comings and goings of trucks. We decided to build a 7,000-square-metre warehouse where we could control the temperature and humidity and store the bottles in perfect conditions.

What to do then with the village of Bages? It was impossible to leave things as they were.

I knew that Lynch-Bages was one of the rare Grands Crus of the Médoc to be identified with a village. If we could revive this one, it could become a singular tourist destination. I was inspired by the idea of Michel Guérard in Eugénie-les-Bains, Georges Blanc in Vonnas and Georges Dubœuf in Romanèche-Thorins. For inspiration, I went to visit all three sites.

In Eugénie-les-Bains, the activities – including the restaurants – are centred around a thermal spa. Transforming a sleepy Landes village into a capital of well-being and gastronomy, Michel and Christine Guérard made it the 'first slimming village in France', as a sign at the entrance to the town proudly proclaims, where visitors flock by the thousands. In Vonnas, the Blanc family created shops, a café, a grocery shop, bakeries and a cinema around the family inn… The 'Hameau du Vin', installed by Georges Dubœuf in the disused Romanèche railway station, focused on vines and wine. Almost like an amusement park, the Hameau attracts visitors of all ages who come from far and wide, in busloads, to familiarize themselves with the Beaujolais region. These projects, which are very different in spirit, have managed to combine intelligent tourism with the development of their promoters' main activity.

An aerial view of the restored village of Bages.

For my part, I wanted to open the doors of our cellars to the public and associate them with the flavours of the world. My visits to the Landes and the Lyon region made me realize that a similar approach could transform the hamlet of my childhood into a welcoming and convivial site, and would give new life to a place that is dear to me. Neither Disneyland, nor a Gallic village, but a place of life, culture and meetings around wine.

At the end of 2002, we launched a renovation programme that lasted several years. We demolished some ruins to create a central square. On the site of one of the old wells, we built a beautiful fountain. We replaced the potholes with old cobblestones from the renovations of the historic centre of downtown Bordeaux. The beautiful stone building that used to house the former Gasqueton haberdashery was the first to be renovated. The building was old, but large and well suited to being turned into business premises. Thierry Marx and I had one thing in common: we both come from a family of bakers. We agreed on the need for a bakery in a village. In the square, I wanted a shop near the Lynch-Bages cellar tour, as I'd seen in Australian 'cellar doors' or Californian wineries. An old, half-collapsed tractor shed would do the trick. Finally, no village can survive without its café. We found its place in the old wine growers' cottages where, in 1945, the group of German prisoners-of-war were housed.

The only thing left to do was to give our establishment a name. In Rueyres, in the Lot, the birthplace of my family, a distant cousin owned a Café Lavinal, named after my maternal grandmother. So now we have our own Café Lavinal… a quick success and a must-visit in the Médoc. I am particularly happy to see all

Above: Where to find bicycles to visit the Médoc? At Le Comptoir d'Andréa on the square in Bages.

Below: No village can survive without its café: on the Place de Bages sits the busy Café Lavinal, in homage to my maternal ancestors, who once ran an inn in the Lot.

Above: On the village square, the Bages' Bazaar is the meeting place for curious tourists and gourmets.

Below: In homage to my grandfather's first profession, we set up a bakery in the restored village of Bages. My daughter Kinou plays the baker…

sorts of people come together there: tourists and professionals of all nationalities, Médoc families, executives from neighbouring estates, Bordeaux wine merchants or brokers… All languages are spoken. It is precisely what I dreamed of.

At the same time, we renovated the substandard housing. In total, 12 abandoned houses were brought back into use. In the village square, we created 'Le Cercle Lynch-Bages', where several rooms equipped with high-performance audiovisual equipment are able to host tastings and conferences.

To complete the renovation of the village, we refurbished the old cellars and vats of Haut-Bages Averous, unused for more than 30 years, for a new venture, VINIV Bordeaux. This company offers wine lovers the opportunity to create their own wine, blending grapes from appellations on both the Left and Right Banks of Bordeaux. To ensure the quality of the wine, each client is accompanied by a renowned winemaker, often including members of the Lynch-Bages winemaking team. VINIV winemakers form a tight-knit, privileged club whose members are able to be a winemaker for a vintage, sometimes longer, and who establish a strong link with Bordeaux and its châteaux. It has become a natural extension of my theory of creating a network of friends around the world, linked by their love of wine.

We completed our accommodation offer by creating six modern guest rooms, a spacious dining room and a comfortable reception area at Les Ormes de Pez, in the 19th-century house surrounded by a vast park. With Cordeillan-Bages, our project quickly attracted attention. The village of Bages has become an essential stop on the Bordeaux châteaux route. You can sit down at the Café Lavinal, shop at the Bages' Bazaar, book a tasting course at Le Cercle Lynch-Bages or blend wine with VINIV. Or hire a bike from Le Comptoir d'Andréa to ride the back roads of the Médoc. The number of tourists is increasing and has been well over 20,000 per year since 2010.

In Cordeillan, Thierry Marx flirted with the third Michelin star for 10 years. We did our best to accommodate his quest for the culinary Grail, but it was difficult to penetrate the secrets of the Michelin inspectors and he did not receive the ultimate trophy in Pauillac. Thierry Marx, who never made a secret of his attraction to far-flung horizons, left our establishment in 2011 for a Parisian palace. His second-in-command, Jean-Luc Rocha, a successful *Meilleur Ouvrier de France*,[1] took over from him. His cuisine is contemporary,

---

[1] The *Meilleur Ouvrier de France* is a prestigious award honouring Frances's finest artisans and craftsmen. In a competition held every four years, contenders must 'reach perfection'.

creative and yet reassuring, and he brilliantly retained the stars he won in 2000. For several years, Jean-Luc delighted our customers… until 2017, when, like his predecessor, he gave in to the attraction of the city lights and chose to leave Pauillac for Paris. His replacement, Julien Lefebvre, a student of Mathieu Pacaud in Paris, kept Cordeillan among the Michelin elite for two more years, but at the end of the 2019 season, he returned to his native Normandy. Covid-19 forced us to close the establishment in early 2020.

The enforced truce imposed by the Covid epidemic has allowed us to reflect on the future. Cordeillan has just celebrated its 30th anniversary… For three decades, we have put significant resources at the service of several talented individuals and have vigorously supported their race to the stars. One after the other, once they had achieved media success, the chefs rushed off elsewhere to exploit the fame they had acquired in Pauillac, leaving us with a feeling of frustration. Once things are back in order post-pandemic, we will continue to promote the combination of wine and the art of the table, enriched by a wine cellar with 1,800 references, built by Arnaud Le Saux, a head sommelier who knows better than anyone how to advise our clients. All the major wine regions of the world are represented. In 2018, the *Wine Spectator* crowned the Cordeillan-Bages wine list with a coveted 'Award of Excellence'.

We are more determined than ever to open our wineries to visitors and let them experience the daily lives of the men and women behind the labels. We will continue to focus on hospitality, comfort and quality of accommodation. We won't forget our goal of putting wine at the centre of the game.

You're almost there! The sign showing you're arriving in Bages…

The vineyards are best explored by bicycle – this way, you won't miss any of the details.

22 In the East, Something New

IN THE 1980s, I TRIED to spread the word. Often accompanied by châteaux friends, I travelled a lot… In the United States and Canada, as I have already described, but also all over Europe. We presented our wines in Brussels, Amsterdam, Munich, Copenhagen, Geneva and more. We didn't forget France, and we sometimes met in Paris, Lyon or Reims. Indeed, in the same way that they drink a lot of champagne in Bordeaux, the people of Champagne are fans of our wines. In 1988, in order to strengthen our relations, we offered a dinner at the restaurant Les Crayères, to which we invited the directors of the main Champagne houses. They all came and welcomed us cordially, a little surprised to see the people of Bordeaux bursting onto their land.

That evening, I made friends with Jean-Claude Rouzaud, president of Roederer, who phoned me a few weeks later: one of his clients, the Cathay Pacific company, wanted to buy Bordeaux wines from slightly older vintages, and they were looking for a Bordeaux contact. Perhaps I can help him?

I had never travelled in Asia, and didn't know Cathay Pacific. Rouzaud told me that it was a British-owned airline based in Hong Kong, and gave me a name and a telephone number. I promised to do my best…

A certain Willi Scherrer confirmed his company's interest in offering wines of various vintages to first-class passengers. Their competitor in Southeast Asia, Singapore Airlines, offered Bordeaux *Crus Classés* which were very attractive to customers. Cathay Pacific did not want to be outdone. The Singaporean airline generally offered fairly young wines, while its Hong Kong competitor was looking for bottles that had aged a few years. Willi Scherrer, who was in charge of the operation, was advised by Roy Moorfield, an Australian specialist journalist who brought his experience as a taster.

We had enough stock to offer around 10 vintages of Lynch-Bages. I sent our samples to the other side of the world, insisting that all the years be selected, whereas the team at Cathay wanted to limit their purchase to only well-noted vintages. Another detail: we would have to accept payment in yen, a Japanese currency that seemed quite exotic to me. The stakes were high, because the volumes envisaged were considerable. Finally, in the autumn of 1989, after a lot of back and forth, we were ready to make an agreement for just over… 22,000 cases! We were successful: the order was spread over all the vintages from 1982 to 1989.

Although I led the negotiation with the client, I did not wish to bypass the Bordeaux trade. A négociant from La Place de Bordeaux would manage deliveries and the possible follow-up of future orders. The wines would be collected over several years, as and when required. Suspicious, the Hong Kong company demanded that the stock be physically isolated in a room where a bailiff from Pauillac, who would hold the key, would be able to regularly check their existence.

The bill was the highest ever issued by Lynch-Bages. It was paid in full and the yen was immediately converted into francs, to our great relief…

In the following years, this transaction proved to be a major asset for the distribution of Lynch-Bages in Asia. From 1990 onwards, the presence of our wine on board Cathay Pacific flights linking Hong Kong to all the major capitals consolidated our position with a select clientele. In Hong Kong, there was a lot of talk about it. The financiers who regularly flew to London (12 hours minimum) invented the 'Lynch-Bages arbitrage'. This involved consuming a volume of Lynch-Bages during the flight to compensate for the higher ticket price. The spin-offs spread throughout Southeast Asia. The reputation of Lynch-Bages accentuated Cathay Pacific's appeal to its customers, and vice versa.

As the contract progressed, our relationship with Cathay Pacific's management grew in confidence. The flight crew, mostly young women of about 10 different nationalities, knew nothing about wine or how to serve it. Our client asked us to train them in this task.

In 1990, for the first time, Thereza and I flew to Hong Kong to teach the flight attendants how to open and serve a bottle of wine properly. This was the first time I had met my Cathay Pacific colleagues in person. The president of the company, the Australian Rod Eddington and his Korean wife Young Sook, received us in their home in a very friendly manner.

This first trip to Hong Kong was like a whirlwind and love at first sight. We admired the city, walked around the bay and discovered a culture that was foreign to us. We explored the Chinese gastronomy in all its trends.

Most of the professionals were English and had relationships with the great London houses. The arrival of a French wine grower did not go unnoticed,

An introduction to wine for Cathay Pacific flight personnel.

which encouraged meetings. The Commanderie de Bordeaux in Hong Kong, run by Vincent Cheung, a well-known lawyer, gave us a warm welcome. We also met Johnny Chan, who presided over the Hong Kong Wine Club. The Commanderie and the Club were both very active and each had about 100 members.

I learned that there was a *Confraria dos Enófilos* in the Portuguese enclave of Macao, of which Filipe Cunha Santos was the *Grão-Mestre*. To reach Macao, it took only an hour to cross the Pearl River Estuary by hydrofoil. We were all the more tempted as Thereza had cousins who had settled there after Mozambique's independence. Filipe Santos introduced us to the sommeliers of the big hotels and restaurants. The rich Chinese players were infatuated with Lafite and Pétrus. A few more modest labels, including ours, were appearing, but the wine market was still in its infancy.

In the mid-1990s, the Asian market was still underdeveloped, with the exception of Japan, which had opened up to our wines towards the end of the 1970s. Bordeaux maintained a modest commercial activity in Hong Kong, but it was weak, even non-existent, in the other countries of the region: Thailand, the Philippines, Indonesia, Vietnam, Cambodia, Taiwan… In continental China, during meals, many alcoholic beverages were served with toasts. Cognac was fashionable, as were beverages made with rice. But they quenched their thirst with tea. In the Middle Kingdom, wine seemed to be a lost cause.

This was without Serge Renaud, an academic whose intervention turned the market upside down. A doctor from Bordeaux, Serge was a specialist in the effects of nutrition on health. His research showed that a reasonable consumption of wine is an effective and pleasant way to prevent cardiovascular disease. In 1990, the echoes of his study reached the United States. Morley Safer, presenter of the popular television programme *60 Minutes*, broadcast the astonishing conclusions: the French population, which does little sport and devours foie gras, confit and cheese, has a much lower heart attack rate than the Americans! A name was given to this anomaly: the 'French Paradox'. Very quickly, the news spread around the world.

The programme contributed to the popularity of wine in the United States. It also had a considerable impact in China, where people are very attentive to all things health-related. In addition, Chinese officials saw the consumption of wine, a moderately alcoholic beverage, as a way to reduce the population's dependence on hard liquor. We were also helped by the fact that, in China, red evokes wealth and happiness… The Chinese began to drink a little wine, red rather than white.

At the same time, new wine distribution companies were emerging. The Hong Kongers were the first to react. Smuggling was the order of the day and many containers of wine ended up on the Chinese coast.

The Chinese market was simmering. Each time I visited Hong Kong, my contacts encouraged me to go and present my wines in 'mainland China' where importers were rapidly extending their distribution network to all the major cities. At the head of the pack were Americans Don Saint-Pierre (ASC), Ian Ford (Summergate), Carl Krug (Montrose) in Shanghai and Beijing, and the Chinese company Aussino which, based in Canton, was enjoying national success.

At the end of 1993, Johnny Chan suggested that I organize a visit to Shanghai and Beijing, where he seemed to know a lot of people. An opportunity arose: a food fair, the HOFEX exhibition devoted to food products and hospitality, was to take place in 1994 in Beijing. Johnny arranged for me to rent a stand where I could present my wines to the visitors.

I didn't expect much from a country where the wine market was still non-existent, but I was excited at the thought of the adventure. Pierre Montagnac, who ran the *Compagnie Médocaine des Grands Crus*, would come with me – as would our wives.

Wherever we went, Johnny was an indispensable guide. In each city on our itinerary, he planned a lecture and tasting. In Canton, our first stop, we wandered through the market, which was said to be one of the most rustic in the country. There were heaps of strange vegetables, improbable fish and all kinds of furry and feathered animals, dead or alive, whole or cut up, including bats nailed to boards. In Canton, almost all animals found their place on a plate. A culture shock, and not exactly appetizing. Nevertheless, we did honour to the local cuisine which harmoniously combined flavours and aromas on steaming plates.

Arriving in Shanghai made a big impression. The city was expanding rapidly; construction sites were everywhere. Day and night, the workers worked in the glow of the spotlights, like scurrying ants… We went for a walk along the Bund, on the banks of the Huangpu. Across in Pudong, on the far side, there rose nothing but the emblematic Shanghai television tower, still surrounded by meadows where cattle grazed peacefully. Another debate organized by Johnny, our mentor, was followed by a tasting and a gastronomic experience where fish, seafood and ginger took centre stage.

We finally arrived in Beijing, where a black limousine awaited us: this was to be our transport for the duration of our stay. On the windscreen, clearly visible from the outside, a sign saying 'State Guest' gave us license to travel anywhere. The welcome dinner brought together about 40 people, all unknown to us. I sat on the right of a lady who seemed to be important. Johnny told me that she represented CEROIL, a giant company specializing in agricultural and food products, which imported wheat, soya, sugar or coffee from all over the world.

Between various meals of lacquered duck, a speciality of the capital, we spent our time sightseeing. At each crossroads, thousands of bicycles would assemble in crowded groups, waiting for the green light to appear. Public hygiene was rudimentary.

After loading a few bottles into the limousine, we set off for the Great Wall, determined to do a public tasting. Once there, dressed as Chinese operetta stars, we offered wine tastings to the tourists walking on the rampart. They all played along and took photos. I think this was the first wine tasting ever organized in this symbolic place. We made friends and had a great time.

The food fair – the supposed purpose of our visit – was held at the World Trade Centre in Beijing, a building complex that included hotels, accommodation and exhibition halls. We had been given a simple stand among other exhibitors. There were various drinks on offer here and there, among which there must have been some wines, but at first glance I could only see us. We

Above: The actress Gong Li (Farewell My Concubine *and many other films*) *appreciates Bordeaux.*
Below: With Pierre Montagnac: we organized the first wine tasting on China's Great Wall.

Above: Bordeaux has found enthusiastic clientele in China…

Below: The imposing barrel cellar at the Great Wall Winery – inspired, no doubt, by the work of architect Ricardo Bofill at Château Lafite.

had a few bottles of Lynch-Bages and Pichon-Longueville for the red wine, and Suduiraut for the white. Assisted by an interpreter, we called out to passers-by who were happy to come and taste. Our visitors communicated their impressions with their faces. We noticed that red wine made people grimace, because the taste of the tannins was so surprising. Sauternes was better received, although most seem to think – and told us – that the alcohol content was very low and that it must be a drink 'for the babies' (sic).

On the plane back home, Pierre and I took stock. The stay was instructive. The people were welcoming and friendly. However, from a professional point of view, the conclusion seemed obvious: maybe one day we would manage to sell some sweet wines in China, but for the reds, there was no significant market.

How wrong you can be!

I TRAVELLED TO CHINA several times, most often accompanied by my wife. We learned to love this huge and endearing country, and its inhabitants who received us with kindness and generosity. With the help of translators, or directly, I was lucky enough to be in contact with wine lovers who wanted to taste our wines or to hear me talk about Bordeaux and my job as a wine grower. The speed of development of Shanghai never ceased to amaze me. On my second visit, there were no longer any meadows or cattle around the Pudong television antenna, but there were buildings, still empty, and the pavements were covered with weeds. The following year, the hotels and offices were fully inhabited and cars had taken over the streets and avenues.

I also visited Chengdu, capital of Sichuan and home of the pandas, where I hosted a wine tasting for the local Communist Party officials. Near Tsingtao, on the China Sea coast, famous for its beer, I discovered the vineyards of Shandong province, which were developing at great speed. I walked through the modern and sometimes overbearingly huge wineries, such as Château Junding. Wineries often owned only a small proportion of the vineyards they operated. The land remained the property of the local farmers who cultivated it collectively. The winemaking centre functioned as a kind of private cooperative, which simply received the grapes at harvest time. The local technicians only gave advice. As a result, the viticultural techniques were not up to the level of oenological science and sometimes peas or cabbages were sown in the middle of the vine rows…

In Hong Kong, I met Judy Chan, a young woman who was actively involved in a vineyard created by her father in the mountainous Shanxi province. We met several times and she invited us to visit her property, Grace Vineyards. I took the opportunity to drop in on the Chans during the 2008 Beijing Olympics, which we attended with Claude Bébéar and some friends. By plane, it was a short hop.

At Judy's, the scenery was superb, the technical facilities good, the accommodation comfortable and the welcome perfect. In contrast to the large estates in Shandong, we were in a family setting reminiscent of a European estate. The property comprised over 100 hectares of well-kept vineyards, and the wine was well known, distributed across both China and Hong Kong. For two days, we rubbed shoulders with the family connections, not least a dozen local party leaders, who bombarded the place with toasts late into the night.

Once we were back in Bordeaux, we received an unusual request: a Chinese company asked us for a quote for 80,000 bottles of red wine to be sold in pharmacies. They provided the label. The French name of the wine, 'Les Amoureuses', was accompanied by two 1900s-style beauties wearing feather hats. Pierre Montagnac did what was necessary.

TOWARDS THE END of the 1990s, in a large hotel in Hong Kong, I presented a few vintages of Lynch Bages and Pichon-Longueville to half a dozen Chinese sommeliers. We had some difficulty in understanding each other and my translators were having difficulty in articulating the names of the wines – the sales prospects were not looking good. 'Repeat after me: Lynch-Bages, Lynch-Bages… Pichon-Longueville, Pichon-Longueville…' The sommeliers played along. I heard: *'Lan Chi Pat, Lan Chi Pat…'* They laughed. They explained to me that this is the name given to our wine by the Hongkongese. It was the name of a famous Cantonese opera singer who died in 1995.

One day I learned from the journalist Lau Chi Sun that the great Lan Chi Pat left his name to a school in Kowloon whose headmistress, Cindy Shi, he knew. Would I agree to offer a few bottles of Lan Chi Pat for the annual meal for teachers and parents? Feeling that I was discharging a moral debt, I agreed, asking to be invited.

I immediately came up with an idea: let's organize a school exchange between Pauillac and Kowloon schools. As soon as Cindy Shi understood that I was ready to finance the operation, she gave me her unconditional agreement. The Master of the local Commanderie de Bordeaux, Vincent Cheung, also helped. Thus, every year, 10 students from the Saint-Jean-de-Pauillac

Above: Thereza and I with Cindy Shi (on my right), director of the Lan Chi Pat school, and Chau Tak-Wai (left), president of Yan Chai, an important Hong Kong organization that brings together hospitals and schools.

school, accompanied by two teachers, head to Hong Kong for a stay of a dozen days. An equivalent group of young Hong Kongers visit us in Pauillac. Since 2007, this exchange has been a success with the pupils of each school and their families, and I am proud of it. It allows young Médoc residents to discover an environment and culture that are very different from their own. As for the Chinese, who live in a crowded city, they rave about the landscapes and the clean air. Unfortunately, we had to suspend the programme in 2020 with the onset of the Covid-19 epidemic, but we are planning to resume it as soon as it is possible to travel again without risk.

The success of the exchange has had unforeseen spin-offs. The Lan Chi Pat school belongs to a network of establishments managed by a Hong Kong charity, Yan Chai, which controls 26 primary and secondary schools, as well as six large hospitals and a dozen retirement homes. This shows its importance at a local level. The board of directors comprises 35 members representing the Hong Kong economic fabric. Its president, elected for only one year, is always an important and generous personality. The members meet every year for a big party, the Yan Chai annual ball, a key event in Hong Kong social life. For the past 10 years, our work in favour of the school has earned us an invitation to host this event. We present our wines to more than 400 guests. Over the years,

Above: Vincent Cheung offers up a Jeroboam of Lynch-Bages at the annual Yan Chai gala dinner.

Below: The great Lan Chi Pat, star of Cantonese opera. In Hong Kong and throughout China, wine lovers use his name, which is easy to pronounce, to refer to our Lynch-Bages wine.

thanks to Lan Chi Pat, we have established friendly relations within social and economic circles that our commercial activity from home would have given us little chance of reaching.

CHINA IS CERTAINLY the Asian country where the demand for Bordeaux Grands Crus has increased the most, becoming the biggest market between 2005 and 2010. But many other markets have opened up to our wines over the last 30 years. The first, from the end of the 1970s, was Japan, where I made several trips. In Tokyo, my first contact was Bernard Leibovich. A French citizen, married to a Japanese woman and perfectly familiar with the local culture, he created Arcane, a company importing quality food products: caviar, champagne and Bordeaux wine. Thanks to Bernard, who knew all the great restaurants of Tokyo, I had the opportunity to get in touch with great Japanese wine lovers, both wine trade professionals and private individuals.

On our first trip, in 1981, we stayed at the Seiyo Hotel, near Ginza, Tokyo's main shopping street. I bought a bicycle at the Takashimaya shop and rode around the city, riding, as is customary, on the pavements among pedestrians. I was impressed by the feeling of safety everywhere, the attention to detail and the friendliness of the Japanese. All the same, it wasn't easy to find your way around the streets, and English signs on the metro were rare.

Shinya Tasaki, Japan's top sommelier, was in charge of the impressive cellar at our hotel restaurant. A few years later (in 1995), he won the competition for the Best Sommelier in the World and became part of the powerful group of Japanese sommeliers that organized regular public wine tastings and competitions and awarded its prizes in baroque ceremonies. Mr Tasaki was one of the country's leading voices and he helped us to understand his country.

During this first trip, I had the opportunity to meet Keizo Saji, president of the powerful Suntory beverage group, producer of sake, beer, whisky, wine and more. A true wine enthusiast, in 1982 President Saji completed the acquisition of Château Lagrange in Saint-Julien, the first Japanese investment in Bordeaux. He then acquired Château Beychevelle, half with the *Mutuelle des Fonctionnaires* (MGF) and half with the group of wine merchants and estates headed by Pierre Castel.

Keizo Saji was the Grand Master of the Commanderie de Bordeaux in Tokyo, where he made great efforts to promote Bordeaux wines. He often stayed at Château Lagrange, and oversaw extensive renovations. Once somewhat neglected, this property became in a few years one of the most beautiful and largest estates of Saint-Julien. Keizo Saji often received his Médoc neighbours, and I saw him regularly during his stays in France.

A perfect host, he became friends with Henri Martin, mayor of the commune and Grand Master of the Commanderie du Bontemps. He helped us to organize many expeditions to Tokyo, Osaka, Fukuoka, Sapporo… I owe him the striking memory of a reception organized by Shu Uemura, founder of the eponymous cosmetics company. This elderly, wise-looking man proposed the most unexpected event ever: dressed in our Commanderie robes, we marched in a procession through the streets of a gigantic shopping complex, splitting the astonished crowd who obviously took us for a mysterious sect and silently moved aside before us. Some bowed in respect.

When we arrived at our destination, we were greeted by Shu Uemura himself, who had opened up for us a beauty institute as large as an airport terminal for our Commanderie ceremony, even while dozens of beauticians were working on their clients. As far as induction ceremonies go, I have rarely experienced a more unusual setting…

FROM 1980 ONWARDS, after Japan but before China, Bordeaux turned its attention to other countries in Southeast Asia. First of all, Singapore, where the wine news was led by a specialized journalist, the influential Ch'ng Poh Tiong, and by the indefatigable Doctor N K Yong, a collector of great wines, always accompanied by his wife Melina, a star cook on local television.

The Commanderie de Bordeaux was very active in Singapore, led by Master Jeremy Ramsay, who represented Rolex watches there. Bordeaux had a beachhead at the Raffles Hotel where a world-renowned week of gastronomy and tastings was held every year. I've participated on several occasions, alongside star chefs such as Frenchman Alain Passard, Swiss Frédy Girardet and American Thomas Keller. I presented my wines and talked about Bordeaux… I sometimes took Thierry Marx, then chef of Cordeillan-Bages, who composed meals inspired by the wines of the Médoc.

In the 1980s, Thailand also opened up to wine. It remained a modest market in terms of volume, but the local high society and the big hotels of Bangkok, the Oriental in particular, under the direction of the legendary Kurt Wachtveitl, became unconditional fans of Bordeaux. Our contacts in Bangkok were facilitated by local importers, first and foremost the IWS company of

Our wine brings joy to life for this Jakarta sommelier...

the Singaporean Seng Tuan Gan and the Swiss Michel Conrad, whose activity extended eastwards to Macao and westwards to the east coast of Africa.

A little later, the rest of Asia began to appreciate wine. There were enthusiastic wine lovers everywhere, including in certain countries with majority Muslim culture such as Malaysia or Indonesia, where important Chinese minorities lived. Everywhere we went we met food lovers who we tried to win over to the Bordeaux cause. In Siem Reap, Cambodia, near the temples of Angkor, I presided over the inauguration of a tasting school where I was asked to prune a vine planted in the middle of the courtyard, in front of the cameras of national television.

To my regret, I have not travelled much in India. There is a wine culture there, inherited from the British Empire, and there is even small production in the Mumbai area and around Bangalore. I can't help but think that India is an emerging market for Bordeaux. From time to time we receive very distinguished Indian visitors who make no secret of their attraction to great Bordeaux. Unfortunately, the Indian government keeps import taxes at a high level, which blocks the development of our exports.

23 Blanc de Lynch-Bages: Villa Bel-Air

LET'S GO BACK to Lynch-Bages, where a new adventure was beginning…

The traditional density of vines in Pauillac or Saint-Estèphe is around 9,000 vines per hectare. Maintaining this density meant that we had to buy large quantities of new plants every year. The deliveries of red grape varieties sometimes included, accidentally, a few plants of white grape varieties (a rare occurence, fortunately), and it was only with the appearance of the first grapes that they revealed their colour.

These vines sometimes escaped being uprooted and remained isolated in the vineyard, where they grew freely. Their fruit ripened a fortnight before the reds, and made us happy when we were children as it was excellent to eat. In September, we would go and hide in the vineyards and, crouching down to escape adult vigilance, we would feast on these bunches of white grapes. The ones that escaped our greed would often be overcome by rot, and when the harvest came, the pickers were instructed to leave them in place, although sometimes they ended up in the vats with the others.

In the 1970s, we used to buy 100 bottles of Château de Launay every summer, a good fruity white wine from Entre-Deux-Mers, which we served to our friends, with oysters and fish, in the family house in Cap Ferret – that is, until 1978, when we had a late harvest with exceptionally good weather in the Médoc.

The weather conditions meant that the white grapes in our Pauillac vineyard, which were usually rotten by that point, remained fresh. On the eve of the harvest, Daniel LLose suggested that I pick the white grapes scattered around the vineyards separately. 'You should make some white wine. Then there'll be no need to buy Château de Launay to accompany your oysters', he suggested. 'I've never made white wine! I have no idea of the technique…' I said. 'I've done a training course at the Duras cooperative. If you want, I'll try!' was his response.

No sooner said than done. Daniel set to work. The white grapes were harvested separately and pressed. The fermentation, carried out off to one side in the vat room, didn't pose any particular problems, and the 1978 harvest produced one barrel, or 300 bottles of the new wine. Keeping things simple, we called it 'Blanc de Lynch-Bages'.

We did the same thing the next year, and soon it became a habit, with a small production of one barrel of Blanc de Lynch-Bages, reserved for family consumption, ready for us to drink the following spring and summer.

We needed to design a label and we took inspiration from Château d'Yquem, where Alexandre de Lur Saluces had the idea of keeping just the name of the château on the front, with all the obligatory administrative data on a back label. I liked its simplicity and Alexandre, with whom I often travelled around the United States, was my friend. I took the liberty of using his idea, hoping that he would not hold it against me.

Ten years passed… In 1988, on the occasion of a routine inspection, the tiny stock of white wine that we kept in a corner of our cellar caught the eye of a particularly zealous customs officer. Despite our protests of good faith (the wine was strictly for family use and was not sold), we were accused of three serious offences: false declaration of grape varieties, false declaration of our harvest, and false declaration of our stock. A triple crime that led to three fines that we paid with great reluctance.

Today, I realize that these fines were a blessing in disguise. The following year, we decided to plant a new vineyard, totally legal, made up of the traditional white grape varieties of Bordeaux.

Lynch-Bages owned a five-hectare plot of woodland in the neighbouring village of Saint-Sauveur, a five-minute drive from our winery, but as it was not located in the commune, it did not qualify for the Pauillac appellation. Moreover, the soil, predominantly clay-limestone, wasn't right for planting traditional Médoc red grape varieties. On the other hand, it seemed to be suitable for the production of excellent white grapes.

Preparing the land was no easy task as it was strewn with large rocks, but we managed to plant equal quantities of Sémillon and Sauvignon Blanc and added a little Muscadelle to flavour the blend. Two years later, in 1990, the small vineyard gave us its first beautiful grapes, and the Blanc de Lynch-Bages was born, officially this time.

At this point, in 1990, there were very few white wines produced in the Médoc, although there had been some in the past. I once tasted a white Lafite, a 1937 vintage I think, which was a little disappointing. Most of the white Médoc vines disappeared with the *appellation contrôlée* laws in 1935, with the exception of Château Loudenne's, an honourable white, and a few small but distinctive productions such as Pavillon Blanc from Château Margaux and Caillou Blanc from Château Talbot, although as there was (and is) no white Médoc appellation, all these wines are simply marked with the name Bordeaux.

We offered our newborn to the Bordeaux brokers, who presented it to our usual buyers. It was received politely, but few took action. Faced with this lack of enthusiasm, I submitted it to Ab Simon in New York. Out of friendship, he placed a timid order, explaining to me that Bordeaux, whether we like it or not, for American customers… was red!

The start was slow, especially as the second harvest, in 1991, was almost totally destroyed by frost. With a normal production in 1992, the quality was recognized and the commercial reception improved. I had the satisfaction, two or three years later, to hear Ab Simon tell me that he had sold the little he had bought from us. He wanted to double or even triple his allocation! Unfortunately, everything was now sold, I told him with a little irony.

But I promised to make an effort in the future – something that was possible when we increased the size of our white vineyard, which now covers about 10 hectares.

IN 1976, I WAS CONTACTED by Dominique Guillot de Suduiraut, owner in the Graves region of the excellent Château Magence in Saint-Pierre-de-Mons, near Langon. He was interested in launching a viticultural research project, harnessing the potential of the private sector to build on work carried out by the National Institute of Agronomic Research at its Château Grande Ferrade estate near Bordeaux. In this, he was supported by Lucien Lurton, from Château Brane-Cantenac, in Margaux, as well as by Jean Perromat, a wine grower in the Bordeaux appellation and one of the leading figures in the *Fédération des Grands Vins de Bordeaux*.

Together, this group – all of whom I greatly respected – imagined a model farm where new techniques in viticulture would be tested. The idea had been in the air for a long time, and an opportunity had presented itself. Guillot de Suduiraut told me that a property was for sale in Saint-Morillon, near La Brède, home of the philosopher Montesquieu, very well situated on a small hill at the exit of the village. The quality of the soil was perfect for growing vines.

It was about 60 hectares in size, not planted with vines, in a single block around the château, a 18th-century Bordeaux chartreuse. Apparently, it had once been an excellent vineyard, but was ravaged by the frost of February 1956, and Gaston Duthuron, its owner and a distinguished intellect, did not have the courage to replant. He now intended to keep the house but sell the land and the farm buildings, the wine storehouses and a beautiful old stable, all in rather poor condition.

Gaston Duthuron's estate seemed ideal to host the model farm that Guillot de Suduiraut and his friends dreamed of. They had the idea, but they did not have the money to make it happen. They therefore organized an En Primeur auction at Christie's (London) of wine from the 1975 harvest. Owners interested in the project were invited to contribute one or two barrels. Seventy-five Bordeaux wine growers, including ourselves, gave their support. Thus, the *Société Civile de Bel-Air* was born. The money collected in London allowed the acquisition of the estate, but was not sufficient to set up operations. This required major investments: preparation of the land, planting, fitting out the buildings, and so on. The instigators of the project then turned to public institutions to finance these operations. For several years, they hunted for subsidies, which proved unsuccessful, and the project slowly fell asleep. We found ourselves co-owners, with 74 other wine growers, of a beautiful, unused estate in the Graves…

In 1987, after years of silence, Dominique Guillot de Suduiraut got back in touch. He announced the death of Gaston Duthuron, and said that his heirs did not intend to keep the house of Bel-Air. The sale opened the possibility of reconstituting the property in its entirety. Unfortunately, the *Société Civile de Bel-Air* was penniless, its managers having long since abandoned their initial project, and there was no longer any talk of a model farm. Guillot de Suduiraut brought the shareholders together. They all agreed: the vineyard land must be sold. Preferably to one of us, who could, by buying the château, restore the unity of the property. Were any of us interested? Two or three of us raised our hands.

It goes without saying that the purchase of the *Société Civile* only made sense if the château could be bought, and vice versa. After a few months of complicated discussions, we signed the purchase of the Duthuron property and the land held by the Bel-Air company simultaneously. More precisely, we bought the shares of 72 of our co-owners. Only two of them were reluctant: Jean Perromat, who said he was interested in remaining part of the adventure, and my friend Thierry Manoncourt who, I don't know why, clung to his only share on the pretext that his mother, who was now in her 90s, never wanted to sell anything!

At the beginning of 1988, we found ourselves the owners of a reconstituted estate, without a single vine, and with a raft of unusable buildings. Our first task was to establish a planting programme, but we immediately came up against an intractable problem: the **Administration (the official body overseeing winemaking), under pressure f**rom certain representatives of the profession, had decided a few months earlier not to accept any more transfers of 'planting rights'. Until then, there had been a real market for these rights, which could be acquired from wine growers who owned them and did not use them. The transfer from farm to farm had been perfectly acceptable – but this was no longer the case.

Without rights, no planting was possible. In Bel-Air, we were therefore stopped in our tracks. Luckily, we had so much to do at Lynch-Bages and Ormes de Pez that I simply decided we should just wait for another, more favourable, administrative environment to come along.

A few months later, I spoke to a wine grower friend from the Graves region, Francis Boutemy, who was a member of that region's chapter of the Commanderie du Bontemps. He recommended that I consult the department of viticulture in Bordeaux. Daniel LLose, who was sent to the offices, returned optimistically: 'The administrative agents say that there is a perfectly legal way to proceed with new plantings. All you have to do is to have recourse to the "farm lease". The farmer plants – or has the land planted – on land he has leased, using rights he owns. The vine follows the fate of the land on which it is planted. If the lease is terminated, the owner of the land then becomes the owner of the vineyard.'

Not only did the officials indicate the correct procedure to be followed, but they offered to put us in touch with owners of planting rights who did not intend to use them. These are generally wine growers who are abandoning their vineyards, either due to age or financial difficulties. All that is needed is to lease the land where the planting is to take place, then terminate the lease a year or two later, before the first harvest. The owner of the land then becomes – in the most legal way possible – the owner of the vineyard. Admittedly, it's a little complicated, but this was the advice all over France at the time.

At Château Bel-Air, as we needed more than the 20 hectares of planting rights in our portfolio, we followed this approach in 1989 for 36 hectares. Approximately half of the vines we planted with white varieties, with the first harvest in September 1991, and began to plan for general renovations and purchasing of equipment for the estate.

A year after planting, the powers-that-be had an about-face and decided that all leases used in this way were 'fictitious', and therefore constituted fraud. They sent agents to every replanted plot and began to draw up infringement

Villa Bel-Air: our vineyard in the Graves where we produce very good white wines!

reports. There were more than 100 in the Gironde department alone. The wave swept through all the French appellations, from Beaujolais to the Loire Valley, where the same problem had been dealt with in the same way, always obligingly, by the representatives of the State.

What happened? A certain number of wine growers took a dim view of their colleagues succeeding in expanding their vineyards, while they themselves were in difficulty. The leaders of certain wine unions, those of the Médoc and Bordeaux appellations in particular, gave in to the pressure of their members.

Other organizations, first and foremost the Young Farmers or the Gironde Wine Growers' League, an association born in the vineyards of Blaye, joined the protest. The debate took an unpleasant turn and became downright political and caricatural: the small guys, who were suffering, set against the big ones, who wanted to expand.

This was the argument presented by a delegation to Minister Michel Charasse. The National Institute of Designations of Origin (INAO) was not neutral. Its president – or rather its presidents, as they changed along the way – tried not to upset anyone but the deputy director general, in charge of the legal department, took a firm stand against the accused. She used the full extent of her powers and insisted that the wines produced could only be sold if accompanied by an approval certificate issued by the INAO, something that prevented an amicable settlement for many years.

In 1991, the reports drawn up by the Administration were transmitted to the Public Prosecutor's Office. The latter entrusted the Bordeaux Regional Criminal Investigation Department (SRPJ) with the task of conducting the investigation. One-hundred-and-twenty-six farmers, as well as the tax inspector in office at the time of the transfers, were questioned. The investigation revealed that, when consulted before the replanting, the central administration in Paris had not expressed any criticism of the validity of our operation. Nor had the services been taken by surprise: everything had been regularly carried out, recorded and checked.

At the beginning of 1992, the conclusion of the police investigation is worth quoting: 'The tax authorities, through their silence, their opinions and even their actions, initially endorsed the procedure. This makes its current approach of denunciation ambiguous, to say the least.' On the basis of this investigation, the Public Prosecutor's Office refused to proceed.

Michel Charasse, however, wanted a public trial – largely because he was in an ongoing dispute with his own agents – and at the end of 1992, disregarding the results of the police investigation, the Directorate General of Taxes used the direct summons procedure in order to prosecute 11 offending wine growers, including myself, in the criminal court. Among more than a hundred wine growers who had used the procedure, we formed a first contingent – largely because we had terminated our leases without waiting for the first harvest, a few months after planting, at the request of the tax officials.

I knew most of my co-accused well. Among them, some well-known personalities in Bordeaux: André Lurton and Pierre Castel. I was in good company. At the Bordeaux courthouse, at the end of 1992, a little intimidated, I went to the dock. The bailiff said to me with a smile and an air of apology: 'Not you, Sir... You stay with the public!' I was naively convinced that the prosecution would turn up short and that we would be acquitted. However, our lawyer, an excellent jurist but a poor pleader, was not convincing enough. In May 1993, after a long deliberation, we were all condemned to pay a fine and, above all, to grub up all the vines we had planted. The thought was devastating. If the judgement was carried out, it would be a major investment reduced to nothing and the financial loss would weaken our entire structure. We had to appeal.

While the wheels of justice turned, the vines kept growing – and wine had to be made. The uncertainty caused by the action of the Administration had obviously blocked our projects, and we had to improvise. Daniel Llose, assisted by Guy Delestrac, recruited to manage the Bel-Air operation, worked miracles. We stored the wines produced in makeshift installations, and even in the homes of our colleagues.

It was not until May 1994 that the case finally came before the Bordeaux Court of Appeal. We changed lawyers and entrusted our case to Monsieur Lecoq, from Libourne, who proved to be brilliant. The debates confirmed what everyone already knew, namely that the Administration was perfectly aware of the practice of using rural leases and that it had never opposed it. Better still, multiple testimonies showed that the wine-growing department officials, armed with instructions from the central services, guided the wine growers to complete the formalities. The climax was reached when a wine grower, whom no one in the room knew, told how the services indicated to him the procedure to follow, before revealing that, as a wine grower in his spare time, he was himself a tax inspector. His office was on the same floor as those who advised him. The president of the court could not hide his amazement.

In its judgment of June 30th 1994, the Court of Appeal acquitted us all. Of course, the Administration, mortified by the image given of its services during the hearings, and accompanied by the INAO, lodged an appeal in cassation.

Jean-Louis Trocard, president of the FDGS, was torn. Only Bruno Prats, then president of the *Conseil des Crus Classés en 1855*, had the courage to defy – in writing – the resentment of some colleagues and advise them to leave it at that. He was not listened to.

At the same time, the INAO maintained the attitude it had had since 1991. Without a shadow of justification, the Institute continued to refuse to issue the documents necessary for marketing the wines produced. Bypassing her president, the deputy director general declared that she would only bow to the order of the administrative court, which was confirmed on appeal. She added that this injunction would have to be obtained for each particular case. And for each vintage.

Eventually, the entire affair began to attract the attention of professional, administrative and political leaders who found it difficult to accept that wine growers who acted in good faith and avoided the disappearance of vineyards and the loss of planting rights (which expired after eight years) should be pilloried in this way. On our side was the new mayor of Bordeaux, Alain Juppé, the president of the CIVB, Jean-Paul Jauffret, then his successor Hubert Bouteiller, the interregional director of customs, Jean Claude Lasserre, and senator Gérard

César, president of the largest cooperative cellar in Gironde. They tried to rally the parties concerned through numerous interventions both in Bordeaux and at the Ministry. I even went so far as to meet one of our toughest opponents at night in the back room of a village café... and eventually these discussions bore fruit. In 1995, a text was accepted by all parties, which put an end to a conflict that had lasted too long. It would serve as a model for the settlement of the dispute in the other wine-producing regions of France.

What did the protocol say? Our opponents were ruthless. The agreement provided for a tax fine of 3,000 francs per hectare per year between the date of planting and the date of the judgement. In addition – and this was the most painful part – the grubbing up of vines on an area equivalent to the planted area, in the Gironde department, but not necessarily in the same appellation, according to complex calculation methods, and within a maximum of five years. In return, the approval certificates would be released by the INAO, thus authorizing the marketing of the 1990 to 1994 harvests.

Strangled for five years, we were prepared to accept almost anything to end the nightmare.

We got on with it. We were able to acquire an abandoned vineyard in Saint-Louis-de-Montferrand, in the Bordeaux appellation, through the land agency SAFER (the *Société d'Aménagement Foncier et d'Etablissement Rural*), a semi-public organization that controls the transactions of agricultural land in France. This allowed us to pay the penalties imposed on us in 1996, and later lease this bare land to a local wine grower who caused us endless problems. But that is another story…

Château Bel-Air took years to get right, but eventually produced very good white and red wines. We built modern cellars and a vat room, recycling metal vats from Lynch-Bages after 1998, and using our own distribution system through the *Compagnie Médocaine des Grands Crus*. Château Bel-Air, renamed 'Villa Bel-Air' after its elegant chartreuse, became a flagship product in its category.

Twenty-five years after the event, I still do not understand why we were targeted by so many people, with so much animosity and desire to harm. What is certain is that the whole episode, which left a deep impression on me, took away any desire I may have had to enter politics.

24 Saint-Emilion, Pomerol, Margaux, Sauternes and Pauillac

AXA-MILLESIMES WAS GROWING fast. Château Franc-Mayne, a classified growth in Saint-Emilion – one of the two properties AXA acquired before Pichon-Longueville – was placed under my responsibility. The second, Clos de L'Arlot, in Burgundy, had remained independent, with Jean-Pierre de Smet in place as winemaker.

Franc-Mayne had a small, well-placed, seven-hectare vineyard surrounding a lovely house tastefully renovated by Claude Bébéar's wife, as well as an old coaching inn – the perfect guesthouse, which would later be opened to the public. Like other properties on the Saint-Emilion plateau, it had a spectacular network of underground galleries, former quarries cut into the thick layer of limestone. This was an underground labyrinth that we used in part for the ageing of the wines and also for touring visitors, who enjoyed their lessons in history and geology.

Franc-Mayne was well managed on site by Rafael Herrera, a solid winemaker. We hardly had to intervene. The wines were good, if a little rustic. With hindsight, I think it's possible that Franc-Mayne was affected by trichloroanisole pollution – a problem that scientists later showed could arise from the treatment of wood used for the construction of cellars and vats, and that could cause certain taste defects in wine. However, in 1987 we had neither the reasons nor the technical means to investigate this. Several years later, after the sale of Franc-Mayne to a Belgian wine merchant, I learned that the latter had decided to rebuild the entire structure of the cellars. I believe that my successor made the right diagnosis and was able to eliminate a weakness that my team and I had not been able to discern.

Meanwhile, the French insurance industry continued its great manoeuvres. The *Compagnie du Midi*, which had succeeded in purchasing Château Cantenac-Brown instead of AXA in 1987, found itself under attack on the stock exchange by the Italian insurance giant Generali.

In 1988, to save his independence, Bernard Pagézy, president of the *Compagnie du Midi*, had no choice but to call his rival Claude Bébéar to the rescue. The association didn't last long. To everyone's surprise, Bernard Pagézy was dismissed at the AGM by the very man whose help he had asked for, and the entire *Compagnie du Midi* fell into the lap of AXA. These Parisian events had little to do with the Bordeaux vineyards, but they had a consequence: in 1989, AXA became the owner of Château Cantenac-Brown and immediately integrated it into AXA-Millésimes.

Since the failed purchase in 1987, Cantenac-Brown had changed a lot. It was no longer the distressed property I visited. During its two years of management, the *Compagnie du Midi* had pulled out all the stops. I found a modern facility: refurbished barrel cellars in refurbished buildings, and, above all, a brand-new vat room. We only needed to improve the temperature-control system. The vineyard was in good condition.

The team, however, had to be reorganized. Bertrand du Vivier's son, Aymar, who had always lived in his father's shadow, took over the management of the estate. Full of good will, but unsuited to the job, he was replaced by José Sanfins, the brother of a wine grower from Lynch-Bages, who had a degree in viticulture-oenology.

In order to improve the financial situation, the *Compagnie du Midi* had recruited Jean Calvet, well known in Bordeaux and unemployed since the collapse of the 'Grande Maison Calvet' a few years earlier. Bypassing the traditional Bordeaux system, he had spent two years developing direct sales, but had achieved little. I felt his approach was inappropriate for an 1855 *Cru Classé*, and as with Pichon-Longueville, was determined to bring Cantenac-Bown back to La Place de Bordeaux.

I therefore entrusted the distribution of the wines to Châteaux & Associés, a structure that we continued to strengthen. Malou Le Sommer, from our offices, began to devote herself full time to commercial analysis and contacts with the trade. After a long period of direct selling, she began to ensure Bordeaux négociants were once again distributing the wines of Cantenac-Brown, and quickly the strategy began to pay off in terms of notoriety and pricing.

I spent quite a lot of time at Cantenac-Brown with its beautiful park, lake and surrounding woods. One day I welcomed courtier Daniel Lawton and his almost centenarian mother, Simone de Luze, a woman of infinite distinction. She had been born in the château, and I remember the three of us in the room overlooking the park, in the very place where she was born.

A Third Growth to be proud of... The two Lalande sisters, distant descendants of the great merchant Armand Lalande, who built the château in 1855, visit Cantenac-Brown in Margaux.

We talked about her family, which embodied the history of the Bordeaux trade on the Quai des Chartrons. On another occasion, I received two sisters from the famous Lalande family in Cantenac, whose ancestor built the château in 1865. They spent their childhood running around the huge building and the park. Snooping in every nook and cranny, they searched for memories of their carefree youth. Under their guidance, we found children's drawings left on the inner walls of the small tower more than 60 years before. The two sisters cried with emotion. They told me how the Lalande family, a large bourgeois family from the Chartrons, used to spend their summers in this place:

'We travelled by train from the Bordeaux Saint-Louis station to Margaux. The servants would arrive first to prepare the house, bringing the essential supplies for a three-month stay. When all the supplies were ready, horse-drawn carriages would be waiting at the Margaux station for the arrival of the family and our guests to take us to the château with songs and laughter.'

At the mention of this vanished society, the ghosts came to life in the eyes of the Lalande sisters.

In 1990, we organized a successful festival of the Commanderie du Bontemps to underline the new life in Cantenac-Brown. Under the eyes of

The oenologist Michel Rolland follows the vinification of Château Petit-Village in Pomerol with Daniel Llose.

guest-of-honour, Sylvie Vartan, the Commandeurs grouped on the lawn cut the wires that held gigantic bunches of grapes formed of coloured balloons. Dozens of them rose into the sky, carried by the wind, then disappeared above the roof of the castle. A few years later, we did it again for a Fête de la Fleur in June 1997, 'Year of the Comet', because a wandering star flew over the vineyard in spring. We received, alongside the mayor of Bordeaux, Alain Juppé, the actor Hugh Grant, whose British charm seduced our 1,700 guests.

IN 1989, AXA-MILLESIMES ACQUIRED Château Petit-Village in Pomerol, owned by the Ginestet family. My friend Bruno Prats was closely involved and kept me up to date with progress, and in the end Claude Bébéar was easily convinced of the interest of this property and the deal was concluded quietly. The winemaking facilities were in good condition, and the vineyard well-kept and relatively young. Having been devastated by the frosts of February 1956, it had been replanted by Prats in the 1960s; he had chosen to use some Cabernet Sauvignon, known well to him at Château Cos d'Estournel, his Saint-Estèphe vineyard. Less well adapted than Merlot to the clay soils of Pomerol, we decided to gradually return to the more conventional grape choice.

Unlike its previous acquisitions, AXA-Millésimes had taken possession of an estate in perfect condition. However, we had little experience of vinification in Pomerol, where the terroirs and grape varieties are different from those of the Médoc, so we called upon Michel Rolland, a renowned oenologist, who was himself a landowner in Pomerol where his family owned Château Le Bon Pasteur. Like Jacques Boissenot, our consultant at Pichon-Longueville, he studied with Emile Peynaud, and got on perfectly with Daniel LLose.

A LITTLE LATER, IN 1992, when I learned that Château Suduiraut, a Sauternes First Growth classified in 1855, was for sale, the contracts were already being drawn up between the selling family and AXA. Claude Bébéar had been seduced by this jewel of the Sauternes region, neighbouring Château d'Yquem. The contracts were prepared in Paris and the negotiations were led by Bernard Robin with his characteristic efficiency. I was only a witness to the transaction and took part in the discussion as a simple technical advisor.

Technically, the vinification of sweet white wines is very different from our experiences in the Médoc, Pomerol or Saint-Emilion, but Daniel LLose was unpeturbed, especially as the team in place seemed solid. The domaine was managed by the Pascaud family, themselves owners in Sauternes, with Pierre Pascaud and his two young sons, Alain and Fabien, sharing the work. We called upon Serge Chauvet, an oenologist and specialist in sweet wines, for consultancy work.

Sauternes wine is made by fermenting white grape juice whose sugar concentration has been increased by the action of a microscopic fungus, *Botrytis cinerea*. This causes what is known as 'noble rot' – as opposed to grey rot, which destroys the grapes. This phenomenon is made possible by the microclimate of the Sauternes region but is heavily dependent on annual weather conditions. The wine growers therefore make their way through every year on a knife edge – good years are the result of a favourable alignment of the planets. It must be said that great vintages are not common.

At Suduiraut, in 1992, the weather for our first harvest was difficult and the picking laborious. Under the guidance of Serge Chauvet, we decided to turn to cryoextraction, a process developed by Chauvet that consisted of cooling the grapes sharply, just before they were put into the press. The less-ripe grapes and those with a low concentration of sugar, where botrytis had not been able to develop, were frozen solid by the cold, which made it possible to separate them from the richer berries, whose juice remained liquid and flowed out of the press. The frozen berries, which cannot be pressed, are thus easily eliminated.

Sceptics claim that this method of pressing was 'industrial' and muted the 'vintage effect'. We felt, however, that cold pressing had the immense advantage of not having to resort to adding sugar – chaptalization – and thus avoiding the concealment that this often accompanies. In a hurry, we installed a cooling unit and two isothermal containers bought second-hand from the SNCF. These were replaced the following year by two large cold rooms.

The debate on cryoextraction, which was heated in the 1990s, is no longer relevant. Since 1997, a great vintage for Sauternes, we have used it less. In the new century, global warming has brought everyone into agreement by making concentration less necessary.

IN PAUILLAC, 1992 WAS MARKED by a small earthquake. In the autumn, Château Latour, a property that had remained in the hands of the descendants of the 'Prince of the Vines', the Marquis Nicolas-Alexandre de Ségur, from the 18th century until 1963, was put up for sale by the drinks giant Allied Lyons, the sole owner since its acquisition of the shares of Pearson's in 1989.

The British group had decided to withdraw from the wine business to focus on spirits, beer and the food industry. At the end of harvest, its directors asked the Lazard bank to look for a buyer. Bruno Roger, one of the managing partners of the bank, submitted the file to Claude Bébéar. It was not an easy situation to assess at the time – the first Gulf War was underway and the economic situation globally was difficult, with wine sales in sharp decline. In order to have the opinion of a professional, Claude Bébéar asked me to study the situation. My assessment was not a scientific analysis, but I did my best and wrote a detailed report. Latour was one of the most prestigious vineyards in the world, and inevitably the figure I suggested was high.

When Pearson's was in the game, I often saw Alan Hare, the chairman of the board of management, at Latour. He even asked me to sit on the board, along with the company's directors and interesting British personalities, Harry Waugh and Hugh Johnson, among others. Somewhat embarrassed now to be involved in the ongoing negotiation, I took the initiative to offer my resignation and wrote an undated letter which I handed to David Orr, Alan Hare's successor, during one of his visits to Pauillac. 'If you feel that my presence on the board may be embarrassing, you date it and send me a copy.'

The next day, I received a copy of my letter in my office by registered post, with the date of my visit added. A small thing, perhaps, but I still regret the loss of the Latour case which I received every year as a thank you for my good and loyal services.

Negotiations progressed. At the beginning of November, the newspaper *Les Echos* ran the headline: 'The French insurance group AXA is set to win.' In the fall of 1992, AXA had to make a decision. Internally, some were surprised that the company was ready for such a serious purchase. The insurance industry, like the wine industry, was suffering from a difficult economic situation. Finally, Claude Bébéar decided: he set the price 20 percent below my estimate. A few days later, Bruno Roger told him that it was not enough.

Claude Bébéar hesitated, but maintained his offer. I was torn. If AXA-Millésimes acquired Château Latour, I was worried that the poisonous social atmosphere that reigned at Latour, under an infamously tough union, would prove contagious for Pichon-Longueville, located directly opposite – and even for Lynch-Bages, less than a kilometre away. I was therefore split between the exciting prospect of having a Médoc First Growth to manage and the fear of seeing Latour's social problems spilling over into my family business and the estates for which I was responsible.

The affair dragged on for several months. I would later learn that the brothers Alain and Gérard Wertheimer, owners of Chanel, were also interested and had the ear of David Orr. Finally, in the spring of 1993, a telephone call informed Claude Bébéar that François Pinault had won the bid.

The property was valued at a price close (within one percent) to that which I had indicated. But I didn't feel any satisfaction, even intellectual. François Pinault, through his holding company Artémis, made a decision at the right time. Bordeaux estates were suffering from a serious crisis, making it a buyer's market. He knew how to put forward the right offer and not to let an opportunity pass that rarely presents itself. The growth of the fine wine market since 1993 has demonstrated the intelligence of his approach.

As soon as the deal was concluded, David Orr disappeared from the Médoc. He resurfaced shortly afterwards in Margaux, where he helped the Wertheimer brothers take control of Château Rauzan-Ségla. The circle was now complete…

By the time 1999 rolled around, the balance sheet for the classified growths was heavy. Family difficulties and repeated viticultural crises had taken their toll on many owners: Pichon-Longueville, Grand-Puy Lacoste, Grand-Puy Ducasse, Pedesclaux, Haut-Bages Libéral, Beychevelle, Margaux, Lagrange, Gruaud-Larose, Saint-Pierre, Cantenac-Brown, Rauzan-Ségla, La Lagune, Cantemerle, Cos d'Estournel, Calon-Ségur, Montrose, Giscours, Ferrière, Pichon-Lalande, Lascombes, Marquis d'Alesme, Desmirail, Branaire-Ducru, Haut-Batailley, Belgrave, Camensac, Dauzac, Pontet-Canet, du Tertre… In less than 40 years, 32 of the 60 Médoc *Crus Classés* had changed hands. And some of them several times…

25 Quinta do Noval

THEREZA AND I OFTEN travelled to Portugal. After Mozambique's independence, her parents, sister and many relatives moved there. We were particularly fond of her first cousin Isabel and her husband Zé Miguel, a young naval officer who had just been promoted to the rank of admiral. They were about our age and shared our walks.

In the autumn of 1985, we were in the northeast of Porto, in the Minho, a polyculture region where the light and sparkling 'vinho verde' is produced, so thirst-quenching when drunk well chilled. We would randomly explore the region, and one evening ended up at a *pousada* in Alijó, called *Barão de Forrester*. Alijó is a small provincial town in the north of the Douro Valley, famous for its wines, which the English in the 19th century – and Baron Forrester in particular – made popular throughout the world. After a quiet night, abandoning our wives who preferred to visit the local churches (it was a Sunday), Zé Miguel and I jumped in the car… I didn't know the Douro at the time. We headed south towards Pinhão, the centre of gravity of the wine region, which was less than 20 kilometres away, along the river.

The first terraced vineyards soon appeared. The further we went, the more they invaded the landscape. Shortly after Vale de Mendiz, at the bend in one of the many curves in the road, we suddenly came across a slope made of drystone terraces that contrasted strikingly with the surrounding panorama. This was, I felt sure, the vineyard of Quinta do Noval, one of the most prestigious in the region. A few hundred metres further on, a wrought-iron sign confirmed my intuition. The gate was wide open… We made our way along an astonishing cobbled path that wound up the side of the mountain under an 800-metre long vine. When we reached a group of buildings, we abandoned our car. A few more metres on foot and we were on a terrace dominated by a giant cedar tree. The view was breathtaking. A gigantic staircase of vines overlooked a distant loop of the Douro River. Sitting on a bench conveniently placed under the cedar, we silently admired the landscape. There was not a soul around. The only sign of human activity was the washing hung out to dry on wires stretched across the terrace. We spent an hour of peaceful happiness before returning to Alijò. I fell in love with the place that day.

Three years later, in the course of a conversation, Hélène Sicet, who headed up communication for our group of Bordeaux estates (Lynch-Bages, Pichon-Longueville, Cos d'Estournel, Ducru-Beaucaillou, Léoville-Barton, Domaine de Chevalier, Figeac), told me that she was beginning to work with Quinta do Noval. The company was owned at the time by the Van Zellers, a family of merchants of Dutch origin who settled in Porto in the 18th century. At the end of the 1980s, the Quinta was run by Cristiano Van Zeller and his sister Teresa. I told Hélène that I would like to meet them if the opportunity arose.

In 1988, I worked with Eric Le Collen on the script for the Fête de la Fleur evening at Lynch-Bages planned for the following year. We decided to add a scene to the joyful musical he was designing: at the end of his journey through the stars, 'Captain Desquet' would land on a planet where a princess offers him a strange wine, different from those of the Médoc. To finish our dinner, we would serve the nectar of 'Princess Antonia' (an evocation of Antonia Adélaïde Ferreira, the great lady of the Douro in the 19th century). This would be my way of paying tribute to my Portuguese wife for her unfailing support.

Now we had to find some port. Through Hélène Sicet, I contacted Cristiano Van Zeller. He immediately understood the interest of presenting his Quinta do Noval in Bordeaux, on the occasion of the Vinexpo trade fair, to the 1,200 guests of a prestigious evening. At Cristiano Van Zeller's invitation, I went to Noval, knowingly this time. On the terrace, the bench had been replaced by a long table where a dozen samples were displayed. The wines were splendid. I fell for a 1966 Vintage, and Cristiano graciously agreed to provide the necessary quantity.

On my return to Bordeaux, I still had to obtain permission from my peers to serve an overseas wine at a Commanderie party. It was unusual, but the agreement was unanimous. In June 1989, the evening was a great success and Princess Antonia's Quinta do Noval was widely celebrated...

After this, I met Cristiano Van Zeller several times. Like me, he travelled widely to promote his wine and he was the personification of port wine. Young, tall, warm, with a well-trimmed beard and a false air of Orson Welles, he represented the Douro and its nectars to perfection. We soon became friends, and he confided in me that the financial situation of Noval was not easy. The company, with shares held by different branches of the family, was having difficulty financing its large stocks, despite the fame of Quinta do Noval.

Cristiano was looking for a long-term solution, and was considering creating a company that would own the stocks. Cristiano was, of course, aware of my links with AXA. For an insurance company, such a structure would be an interesting investment, he told me. For my part, I started to dream. I hadn't forgotten the love at first sight I felt at Noval and the prospect of taking a stake was very tempting…

For a year or two, we explored the possibilities but came up with nothing concrete: Cristiano wanted to sell his stocks without giving up anything on the management board or the land. Our conversations were courteous, but did not progress. In Portugal, the company's situation was getting worse. Finally, in 1992, Cristiano told me that his uncle Fernando Van Zeller, who had a decisive voice in the family council, had decided to sell Quinta do Noval.

To my great regret, I didn't have the means to buy it myself. Instead, I suggested to Claude Bébéar that we took a trip out to the estate. His time was precious, but it so happened that he had to go to Lisbon for a meeting and there was an airfield an hour's drive from Noval. A quick round trip with Bernard Robin was possible.

When the day came, Thereza and I explored the area around Vila Real in search of the famous landing field, which we eventually found between two hills. There was no control tower and the runway looked modest, at best. The only building visible, at the edge of the runway, was a bistro whose owner was setting up the tables on the terrace. I asked for a radio contact to communicate with the pilot. There was no radio. We waited… After a few minutes, a small plane appeared in a cloudless sky, made a first pass over the runway to check that no goats were walking around and landed smoothly. The four of us flew to Noval.

Cristiano welcomed us on the terrace, in front of the landscape that had so seduced me. He told us about the Quinta, its history, its vineyard, its wine, its family. It was a packed day, and before we knew it, we had to leave for Porto where we had onward flights to Paris. On the plane, Claude Bébéar admitted to being won over by the place, the wine and the personality of our host. Bernard Robin shared his enthusiasm. Both were aware that Noval would be a magnificent addition to the AXA-Millésimes portfolio, and Claude gave the immediate green light to begin negotiations.

Things were completed in early 1993. In the Van Zellers' case, the family agreement broke down during the negotiations. When the time came to sign the deed, the atmosphere was heavy, with different branches of the family meeting at the notary's office at arms length, keeping away from each other in separate rooms. And while we waited, a clerk passed from one group to another to collect signatures.

The day after this meeting, it was my turn to take charge of the company, starting with an inventory of fixtures. From then on, I often travelled to Portugal. In Porto, the people in the trade were very welcoming, especially Francisco (Vito) de Olazabal, head of the Ferreira house and president of the exporters' association. He did his utmost to make me feel at home and introduced me to his colleagues, with whom I established excellent relations. Thanks to their kindness, I soon felt at ease.

Like all the great port houses, Quinta do Noval's offices and main winery were located in Vila Nova de Gaia, opposite the city of Porto, on the left bank of the Douro River. But the heart of the company remained the estate itself: 145 hectares of vineyards located a few kilometres north of Pinhão, about half of which were terraced.

A small part of the vineyard was ungrafted and produced a rare wine marketed under the name Quinta do Noval 'Nacional'. A unique, almost mythical wine, the Holy Grail for connoisseurs. Noval acted as a trading company and used its brand on a variety of labels. Among the constellation of 'English houses': Taylor, Graham, Delaforce… or 'Portuguese' companies: Ferreira, Calem, Ramos Pinto… Noval shone with a particular brilliance thanks to its vineyards, and its ability to deliver quality time after time.

In the interests of continuity, I suggest that Cristiano Van Zeller took on the role of general manager. His sister Teresa, a fierce defender of the family brand, did not wish to continue working with us. The technical responsibilities remained in the hands of Antonio Agrellos, who lived in Porto but commuted to the Douro. A talented taster and blender, Antonio compared the creation of a great port to the work of a composer bringing together musical notes into a harmonious whole. He was unrivalled in his ability to create the wines that made the house famous.

As with most port houses, Noval's production was divided into two types of wine:

Tawny, an oxidative wine aged in *pipas* (550-litre chestnut barrels) in contact with the air, before being blended and bottled. Tawny port can be made from a single harvest, in which case it is called Colheita. If it is the result of a blend of wines of different ages, it is then given an indication of age: 10

Above: *Quinta do Noval, clinging to the side of the mountain, occupies a dominant position over the Douro Valley. This beautiful estate made a fine addition to the portfolio of AXA-Millésimes in 1993.*

Below: *Ancient port* foudres *resting in the Noval cellars.*

years, 20 years, 40 years, and so on. It is a product of great finesse; Antonio Agrellos' talent as a blender was particularly evident in the development of Noval Tawnies.

Vintage is considered to be the best of the port wines. I believe that it differs from Tawny port more in its structure than in its intrinsic quality. Made from a specific harvest, the quality of which is officially 'declared', Vintage port is bottled after spending two years in cask. It has great ageing potential and reflects the character of the vintage. LBV (Late Bottled Vintage) comes from the same harvest, but spends five to six years in *pipas* before being bottled. It is not intended to be aged further on release.

In Noval, there was a certain amount of uncertainty about the management of the company. The lack of investment was obvious, but I was counting on Daniel LLose to work with Antonio Agrellos on technical improvements. The human resources situation was no better and reminded me in some ways of Lynch-Bages in the late 1960s. I hoped that Cristiano, who now had a free hand and more resources, would be able to dust off the house. Unfortunately, we soon had to face the fact that he was not the right man for the job, and I had to find a replacement for him.

Since the British market was important for port wine, I thought of recruiting a British citizen. There were a lot of them in the port trade. James Seely, an English journalist and author of books on wine, who often visited Bordeaux, told me about his son Christian, who was 33 years old, knew wine, had management experience and seemed to be looking for his way. A few days later, I saw a young man in a smart bow tie arrive in my London hotel room with an umbrella on his arm. The conversation went well, and it would have been hard to find somebody more English than Christian! It seemed to me that he had all the necessary skills, and he was happy to move to Portugal.

Christian Seely became the new manager of Quinta do Noval. He adapted quickly. He naturally frequented the town's English club, where he met Maria Ascunção Calem. Her family controlled the Villanova de Gaia company that bore her name, and in Pinhão, not far from Noval, the Quinta da Ponte, on the banks of the Douro. The two young people liked each other and their marriage was celebrated after a few months, anchoring the Briton to his adopted country.

The production and trade of Portuguese wine was regulated in the 18th century by the Marquis of Pombal, prime minister. He imposed strict conditions on the port houses. It was he, Pombal, who obliged them, in order to facilitate controls, to keep their stock in Villanova de Gaia.

In the 21st century, legislation changed and it became possible to hold stocks at the place of production, but few companies made use of this flexibility. For the most part, they remained rooted in the small, sloping streets of Gaia, where they had large, picturesque but very inconvenient warehouses. Noval had one imposing building, but it was practically abandoned. Indeed, the Van Zellers, taking advantage of the new regulations, had started a movement back towards the vineyard and built a large ageing cellar on the quinta land where they housed almost all the company's stocks. However, they kept the bottling and shipping at Gaia.

The movement back towards the valley seemed irreversible to me. I decided to continue the policy of our predecessors. We would not return the stocks to Gaia, so we had to decide what to do with the old Gaia cellars, which were well placed in the middle of the city. The Van Zeller family offered to buy the site; and the deal was quickly finished.

This meant we had to equip the quinta with a bottling and logistics centre. Most deliveries were no longer made by ship as in the previous century, but by road transport, so it seemed logical to look for a solution near the IP4, which serves the north of Portugal and connects it, through Spain, to the whole of Europe. In less than two years, we built a bottling and storage centre in Sabrosa, close to the motorway.

At the quinta itself, new steel vats made vinification easier. For the highest quality grapes, we chose to return to tradition, with grapes pressed by crushing them in *lagares* – shallow presses where the grapes are collected after harvest and crushed by foot. Fermentation is stopped by *mutage* with alcohol, and the half-fermented juice is then poured into wooden tuns. The process offers great quality results, but it is laborious, difficult to implement and requires a large workforce and suitable equipment.

At Noval, the method had been virtually abandoned over recent years but the *lagares*, although in poor condition, still existed. To facilitate the movement of the wine, the natural contours of the land were used, with the *lagares* placed overhanging the casks in a building separated from the house by a small chapel.

From our first harvest, we put teams together. At regular intervals, the pickers entered the *lagar* to tread the grapes. First in rows, side by side, holding each other's arms, then 'freely', each one independently engaging in a sort of bacchic dance. This exhausting work was carried out by the men and ended late in the evening. In a corner of the room, between two small glasses of *bagaço* (local brandy), an accordionist accompanied the workers, while at the edge of the *lagar*, there was a foreman with a long cane ready to hit the head or shoulders of the *pigeur* (the person treading the grapes) who failed or was not conscientious enough.

Daniel LLose, never short of ideas, was convinced that he could design an automatic *pigeur*. The following year, on his instructions, the plans for a prototype were drawn up by the technical college in Bordeaux. We were the first to successfully test a robot *pigeur*. We had several examples manufactured in Portugal and installed them in Noval.

Since the transfer of the warehouses, we no longer owned anything in Villanova de Gaia. However, we thought it could be useful to have a place in Gaia where we could receive tourists and possibly sell some bottles, so I bought a pretty house on the river to be our showcase.

Back at La Quinta itself, the main 19th-century house was also fully restored, fitted out with reception rooms and a few comfortable bedrooms, in keeping with the Douro style: *azulejos* and woodwork. Maria Ascunção Calem-Seely gave soul to the house where she received our guests with great warmth.

For his part, Christian Seely managed the company, travelled widely and organized distribution by nurturing contacts with customers, especially in the United Kingdom and America, which were the most important markets. For the technical side, we relied on Daniel and Antonio Agrellos and hired José Eduardo Costa, a young and talented vineyard manager. Absenda Matos, previously in charge of the modest analysis laboratory, took on the responsibility of the winery.

The crew was finally complete. In 1993, the estate was near the end of the road, having lost much of its soul and energy. In five years, thanks to everyone's efforts, we brought Quinta do Noval back to life and I am very proud of that.

26 The Hungarian Parenthesis

IN NOVEMBER 1991, I FLEW to Hungary. The Soviet Bloc had collapsed like a house of cards and, without any transition, the Magyar country was moving towards a market economy with its share of privatizations and openings for foreign investors. The famous Tokaj vineyard did not escape this troubled and violent changeover.

Once again, Claude Bébéar was at the forefront of the adventure. During a hunting trip, he met Hector de Galard, from an aristocratic family in Gascony, who was heir to the Terraube manor. This likeable man, who elegantly wore his title of marquis, was known as an agricultural expert and often advised on the investment operations of Clinvest, a subsidiary of Crédit Lyonnais. He advised, among others, the president of the *Garantie Mutuelle des Fonctionnaires* (GMF), owner of Château Beychevelle in the Médoc, in matters concerning forests and wine estates.

Hector de Galard told Claude Bébéar about a project to privatize the Tokaj vineyard, to which Clinvest was contributing. He talked about the historical reputation and the quality of the wines, and the proximity of the immense Zemplén forest next to the vineyard that abounded in game. For Bernard Robin and myself, a visit proved impossible to resist!

In Hungary, the man in charge was called Jean-Claude Bras, and he brought Hector de Galard and Clinvest into the loop. A former football international, born in Saint-Ouen, he couldn't have been more different from the marquis. Nicknamed 'The Red' in sports circles, he revived the revolutionary socialist organization Red Star, which he chaired for 20 years, and was elected on the communist list in the Seine-Saint-Denis department. He went into business in Budapest, where his political background made things easier. Warm and opportunistic, in the style of Bernard Tapie, he was involved in a wide variety of projects, from the construction of the Hungarian capital's metro to being part sponsor of Ferencváros, the city's legendary football club.

In Budapest, Hector de Galard, Bernard Robin and I met Jean-Claude Bras' representative, a Hungarian engineer named János Mikulecs, who offered to drive us to Tokaj. We set off eastwards in thick fog. We passed a few broken-down Trabants on the side of the road... and drove through sad and icy villages where the carbon dioxide fumes from the burning of coal briquettes used to heat the houses constricted our throats.

ROBIN AND I KNEW almost nothing about Tokaj and Hungary, and eagerly listened to Mikulecs and Galard's explanations. Two-hundred kilometres east of Budapest, the Zemplén mountain range, covered with dense forests, forms a sort of V, the southeastern tip of which is marked by Mount Tokaj, a focal point for travellers. The perfect cone of this ancient volcano dominates the plain. At the foot of the mountain, Tokaj is a large town located at the confluence of the rivers Tisza and Bodrog, which meander across the plain. Tradition has it that the body of Attila, king of the Huns and hero of the Hungarians, was immersed in the Bodrog nearby.

The region, the Tokaj-Hegyalja ('foothills'), is dotted with villages with often unpronounceable names: Tarcal, Mád, Tolcsva, Sárospatak and Sátoraljaúhely, the administrative capital. The vineyards were located on the slopes of Mount Tokaj itself and in the foothills of the Zemplén.

The wine civilization here is ancient, dating back to the Romans, and focuses on local grape varieties: Furmint, **Hárslevelű and** Oremus. In the 17th century, Tokaj's wine growers discovered late harvesting and sweet wines. Just as in Sauternes, where the river Ciron plays a fundamental role, in Hegyalja, the mist rising from the rivers generates a very special microclimate favourable to the development of botrytis. In 1630, Abbot Szepsy, the local Dom Pérignon, was the first to use the '*aszú*' grapes, highly concentrated by noble rot or *passerillage*, to produce a special wine.

Long marketed to Poland, the Baltic, Scandinavia and Russia as a wine for mass, or as an elixir of long life, Tokaji could be found on all the great tables of Europe. At the time, Greek merchants were the main players in the town of Tokaj, while 15 kilometres away, the village of Mád saw the wine as a popular commodity among Jewish merchants centred around its synagogue.

To raise their nectar, the wine growers dug labyrinthine cellars in the volcanic tuff. Little by little, they refined their range according to the sugar concentration of the wines. In 1737, a royal decree delimited the production area. In 1772, 80 years before the Bordeaux Classification of 1855, a notary from Zemplén drew up an official list of the best Tokaji wines. Over the years, the appellation area took shape, eventually extending to nearly 8,000 hectares.

In the 1880s, with the attack of phylloxera, the region was devastated, until being gradually reborn – as it was in France – with the help of grafting. During World War II, Hungary was invaded by the Wehrmacht, and from 1945 onwards, the Soviet takeover continued to impoverish the country.

The wine estates became the property of the *kolkhozes*, and the sale of Tokaji was placed under state control. To make life easier, the vineyards were replanted down on the plains (working the mountain slopes was time-consuming and expensive). Rows of vines were spaced out to allow the passage of Russian tractors. Productive, generously cropping grape varieties were favoured. Lack of concentration was compensated for by adding sugar or alcohol, and the farmers were asked to adapt and change. Volume was critical for supplying the communist neighbour, who in exchange provided electricity, gas and timber.

The government state farms, most of which were of the Soviet type, employed salaried peasants. Some of them allowed wine growers to retain ownership of their vineyards, provided they pooled their means of production. The final touch of the reforms was brought about in 1971 by the creation of the Borkombinat (*bor* means 'wine' in Hungarian) which grouped together all the farms belonging to the state. A giant winery was set up in Tolcsva, which became the winemaking centre for the whole region and produced wine on an industrial scale. In the 1980s, the Borkombinat owned one-third of the vineyards and vinified and marketed 85 percent of the production.

Things went wrong in 1989, after the fall of the Berlin Wall and the collapse of the USSR. Suddenly, there was no market for Tokaji wine. The country entered a new world. Some 30 million bottles of Tokaji had been sent to the Soviet Union every year. From 1989 onwards, that figure dropped to one million, maybe two. In 1993, the Borkombinat employed only 650 workers, far from the 2,500 there had been before the crisis.

In early 1989, one of the first to see the potential in post-Soviet Tokaj was Danish winemaker Peter Vinding-Diers, who I knew well from our Médoc meetings at Château Loudenne. He was the owner of Château Rahoul in the Graves, near Bordeaux, and advised several estates throughout the world, in France, Chile and Spain. Considered an authority on white wines, he became interested in Hungary very early on. He told me about his first trip, in the company of a Danish businessman and a Swedish banker. A Russian helicopter brought them to the village of Mád where they were received in the school by the mayor, the director of the cooperative, members of the Party and even a KGB representative who squinted at the buffet served for the occasion. While touring the region, they were seduced by the wines of a local winemaker, István Szepsy, and convinced him to bring together the members of the Mád cooperative who still owned their plots. A joint venture was born in the form of a 'private' cooperative of which István Szepsy agreed to be the president…

The founders involved another Dane, Vum Kai-Nielsen, director of the Dubos house in Bordeaux, and, above all, the influential English journalist Hugh Johnson. The latter proposed to name the company The Imperial Tokaj Wine Company, but the adjective reminded the Hungarians of Austrian domination. The name finally chosen was Royal Tokaj Wine Company. Peter Vinding-Diers recruited Samuel Tinon, a young oenologist from Bordeaux, who worked within the limited budget available. When I met him in 1992, during my first trip, he was at the back of a garage where he was making do with a makeshift installation… For the first year, in 1989, he had no premises and vinified 240 batches of grapes in 100 different cellars spread over four or five villages. A lacemaker's job!

The Royal Tokaj was quickly transformed into a joint stock company, to which each small owner contributed his land in exchange for shares. The total surface area of the farm stabilized at around 100 hectares. However, the material difficulties remained considerable. The coffers were empty and the agreements made were not respected. The relationship between the shareholders and the company's management gradually deteriorated. István Szepsy distanced himself from the company. At the same time, in London, new investors, brought together by Hugh Johnson and Jacob Rothschild, gave the company the means to put a new team in place.

IN THE BORKOMBINAT, it was obvious that the whole structure had to be reformed. The architect of the revolution was György Raskó, a former World Bank official who became director of the national privatization agency for the food industry and agriculture. He played a major role in the sale of state assets.

Already a German industrial group, Underberg, manufacturer of the digestif that bears its name, had offered to acquire 49 percent of the shares of the Borkombinat that was by now a limited company. Laszlo Mitro, president of the state farm, was in favour of this solution, but not everyone was happy.

The deputy technical director of the Borkombinat, the young oenologist András Bacsó, made his disagreement known. He could speak French and travelled to Italy and France, where he attended the Vinexpo exhibition in Bordeaux. Inspired by the French vineyards, Bacsó pleaded for a partial opening to foreign capital which would allow the redrawing of the terroirs and the revival of the older estates. At the same time, György Raskó made it clear that simply turning the Borkombinat – a state monopoly – into a single private company would defeat the purpose of opening things up.

In September 1990, György Raskó had had enough. He dissolved the Borkombinat board and organized new elections. To everyone's astonishment, the incumbents were swept aside by a general assembly of the staff, which elected András Bacsó as its president and approved the main lines of the privatization plan he had presented. Bacsó was suddenly placed at the head of the company and became higher in ranking than his former boss, Sandor Bodnar, who remained in place as technical director. It was a power grab, but not without its perils. Perceived by some as a 'foreign agent', the new president had many detractors.

Bacsó had to deal with the inevitable bankruptcy of the Borkombinat and redistribute the land without giving too much to foreigners. He also had to compensate the families who had been robbed during the nationalization process through 'reparation coupons'. At the same time, he had to identify the great terroirs, which was no easy task. He dreamed of creating pilot farms, 'capable of reconstituting an entire terroir and replanting it', he explained. He wanted to 'create modern companies capable of transforming the grapes into quality wine and of presenting wines on the Hungarian and foreign markets that are in keeping with the reputation of Tokaj'.

He needed money to achieve this. The Hungarians eventually accepted the idea that some of the best terroirs could be transferred to foreign hands. After all, in France, châteaux Haut-Brion, Margaux, Lagrange and Latour were in English, American and Japanese hands at the time. On the other hand, the historic Szarvas-Dülö estate, near Tarcal, had to remain state property, as it was part of the national heritage. This was non-negotiable.

On his first trip to Hungary, Hector de Galard met Jean-Claude Bras at Kokapu Castle, his property in the Zemplén forest where he entertained friends for hunting parties. The former footballer explained the whole thing to de Galard, and the unlikely meeting of these two very different characters would shape what happened next.

Initially, Hector de Galard approached Aymar de Baillenx, head of *Grands Millésimes de France*. Baillenx and Galard suggested that András Bacsó set up a study for the contribution of foreign capital. The idea was accepted and Clinvest, the subsidiary of Crédit Lyonnais, was retained to research the conditions for the successful privatization of Tokaji production.

After some trial and error, the experts came up with a plan: they proposed the creation of three pure trading companies in which foreign investors would contribute 50 percent of the capital. At the same time, a dozen autonomous production units of 16 to 50 hectares, of high quality, would be set up. Each one was to be majority controlled by a foreign operator up to 70 to 80 percent. The 12 estates would be the showcases of the appellation and bear the name 'château'.

In 1991, GMF was the first company to put this plan into practice by setting up a joint venture at Hétszőlő, a former Habsburg estate at the foot of Mount Tokaj. The estate had 45 hectares of vines before the war but by this point only one hectare was planted. The initial agreement took the form of a long lease for 99 years. At the same time, GMF acquired Château Dessewffy, an early 18th-century palace on the banks of the Tisza, as well as the historic Rákóczi winery in the heart of downtown Tokaj. The signing was celebrated at the Budapest Hilton. Aymar de Baillenx told me later that between two spoonfuls of caviar, András Bacsó asked him: 'Which fellow civil servant are you going to put in charge of the company?' Aymar almost choked.

In Paris, Bernard Robin learned about the operation from an article in *Le Point* and Claude Bébéar met Hector de Galard. This is how we found ourselves in Hungary, at the end of 1991, in freezing cold and fog, at the mercy of a reckless driver who we quickly nicknamed 'Jean-Manuel Fangio of the Carpathians'.

ANDRAS BACSO LAID OUT his plan and the composition of the properties he wished to privatize. The proposed division of the estates did not suit us – our reluctance was hardly helped by the fog, which meant we hardly saw a single vine during our short stay, and what we *did* see seemed abandoned by 45 years of communism. We were not convinced, to say the least. Back in France, I told Daniel LLose about my trip and concluded: 'I would be surprised if I ever set foot in that fridge again!'

How wrong I was. A few months later, Claude Bébéar called me. He had seen Hector de Galard again and the two were still convinced that Tokaj was of interest. It would be good if I went back there…

I proposed a technical mission to select the four or five most interesting vineyards. Daniel LLose would be in charge of the technical evaluation accompanied by Claude Dulhoste, former director of Pommery, who for a time looked after Château Phélan Ségur on behalf of my friend Xavier Gardinier. In February 1992, our two experts spent about 10 days on site and drew up an inventory of the vineyards, the terroirs, the quality of the plantations, the yields, the vinification techniques, and so on.

Armed with this information, Bernard Robin and I made an appointment in May with the Borkombinat leaders. Hector de Galard accompanied us. Tokaj seemed transformed. Spring had arrived, and the landscape was dotted with poppies and multicoloured wildflowers. The people seemed open and rather friendly. We got back in touch with András Bacsó, and were recommended Béla Barati, a local lawyer, as an interpreter. With his coloured shirt and fluorescent tie, he looked like something out of a Soviet film.

The negotiations began on the morning of May 20th 1992 in Sátoraljaújhely, at the Borkombinat headquarters, whose large, glassed-in entrance hall, lined with incongruous green plants, resembled a sad winter garden. The hours ticked by, the negotiations made little progress and the discussion went round in circles. Our field study showed that the plan proposed by Clinvest was more of a general framework than a practical and concrete project. András Bacsó, on the other hand, was coming up with figures using prices based on Soviet-style accounting that bore little relation to reality.

Again, we were not impressed with the offer. Bernard Robin became impatient and kept looking at his watch. He suddenly called for a break and asked me to follow him out of the room: 'If we don't move things along, we'll never get to Budapest airport on time. I have to be in Paris tomorrow...' When the meeting resumed, the atmosphere had changed, and it was clear now that there was a deal to be done. Bacsó concluded: 'Everything is for sale, make your choice!'

We chose one of the terroirs identified by the LLose-Dulhoste report, the Disznókő estate. Its name, the 'boar's rock', sounded good, for a start. The vineyard – nearly 100 hectares – was located at the southern tip of the Zemplén massif, very close to Mount Tokaj. It was in poor condition, but had a southern location ideal for ripening grapes, and was close to the main road from Budapest, making it full of potential for developing wine tourism. The property also included Sárga Borház – the 'Yellow House of Wine' – a restaurant in an old cellar.

In the end the discussion came down to an unusual provision: we were asked to make a substantial payment to a fictitious 'Tokaj Foundation' that András Bacsó wanted to create to promote the region and its wines. I proposed another rule of the game: the company would commit itself to paying the future foundation of one *forint* per bottle sold, for 10 years. An amendment that would prove very useful over the years to come.

Bernard Robin asked for a few blank sheets of paper, sat down at a table in the next room, and wrote a contract of five pages and eleven paragraphs in one go. I was impressed by the clarity of the document that he had put together so rapidly.

We submitted the draft to András Bacsó: 'You'll like it and we'll sign it, or we'll leave.' Miracle! A few minor amendments were proposed and everything was sorted. Of the 120 employees that the Borkombinat asked us to hire, we agreed to retain 30 or so, the choice of whom we would approve later. To avoid any issues, the memorandum of understanding was immediately translated into Hungarian.

The final deed was signed a few months later, in September 1992, in AXA's offices on Avenue Matignon. AXA-Millésimes became the 'owner' of 150 hectares of land and vines, and a restaurant. On top of that, the company purchased a stock of 23,000 hectolitres of wine, across the ascending range of sweetness that is categorized in Tokaj from Dry Furmint through Szamorodni, Aszús 3, 4, 5 and 6 Puttonyos, and right up to Eszencia (an extremely concentrated wine that almost tastes like liquid honey and is very low in alcohol).

We were allowed to select the wines from Tarcal's cellar, during a memorable tasting session to which we invited the journalists Jean-Paul Kauffmann and Thierry Desseauve. In semi-darkness, the wines were presented to us by the technical director of the Borkombinat, Sandor Bodnar, who accompanied them with impassioned comments. Some of the wines had been in the wrong barrels for too long and all had suffered from excessive oxidation.

The gap between the description and the reality in the glass was so wide that amazement soon gave way to outright hilarity. The Hungarians' discomfited looks sent us into fits of laughter. But we had to choose… We later managed to pass on the purchased wines to the Canadian monopoly of the *Société des Alcools du Québec*, which integrated them into its 'Cuvée du Patriarche', a low-cost, high-volume production.

But let's not get ahead of ourselves, and return instead to the 1992 harvest. One hundred hectares had to be harvested and above all vinified. But we had neither the premises nor the necessary equipment. Daniel LLose organized an invitation to tender in July for a vat room to be built within two months. Finally, the company Julien, a vat manufacturer in Béziers, supported by competitive Italian colleagues, took up the challenge. We were to have 40 vats: 15 with a capacity of 200 hectolitres and 25 of 150 hectolitres. But we still had to find a place to install them. Daniel and I shuttled back and forth between France and Hungary, first to a former military barracks in Tokaj, then to a disused college near Tarcal... Driving one day in the streets of Tokaj, I saw a large, beautiful building with yellow walls, and asked my guide what it was: 'This is the old synagogue. There are no more Jews in the region, it is used for storing agricultural equipment... We can sell it to you...' The conversation ended there.

The Borkombinat offered to rent its own facilities, but they were in a poor state. Finally, thanks to our interpreter, we visited Ond, about 10 kilometres from Tokaj on the road to Budapest; there, we found a large concrete shed measuring 30 by 30 metres, with a 6.5-metre-thick ceiling and a vast grain silo. First of all, the latter had to be emptied of its grain and rid of the rats it was infested with; then, the green light was given for the delivery of the tanks, which arrived during the harvest and were filled as quickly as they were installed.

We needed someone we could trust to lead the Hungarian team in what was a difficult harvest, and on the recommendation of Guy Guimberteau, a professor at the faculty of oenology in Bordeaux, we recruited Nicolas Godebski. Originally from Costières de Nîmes, he looked after a family estate, but was experiencing some difficulties with his partners and looking for work elsewhere. Our proposal came at the right time and Nicolas moved to Tokaj just before the first grapes were picked.

Our team was formed around two Borkombinat alumni, János Arvay, cellarmaster, and László Kóródi, vineyard manager. In Hungary, vineyard work is mostly done by women. Although János and László knew a few words of English or French, the accountant, Ilona, spoke only Hungarian. To overcome the language barrier, we recruited Krisztina Palágyi, who was perfectly bilingual and smoothed our communications with ease.

We began experimenting in a very practical way with how to vinify the *aszú* style, following the sometimes confusing explanations given by the Borkombinat oenologists. Our specialist in sweet wines, Serge Chauvet, was there, learning with us. The icy cold did not help the vinification. In the former silo, now a vat room, the wash water froze in a few minutes. Our technicians carried out fermentation tests in small plastic containers: into 300 millilitres of fermented must or white wine, they mixed 300 grams of *aszú* grains reduced to a paste using a mincer normally reserved for sausage meat.

On day two, they filtered the liquid through a cloth, tasted it and sent it for analysis to the only laboratory in the region, which belonged to the Borkombinat. After a few weeks of going back and forth with no results, Daniel LLose and Serge Chauvet exploded in front of András Bacsó: the explanations served up by the local oenologists bore no relation to reality!

Our experts finally understood what had been going on: their counterparts in the Borkombinat had been adding alcohol instead of completing the secondary fermentation, which was always difficult to assure. They had been doing it for years, as it was faster and easier… but hadn't told us. When confronted with the evidence, Bacsó didn't deny it. The problem was that this practice was not covered in the official Hungarian texts – in fact, it was forbidden, no doubt accounting for the discretion of our new colleagues.

While the technicians were busy in Ond, I visited the town halls of the surrounding villages to present our company and explain its objectives. The Hungarians looked at us with curiosity. For them, we were a bit like settlers whose resources must be used to restore their own heritage. Some visits resulted in dialogue through an interpreter. Everyone was concerned about one thing: were we going to buy grapes, as the Borkombinat used to do, and above all, were we really going to pay for them, in good money, and quickly?

I explained to everyone that our purchase price would depend on the price at which we could sell the wine. In this country, which was communist for 50 years, the notion of cost price was unheard of. But we were generally well received, even if I sometimes noticed the slightly mocking look of those who were waiting for our first slip-up.

We managed to get through the 1992 vinifications as best we could. The size of the harvest, which exceeded our forecasts, surprised us. We learned that some workers cheat. They were paid according to the yield for the piece of vineyard assigned to each of them. But many of them were also owners of plots close to their homes and usually delivered their grapes, all together, to the Borkombinat. They now preferred to bring their harvest to us – and our neighbours – rather than deliver it to an institution that no longer had the means to pay them. We returned from the bank with bags filled with the local currency, the *forint*, and paid for everything in cash.

The vines inherited from the 'kombinat', which were high and sparsely planted, were not conducive to quality viticulture, so we embarked on a major replanting programme. Our new vines were laid out in narrower rows, perpendicular to the hill-slope. When they saw us doing this, the Hungarians understood that we were investing with them for the long term and finally took us seriously.

For three years, we continued our vinification in the Ond premises. Little by little, mentalities changed, and everyone got used to each other. Bernard Desmartis, former general secretary of the *Girondins de Bordeaux Football Club*, who had already worked for us in Portugal, briefly replaced Nicolas Godebski who had to return to France after the first harvest. The following year was marked by the arrival of Dominique Arangoïts, a young oenologist from the Bordeaux faculty. A native of Saint-Etienne-de-Baïgorry in the Basque region, the grandson of a shepherd and wine grower in Irouléguy, he wanted to do his military service abroad as a National Service Volunteer (VSN). Dominique stayed in Hungary for seven years, until 2000. With him, our team gradually found its feet and its cohesion.

IT BECAME OBVIOUS that we had to build new vinification facilities. As with Pichon-Longueville in the Médoc, I wanted the project to combine functionality and aesthetics. The new buildings had to spark curiosity and one day welcome visitors. I spoke to Jean Dethier, who had been key to the decision-making process for Pichon-Longueville. He mentioned Imre Makovecz, the in-vogue architect in Hungary, whose impossible character was as famous as his name. But he directed me instead to one of his students, Dezső Ekler, whose work he appreciated at the Venice Biennale (the international cultural exhibition based in Venice), and who he believed spoke English. I called Ekler on the phone and explained the project to him, and the architect immediately gave me his agreement in principle.

The plans were drawn up in record time. In two months, everything was thought out. **Dezső** Ekler understood our objective and he got on extremely well with Daniel LLose.

He constructed a long, slightly rounded building near Sárga Borház, our 'Yellow House of Wine', which became our restaurant and was built to reflect our surroundings. Three perpendicular aisles emerged from it, reminiscent of the entrance to the Tokaj Hegyalja cellars. Inside, the visitor had the impression of walking down the street of a local village. The architect made extensive use of wood, an essential material in the region, which gives the buildings

Above: With András Bacsó in Disznokő. At the beginning of the 1990s, after the fall of the Berlin Wall, his actions made possible the resurrection of around 50 historic estates in Tokaj, breathing new life into the region.

Below: In the cellars of Tarcal... a tasting of the Borkombinat stocks with journalists Jean-Paul Kauffmann and Thierry Desseauve... and some of our Hungarian friends.

warmth. A little further away, in the middle of the vineyard, Ekler built a tractor garage inspired by local buildings. It was a real work of art.

But before inaugurating, we had to build. During the winter, our construction site looked like an ocean of mud. We had a lot to do with the masonry company and its Roma workers (30 percent of the population of the region was Roma at the time). All the work was done by pulleys, as there were no cranes. No trucks for the concrete either; and the taps had to be thawed with a blowtorch. Concerned about the quality of the foundations, we had them rebuilt. To dig the cellar in the rock, the company used dynamite. The workers prayed to the heavens before each explosion. Everything was done the old-fashioned way, except for the construction of the vaults. To be on the safe side, I asked an engineer from the Nancy School of Mines to check the work.

Daniel LLose and I went to Hungary every two weeks. We stayed with locals, before finally buying a house in Tarcal for the French executives, as the living conditions were so harsh. Even in our house, running water did not always reach the tap. In February, night fell at 3pm. On top of that, the Hungarian language was complicated, and it was impossible to understand anything on the restaurant menus. We would grunt like a pig to order pork, or cluck like a chicken to get poultry.

Our technicians by now had mastered the vinification process, and we produced dry white wines, dry and sweet *szamorodni*, and finally *aszú*, the nectar that made Tokaj's reputation. But our *aszú* had to obtain the approval of a commission, a sort of Hungarian National Appellations' Institute based in Budapest and directed by an official oenologist, Daniel Szabo, who was an old hand in the system. He was totally biased. He considered it normal for *aszú* to be mutated with alcohol to shorten fermentation, before being oxidized by a long stay in the barrel. The addition of alcohol prevented complicated fermentations and the oxidation hid the misery. This was the method of the Borkombinat.

We were not going to give up. Our research had shown that the *aszú* of the past was not oxidized and we wanted to preserve the fruit of the ripe grape in our wines. The Szabo commission did not see it that way and one of our 1995 *aszú* wines was refused 13 times… We were beginning to worry about the future and we were not the only ones… One day, a journalist wrote that the control commission had refused one million bottles. The publication of his article caused a minor scandal and unblocked the situation.

The year 1995 was when László Mészáros arrived at the estate. László was originally from western Hungary, on the Austrian border. His grandparents were farmers, his father a soldier and his mother worked in the bank. He had learned German and Russian – as was compulsory at school – but also English. In 1990, with a friend, he travelled to France, where he appreciated the culture, and enjoyed the gastronomy and the wines, and on his return to Hungary, he began to learn French.

Thanks to a European scholarship, he was accepted at the Purpan Agricultural College, near Toulouse, where he obtained a degree in agricultural engineering. In 1995, during an internship with us in Disznókő, he became familiar with the techniques used by Dominique Arangoïts and Daniel LLose. He was looking to make quality wines, and had an obvious talent for management and human relations. In 2000, I appointed him director of Disznókő, where he succeeded Dominique Arangoïts.

The new Disznókő winery was inaugurated in 1997 by Claude Bébéar, whom I picked up near Debrecen, about 50 kilometres from Tokaj, where his small plane landed on the runway of an abandoned former Soviet military base. It was from here that the tanks that crushed the Budapest revolt left in 1956, but by this point the site was deserted and looked like the setting for a James Bond film…

The next thing to do was recreate a market for dry wines as well as for *aszú*. Thanks to the *Compagnie Médocaine des Grands Crus*, we travelled the world trying to work out what would be successful. At first, I imagined that we would sell mainly dry white wines, from the Furmint grape variety, a type of wine to which Western palates were accustomed and which could be drunk immediately on bottling. I was also hoping that a small production of *szamorodni* and *aszú* would improve the company's finances. I was wrong. Our dry wines faced competition from similar products made from better-known grape varieties such as Sauvignon and Chardonnay, offered at low prices all over the world.

So we explored new avenues. When the Antwerp rabbinate asked us for kosher wines, we decided to try. Our employees were allowed to handle the grapes, but they were not allowed to work on the wine, which only a rabbi was allowed to touch. Vats and barrels had to be washed with water all the time, and all products and materials in contact with the wine had to be approved by this same rabbi. We were not able to taste the wines because, once filled, the barrels were not to be handled – we did not try again the following year.

I gradually understood that our efforts had to focus on the traditional wines of Tokaj, *aszú* and *szamorodni*. These were products that could not be found anywhere else – not that this made our task any easier. The name Tokaj might have been known to wine lovers, but the wines themselves had disappeared from the market decades earlier and were unknown to the wider public. Even so, we broke even in just under 10 years, and I never felt any pressure from our shareholders. For AXA-Millésimes, the acquisition of Disznókő was a long-term investment.

WE WERE NOT THE ONLY ones to have bet on Tokaj. After the English of Royal Tokaj and the GMF of Hétzőlő, which were the first two companies to be placed under a foreign flag, Jean-Michel Arcaute, son-in-law of the Bordeaux merchant Audy, owner of Château Clinet in Pomerol, bought Château Pajzos from the Kombinat. Supported by the insurance company GAN, he repeated the operation with Château Megyer, located near Sárospatak.

A little earlier, in 1991, the CANA, a French agricultural cooperative based in Ancenis, represented by one of its member wine growers, Jacques Carroget, was interested in the cooperative in the village of Bodrogkeresztúr, about 20 kilometres north of Tokaj. He liked the wines he discovered there, and appreciated the mentality of the local wine growers, which seemed to him to be close to that of the French cooperative members. The directors turned down his proposal, but in 1993, Jacques Carroget succeeded in bringing together 200 wine growers in a company – Bodrog Varegy – which worked an area of about 120 hectares of vines.

Finally, in 1994, the Spanish Alvarez family, owners of the famous Vega Sicilia estate in the Ribera del Duero, acquired Oremus. The vineyard was very small and the winery, located in Sátoraljaújhely, was in poor condition. Rafael and Pablo Alvarez cleverly moved the winery further south to Tolcsva, where Borkombinat also had vines for sale and the terroir was of much better quality. They built a spectacular winery there, which retains the name Oremus, and bought labyrinthine cellars beneath the village. To manage their Hungarian *bodega*, they call on András Bacsó, who had been unemployed since the decaying Borkombinat gave way to another state body, the Kereskedöhaz, which was only involved in trading.

Overall, the foreign financial contribution to the Tokaj vineyards has remained small, concerning only a few estates. But it has been decisive, because these estates have become quality locomotives for the region and have led others towards significant progress.

RATHER THAN THE 'Tokaj Foundation' wanted by the Hungarian authorities to help the development of the region, and whose funds we feared would be misappropriated, we proposed to create a 'Union des Grands Crus de Tokaj' whose objective would be to promote the product. I proposed to model its operation on that of the *Union des Grands Crus de Bordeaux*. Each member would contribute in proportion to the size of its estate.

In February 1995, 'Tokaj Renaissance' was born, a name suggested by András Bacsó because the word 'renaissance' has the same meaning in Hungarian, French and English. We copied the statutes from those of the *Union des Grands Crus de Bordeaux*. The overseas owners were joined by a dozen Hungarian wine growers. In the same year, the association took a stand at the Vinexpo exhibition in Bordeaux.

I STOPPED WORKING for AXA-Millésimes on January 1st 2001 and did not return to Hungary until 2019. I wanted to go back and see Disznókő and some of the people I had met there. My daughter Marina came to keep me company, as well as my usual travelling companion, Daniel LLose. We also took advantage of the trip to make a diversion to Germany, to follow in my father's footsteps to the Oflag IV-D Elsterhorst and the Zeithain camp, near the Polish border, where he was detained.

In Hungary, the wide road took us in three short hours from Budapest to Tokaj and was nothing like the one I knew 25 years earlier – but Disznókő remains the first property that one encounters when arriving in the vineyards. Behind the buildings built by Deszö Ekler, the vines climbed the hill in the sun. Newlyweds were being photographed on the belvedere in the centre of the vineyard with its stunning view plunging southwards over the plain towards the capital, Budapest.

We met up with László Mészáros, who by this point was welcoming 5,000 visitors to Disznókő every year, half of whom were Hungarians. Foreign tourists come from Poland, Slovakia, Austria, Russia, Germany, France…

Disznókő, with 117 hectares of vineyards, has become the largest estate in the region. László Mészáros was now president of 'Tokaj Renaissance', focusing on sweet wines (Tokaji Aszú), which were sold in England, the USA, France, Scandinavia and Asia. China's share was growing strongly (which reminded me of my tasting at the Beijing Food Fair in 1994). The Russian market remained almost non-existent. In the traditional Bodrogkereszúr restaurant, where we

Above: The new winery at Disznókő, designed by Deszö Ekler, and the mausoleum overlooking the vineyard.

Below: The barrel cellar at Disznókő makes extensive use of wood and is reminiscent of old Transylvanian buildings – it was important to mirror the traditional architecture of the region.

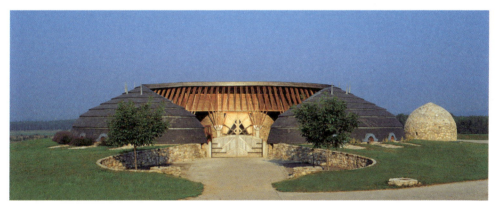

dined on an excellent goulash, a portrait of Admiral Miklós Horthy, Hitler's dictator friend, in uniform, still hung on the wall as it had done years ago.

The privatization of the Borkombinat lasted two years, before the state decided to 'protect the Hungarian heritage'. From that point on, no foreigner from the European Union could buy more than one hectare. To acquire more, he or she had to register as a Hungarian farmer, which imposed very specific conditions and often blocked transactions.

Sandor Bodnar, the former chief oenologist of the Borkombinat, our one-time adversary, now 80 years old, welcomed us to the six-hectare estate he now ran with his daughter and son-in-law. He seemed to have forgotten his former hostility. He acknowledged that the Disznókő project had been successful, but talked about the commercial difficulties he was personally experiencing. Obviously, he had difficulty selling his production. The free-market economy had not convinced him and he said that he missed the time when wages were low, but there was work for all, with cultural spaces, cinemas and libraries in the villages. Nostalgia can be a powerful force.

We went to Tolcsva to meet András Bacsó. And to Oremus, now with a hundred hectares of vineyards scattered throughout the Tokaj region. The Alvarezes were right: Bacsó was a good manager and an excellent ambassador. He welcomed us in the park with his elegant courtesy, in impeccable French. I explained to my fellow travellers that the Tokaj region owes its current development to him. 'The people of Tokaj should erect a statue to him,' added Daniel LLose. András, while showing some embarrassment, ironically said that in Hungary the era of statues was over… In the end, András Bacsó has achieved his dream. Although the Hungarian government had rather quickly abandoned the liberal opening up of the 1990s, his actions had nevertheless made it possible to resurrect some 50 historic Tokaj estates.

In Olaszliszka, about 20 kilometres from Tokaj, we met the Frenchmen Samuel Tinon and Mathilde Hulot. Both passionate and well-integrated in the country, they had been producing wines for 20 years whose quality was recognized by the best sommeliers. Their *aszús* were rich and expressive and their dry *szamorodni* extremely finessed, the best I have ever tasted.

In Mád, the Royal Tokaj Wine Company now occupied brand-new premises. Its current director, Zoltán Kovács, a former member of Disznókő, welcomed us in French. In the middle of the courtyard stood a bronze bust of Hugh Johnson. Hugh rarely came to Hungary, but in London he was an influential spokesman whose judgement carried considerable weight. He had a lot to do with the success of the 'Royal' which, after a difficult start, became a successful company.

This company, which grew out of the juxtaposition of the many small terroirs of the former Mád cooperative, continued to be inspired by the model of the Burgundian 'climats' and their many labels. On the other hand, the strategy of the 'châteaux' where the French have intervened, Hétszőlő or Disznókő for example, were rather inspired by Bordeaux: these are vast estates producing a range of wines based on 'blends' of well-managed plots.

The Hungarian adventure remains one of the most exciting experiences of my professional life. I am happy to have had the chance to contribute to the resurrection of Tokaj, whose vineyard is now a UNESCO World Heritage Site.

27 Chess and Success

CALIFORNIA

EVERY TIME I TRAVELLED to the United States, Miklos Dora tried to convince me to try my hand at winemaking in California. He had been closely involved in the connection between Philippe de Rothschild and Robert Mondavi and hoped to be able to broker a deal between me and a Californian wine grower.

When I visited the region in the summer of 1984, he told me he had found an ideal candidate for a joint venture. The name of this rare bird was Gary Andrus, founder, a few years earlier, of the Pine Ridge Vineyards in Napa Valley, located on the Silverado Trail in the Stags Leap District, one of the highest quality enclaves in the region. Miki, never short of ideas, put the cart before the horse and even suggested an evocative name for the future wine: 'Duet'. We decided to make a diversion to Napa during our usual stop in San Francisco.

The winery was a little isolated, in the middle of the woods, but close to two other vineyards I knew well: Warren Winiarski's Stag's Leap Wine Cellars, whose triumph at the international tasting organized in 1976 in Paris by Steven Spurrier made him famous in the United States, and Clos du Val, another well-known property, managed by Bernard Portet, son of the former director of Château Lafite in Pauillac. Very good wines and an auspicious neighbourhood…

Before becoming a winemaker, Gary Andrus was a member of the US Olympic ski team… At least that's what he said. I expected to meet a sportsman, but his heavy figure and firm tread surprised me. In any case, it was not his past as a champion that interested me… Gary gave us a quick tour of his facilities. He introduced us to his gracious and welcoming wife, Nancy. We shared a glass of excellent Chardonnay and talked about a possible collaboration. Without being very demonstrative, Gary seemed interested. We did not decide anything that day. I merely suggested that Daniel LLose come to spend a few days at his place to assess the quality potential of the Pine Ridge Vineyards and to advance what was still a vague project.

The California climate allowed an early harvest, so Daniel made the trip in September 1984. His objective was to make a pre-selection of Cabernet Sauvignon plots that could be used to make a wine with a Franco-American signature. On his return to Pauillac, he was quite positive. I got back in touch with Gary Andrus.

Gary and I met again at Lynch-Bages a few weeks later to establish the basis for our future cooperation. Once the broad outlines were defined, we agreed to keep the project confidential until the signing of our agreement, which we planned to formalize during a forthcoming trip to California.

Three weeks after this conversation, I was stunned to discover an interview with Gary Andrus in *Wine Spectator*. Without consulting me, my potential partner announced – *urbi et orbi* – the creation of our joint venture! The article was illustrated by a photo of Daniel LLose taken in the Pine Ridge Vineyards.

How can you trust someone who so casually breaks his word? I wrote to Gary Andrus and told him that I was ending our conversations. I would not hear from him again… until 1988.

A Washington DC distributor wanted to know about a new wine from the owner of Pine Ridge. 'Duet' (as it was called) was said to be a joint venture between Pine Ridge and Lynch-Bages. Of course, neither Daniel nor I had tasted it… When I enquired with other American contacts, I found that the offer was being circulated throughout the United States. This was unacceptable. A Californian lawyer intervened at my request. Gary Andrus did his best to evade the issue. It took several months and threats of legal action to finally put a stop to what I could only consider a deception…

My California adventure ended there. In a way, it was an enriching experience that taught me prudence and, incidentally, gave me a better understanding of American legal culture.

ARGENTINA

ONE DAY IN AUGUST 1999, a visitor knocked on the door of Lynch-Bages. Slim, elegant, speaking in English, he introduced himself: Federico Benegas Lynch. Obviously, the bearer of such a surname can only be welcome here. He was of Argentine nationality and told me that he was a direct descendant of a

Patrick Lynch, born in 1715 in Galway, Ireland, nephew of John Lynch, who settled in Bordeaux in 1691. Like many members of the Galway Tribes, this Catholic Patrick fled the Protestants from England.

After a tour of the Pauillac estate with him, I listened to him talk about his country… and his projects. Without giving too many details, Federico presented himself as being 'in business'. He lived in Buenos Aires and had, it seemed, a foot in Montevideo in neighbouring Uruguay. He also had a special mission. Passionate about vineyards, he enthusiastically told me about his intention to acquire a property near Mendoza. The *finca* (farm) Cruz de Piedra consisted of some 40 hectares well placed on the banks of the Rio Mendoza. But Federico had no experience of viticulture or winemaking. He needed help. We discussed the possibility of building his project together. Lynch-Bages was obviously the ideal partner for him. Not only could we bring our technical expertise, but a partnership would greatly facilitate the marketing of a new label.

After my visitor left, I did some research… Patrick Lynch was 25 years old when he left Galway. He made a first stop in Bilbao, crossed the Atlantic to the Rio de la Plata, and settled in Buenos Aires where, as Patricio Lynch, he became '*Regidor*' (royal representative) commanding the militia.

In Argentina, Patricio married a wealthy heiress who gave him nine children. The Lynches were prolific: generation after generation, they always seemed to have around 10 children and the family expanded quickly… Some of them we have talked about: in the family tree of the Argentinian Lynches, there is an Ana Lynch y Ortiz who married Roberto Guevara Castro, grandmother of little Ernesto Guevara. My visitor was the cousin of 'Che Guevara'!

A cousin, Marta Lynch y Ortiz, married Alberto Benegas, son of Tiburcio Benegas, a considerable figure in Argentina, who was governor of the province of Mendoza. While working as a banker, and with a passion for the vine, Don Tiburcio promoted the development of vineyards through his writings and the advice he gave to those around him. He was responsible for the creation of 'El Trapiche', today one of the oldest and most important wineries in the province. I would later note that the main public square in Mendoza is named after him.

My visitor was therefore connected to a family that has left its mark on the history of wine, thousands of kilometres away.

I didn't know much about Argentina, where Carlos Menem had been forcing the economy to liberalize and privatize at every turn for the past 10 years. The country's growth and modernization followed. In order to stabilize the national currency, the president aligned the peso with the US currency. One peso became equal to one dollar. This ultra-simple arithmetical relationship made calculations easier, but it was largely artificial and did not increase investment.

I also didn't know much about Argentine wines, but having witnessed their rapid commercial introduction in the United States and England, I knew that, relatively inexpensive and of good quality, they were becoming fashionable. The influential columnist Frank Prial had written a notable article on them in the *The New York Times*. France's Pernod Ricard, Britain's Allied Domecq and California's Kendall Jackson had already taken an interest in the vineyards, which were said to be undergoing a quality revolution. Since 1990, national consumption had dropped by half. In the Mendoza region, the vineyard had lost about a third of its surface area, but this reduction had been accompanied by an explosion in exports, the amount of which had increased fivefold in the last three years.

Some Bordeaux colleagues had already made inroads in Mendoza. Jean-Michel Arcaute, from Château Clinet in Pomerol, had shown the way by creating the bodega Alta Vista. In the same region, the most ambitious project was that of Dany and Michel Rolland. With the help of five friends, they planted the 800 hectares of vines that made up Clos de Los Siete, and brought in partners who all had vineyards in Bordeaux: Benjamin de Rothschild, Catherine Péré-Vergé, heiress of the Arques crystal factory and owner of Château Le Gay in Pomerol, Laurent Dassault, the Cuvelier family of Léoville Poyferré in Saint-Julien, and the Bonnie family of Malartic Lagravière in Pessac-Léognan.

Having learned a lot with my Hungarian experience, I was tempted. During the following weeks, I kept in touch with Federico. Our exchanges, by telephone or by mail, were helped by the early days of the Internet. Federico informed me one day that he had bought the vineyard of Cruz de Piedra, which was immediately renamed with the evocative name 'Finca Libertad'.

There was, of course, no question of concluding a formal agreement over the telephone 12,000 kilometres away. After considering several possibilities, we decided to take advantage of the *finca's* next harvest, which was due to take place around March 2000. During the winter of 1999–2000, the outlines of our joint venture gradually took shape. The aim was to create a company where, as equal partners, we would produce a quality wine.

Federico was to provide the vineyard. We would provide additional investment and our technical capabilities. The vineyard would have to be rehabilitated and the necessary winery built. I asked Daniel LLose, who spoke Spanish fluently, to prepare for his first harvest in Argentina, and I would join him in

Mendoza to draw the first conclusions and, if everything went well, to move forward with the project.

As soon as he got settled in Cruz de Piedra, through daily emails, Daniel kept me updated me about his days. Everything was new for the Frenchman. In the first few days, he visited the vineyard and met Mario Toso, a winemaking contractor and solid winemaker to whom Federico has entrusted the maintenance of his vineyard. The plots were in poor condition and the wide variety of grape varieties disconcerting. Besides Malbec, which was very common in Argentina, there was Cabernet Franc, Cabernet Sauvignon, Merlot, Tempranillo and even Sangiovese. A real rainbow… There was work to be done. Toso made a good impression on Daniel, but the situation in the winery was more complicated.

As soon as he arrived, Daniel planned to meet Jean-Michel Arcaute. Thanks to Michel Rolland's intervention, he agreed to make part of his Alta Vista vat room available to us, installed in an old bodega containing about 50 vats, all of which were equipped with a cooling system. But no one could reach him – this was particularly annoying because he hadn't told the site manager, Juan Argerich, about the arrangement he had made with us. Daniel was persistent and eventually convinced Argerich to set up our winemaking at Alta Vista. For his part, Mario Toso recruited harvesters and set the picking schedule. Hail, which is common in the Andean foothills, took its toll, and heavy rainfall in February compromised the health of the harvest. As a good winemaker, Toso feared an attack of botrytis and was keen to begin bringing in the grapes, but Daniel had stronger nerves and preferred to wait a while to ensure they were harvesting quality fruit. At Alta Vista, after a chaotic start, the fermentations were proceeding normally. When he had a moment, Daniel visited the bodegas in the region and got to know their managers, and the days passed slowly, always too short.

April was already well underway when Thereza and I arrived in Buenos Aires. Federico showed us around the city and its surroundings, and we fell in love with the Argentinean capital.

It was just a few days before Easter, and the city was in full swing. Traditional buildings stood next to majestic palaces. The wide avenues that crossed at right angles gave the city a very organized Haussmannian character. Thereza returned to Europe after visiting the city and dancing the tango in San Telmo; I then headed to Mendoza, where the eponymous Rio meanders and spreads its alluvial deposits in vast plains occupied by vineyards. The landscape would be flat and unrelenting if not for the snowy summits of the imposing Andes mountains which are visible everywhere.

Thereza and I in Argentina: the vineyards of Mendoza have spectacular views of the Andes mountains; the peak of Mount Aconcagua (6,961 metres) is the highlight of the range.

Daniel LLose, who had returned to France, prepared the ground. I met Mario Toso and Juan Argerich. The vinification of our first harvest was finished, and everything was going well. Thanks to the contacts Daniel made during his stay, I was lucky enough to visit several bodegas. Impossible to name them all, but some made a strong impression on me: Terrazas de Los Andes, with its modern equipment and renovated old buildings of great architectural quality, and Catena Zapata, where Nicolás Zapata, a visionary winemaker, welcomed me with warmth and simplicity… And, a little further south, the Clos de Los Siete of Michel Rolland and his friends.

Back in France, with our legal and financial director, Pierre Doumenjou, and the assistance of the Francis Lefebvre law firm in Buenos Aires, which ensured contact with Federico Benegas, we studied a business plan and put our project in black and white: articles of association, partners' agreement… The documents crossed the Atlantic at lightning speed. But the Argentine business culture seemed to accommodate a certain amount of opacity that I was not used to, and it became clear that I needed to go back to Argentina for another meeting.

I returned to Argentina in early December for a whirlwind trip. My son Jean-Charles, who was then working in São Paulo, Brazil, for the French company Valeo, met me in Buenos Aires on a Sunday.

The day after our arrival, our law firm organized a working session with the lawyers who represented my future partner. He was away from the capital and was to meet us a few days later in Mendoza. We discovered that Federico's representatives had hardly prepared anything. However, we set to work. As is only natural, the lawyers split hairs, and it was almost midnight when everyone finally came to a rough agreement. We agreed that the Argentinians would put the result of our meeting in black and white for the final meeting in Mendoza a few days later, this time in the presence of Federico.

On the fateful day, I met our lawyer in the hotel lobby. He explained that our future partners had turned up in the morning, as planned, but empty-handed, without having done any of the work they had undertaken to do. Our lawyer regretted that he could not recommend continuing with these discussions, which had already gone on too long. Argentina, he told me, was a country where the law was less clear than in Europe… and he urged me to be careful. He was aware of my disappointment, but he no longer trusted the other side, Federico in particular, and urged me to leave it at that. I immediately felt that he was right.

The meeting with Federico and his advisors that followed this conversation was brief. I explained the decision I had just taken and the reason for it. In a few words, everything was said. My ex-future partner was speechless. All I had to do now was go back to France.

Later, in Pauillac, I received a convoluted letter from Federico. He was sorry for the way things turned out, and spread recriminations against his own lawyers who had not been able to convince us of the purity of his intentions. And also, against mine, who he felt had been overly rigorous… He ended by insisting on his sincerity and reaffirmed his desire for a partnership.

But by that point I had moved on… with a few regrets, and many memories.

AUSTRALIA

ON DECEMBER 31ST 2000, leaving my position at the head of AXA-Millésimes led me to take a step back. I decided that the time had come to sell the insurance portfolio created by my grandfather in the 1930s. On January 1st 2001, I only had to worry about the family vineyards.

My schedule was suddenly cut in half. I transferred my office, which had been located, since 1973, at the AXA agency headquarters on rue Jean-Jaurès in Pauillac, to Lynch-Bages.

I had resisted this move until then, preferring to remain close to a profession that had helped my family get through crisis periods without irreparable damage. I can still hear my father's voice telling me: 'Never sell your portfolio. With insurance, you are sure to be able to feed your family!'

At the end of the 20th century, wine growers from the southern hemisphere, led by the Australians, arrived on the market in force. In 2001, I suggested to my son Jean-Charles that he go and see for himself. My contact down under was Len Evans, a tireless promoter of Australian wines (as well as a maker, teacher and judge of them), who I had met in the United States.

We visited him in the Hunter Valley, about 50 kilometres north of Sydney, where he owned a wine estate that was also his home when he wasn't travelling the world. I told him about our programme, which would take us to the Yarra Valley near Melbourne, then to the Barossa Valley near Adelaide, and finally to Margaret River south of Perth, at the tip of the continent. We were there as tourists. I'd already made a few appointments, but Len completed our programme with authority.

Despite my denials, he was convinced that we were looking for an investment opportunity in the Australian wine industry. 'You absolutely must,' he said, 'meet Brian Croser in Adelaide.' Good thing we already had him on the agenda. Len Evans gave us a flattering portrait of the man, assuring us that he would be the ideal partner, and then called him on the spot to recommend us.

After visiting a couple of wineries in the Hunter Valley, we flew to Melbourne. In the Yarra Valley, we felt as if we were entering a different, bigger, bolder country. The Bortoli family, owners of some of the biggest vineyards of the region, received us with great warmth, Italian style. All the estates sold their wines directly. They put a great emphasis on tourism and offered perfectly organized tours, which invariably ended in a restaurant or a shop called the 'cellar door'. Here, visitors could buy wine and all sorts of objects, clothes, trinkets, caps, and so on.

In Adelaide, we first headed for the Barossa Valley where an industrial winery impressed us with the rigorous organization of its work, even more than its modernism. After a diversion to Jacob's Creek (Pernod Ricard) where we felt overwhelmed by the giant installations that produced several tens of millions of bottles per year, we continued towards Adelaide Hills to meet Brian Croser.

Partners and friends: Portuguese Jorge Roquette of Quinta do Crasto and Australian Brian Croser.

Brian was waiting for us at his home in the green hills of Piccadilly Valley. He told us about his career. Born into a family of farmers, he turned to the science of wine very early on. He completed his training as an agricultural engineer in the United States. After travelling in Europe, he returned to Australia where Tom Hardy, heir to Australia's oldest wine-growing family, gave him positions of responsibility. He quickly rose through the ranks to become chief winemaker at Hardy's. At the same time, he lectured at local universities. His knowledge of grape varieties and terroirs made him one of the leading figures in Australian wine.

In 1976, Brian left Hardy's. In partnership with Len Evans and with the support of his wife Ann – owner of Tiers Vineyard in the Piccadilly Valley – he created Petaluma Winery; Tiers became the core of the new unit.

To speed up the growth of the company, the partners had to ask for outside investment, and ended up as minority shareholders. As a result, they were not really in control. All went well for 20 years, but the success of the business led to an unhappy ending for the Croser family and their friend Evans.

In 2000, Petaluma, whose value had risen significantly, was acquired by the Lion Nathan group, whose products ranged from fruit juice to yoghurt and beer. The timing was right for a profit and the majority shareholders decided to sell. Petaluma changed hands. The industrial universe of the new owner was the opposite of that of Brian Croser and Len Evans, who had no choice but to go along with it. The deal closed in 2001. When we met the Crosers, they were scarred by all this. Their 'baby' had been taken away from them and their disappointment was immense. But they had not lost heart and now, having some financial means at their disposal, they wanted to bounce back.

Len Evans' glowing portrait of Brian Croser was no exaggeration. He described the project that was now taking up all his energy: the starting point was the Koppamurra estate, located in the Wrattonbully region, about 100 kilometres south of Adelaide, near Coonawarra. It was a 30-year-old vineyard, renowned for the quality of its Cabernet Sauvignon.

Brian proposed to start a three-way venture. The third partner would be the French company Bollinger, with whom he had already established contact. This was a positive argument for us, as we already had excellent relations in France with this Champagne company. Brian had already come up with the name 'Tapanappa', which means 'follow your path' in the Aboriginal language. The Croser 'path' was to plant vines that were adapted to the climate, the soil and the geology, in renowned sites. As he did at Petaluma, Brian wanted to produce wines marked by their terroir – a different approach to that of the Australian industrial wineries.

We made good progress, and by the time we left Adelaide, we were committed to the idea of getting involved with Tapanappa. We still had to finalize the partnership documents, and agreed to do this remotely, as soon as we returned to France, in conjunction with Bollinger and with the help of an Australian lawyer.

Our Australian exploration ended 250 kilometres south of Perth – it felt like the end of the world – in the Margaret River region, whose oceanic climate was said to be somewhat reminiscent of Bordeaux. The neighbouring areas were a surfer's paradise. The road wound between hills covered with immense trees and fertile valleys where vineyards were dotted here and there. The structure of the vineyards was somewhat similar to that of the Médoc, as was the size of the properties and the omnipresence of Cabernet Sauvignon.

At Voyager Estate, we met Michael Wright, heir to a huge mining fortune, who ran the property with his daughter. This colourful character, although a teetotaller, was passionate about his vineyard. At Cullen, a family estate created some 30 years earlier, the succession was assured by Vanya Cullen, a deep-rooted Australian and passionate oenologist who had just been awarded the prize of Best Australian Winemaker. The Cabernet Sauvignon on this site, on the shores of the Indian Ocean, expressed itself well, and her wines made a good impression on us.

A little further south, the Horgan family's Leeuwin Estate also produced great wines from a vineyard of about 60 hectares. They had invested generously in wine tourism and ran a large restaurant and cellar door. Every year at Leeuwin, the Horgans successfully held musical events featuring world-renowned artists. Our last stop in the vineyard was at Cape Mentelle, a beautiful estate of about 100 hectares that was one of the pioneers of the region. Renowned for the quality of its Cabernet Sauvignon, it is now owned by the French luxury goods company LVMH.

We were coming to the end of our time in the south, having crossed the continent from east to west and visited four major wine regions, each with its own character. **We had discovered exce**llent wines in many places. If I had to single out one region that I admired most, I would choose Margaret River because of the beauty of its landscape, its beaches and the personality of its winemakers, whose youth and boldness we loved.

DURING HIS EXPEDITIONS TO WRATTONBULLY, Brian discovered a massive 35-million-year-old whale jawbone in a limestone cavern beneath the vineyard… and renamed the vineyard the Whalebone Vineyard. This name, along with a drawing of the fossil, appeared on the label of the wine from our first harvest, the 2003 vintage. Brian Croser, Bollinger and Lynch-Bages would be partners in the Tapanappa company for 10 years.

Brian advanced rapidly. A winery was built, initially quite modest. We put a Whalebone Vineyard Cabernet Sauvignon on the market, in addition to the 'house' Chardonnay from Tiers Vineyard. We needed a Pinot Noir, and selected Foggy Hill vineyard on the Fleurieu Peninsula where the Burgundian grape thrived in a benevolent climate and where the Crosers had a second home by the ocean.

After showcasing our initiative in Bordeaux at Vinexpo in 2001, Brian and I decided to divide up the commercial side between us: the Crosers, the Australian market, and Bollinger's British subsidiary, the UK, where the company was well established, and where Australian wines were warmly received. Our Médoc trading company was entrusted with the rest of the world. In France and Europe, the success was… measured. In New York, we were the object of polite interest, but without convincing a powerful distributor, our sales in the United States remained weak.

Commercial development was slow and unsatisfactory, but Tapanappa made rapid progress on the technical front and the wines, both white and red, were excellent. Despite this, communication proved difficult, with distance complicating matters. The division of labour, which was clear at the beginning of the adventure, did not work as planned.

Brian's son-in-law, Xavier Bizot, a member of the Bollinger family, was by this point helping him manage the property. He proved to be a difficult partner, only grudgingly respecting our agreement to share the marketing. The Australian domestic market remained limited and the results of our marketing efforts in Europe and the rest of the world were frustratingly slow.

Xavier, who probably wanted to do the right thing, tried hard to sell, and sometimes would end up directing his efforts in areas that were in theory allocated to us, most often without warning us. Things got worse, and although Brian was unhappy to see our relations deteriorate, there was little he could do about it. He added a sparkling *'méthode champenoise'* wine to his output, and after a few more years we felt it was time to pull the trigger on the ejector seat – as did our friends at Bollinger who were experiencing similar difficulties. We sold our shares to Brian, who became the sole shareholder… and we remained good friends.

Neither Jean-Charles nor I have returned to Australia.

28 The Call of the Languedoc

SINCE THE 1996 and especially the 1997 harvests, the prices of land for the Bordeaux Grands Crus had risen in a way that many consider unsustainable. Around the same time, the Languedoc joined the party… Its vineyards, 2,000 years old but with much of the past century spent producing high-yielding, mass production wines, were the object of renewed commercial interest.

Its favourable climate for vine growing and the quality of some of its soils had attracted attention. The first to point this out, in 1997, was the English journalist and Master of Wine Jancis Robinson, who had high praise for James Herrick, a British national who had planted 200 hectares of Chardonnay near Narbonne for a major Australian company. For Jancis, the Languedoc was the 'New Frontier' of wine.

In fact, James Herrick was preceded by some visionaries – among them one of my namesakes in the Cazes family, with whom I had long maintained friendly relations. André and Bernard Cazes were among the first, at their eponymous estate in Rivesaltes, to really focus on quality.

Another precursor was a former rugby player from Narbonne, Yves Barsalou, who became the powerful president of the *Caisse Nationale de Crédit Agricole*. From the 1970s onwards, he supported numerous initiatives that gave lasting structure to the Languedoc vineyards, such as the creation of the Val d'Orbieu producers' group, whose objective was to develop the production of bottled wines in a world that had until then been dominated by bulk sales. Since my conversation with Jancis Robinson, I had made several trips to Languedoc-Roussillon and met many of the regional players, starting with Yves Barsalou.

Robert Skalli was also part of the avant-garde. Heir to a family that was involved in vineyards in North Africa, in the wine trade in Sète and in the food industry (Panzani pasta and Lustucru most famously), he crossed the Atlantic in the early 1980s and bought a ranch in Napa Valley. The climate of California reminded him of the South of France and this experience led him, with the help of Yves Barsalou, to become the champion of French 'varietal wines' with his brand 'Fortant de France'. From his stronghold in Sète, he criss-crossed the Languedoc to convince wine growers to commit themselves to quality wine and to dare to plant Chardonnay, Sauvignon Blanc, Syrah and Cabernet Sauvignon. It was the beginning of a revolution.

The terroirs of the Midi also attracted passionate winemakers in search of new horizons. Aimé Guibert left his native Millau and fell under the spell of an old abandoned farm near Aniane. Advised by Henri Enjalbert, a Bordeaux specialist in terroirs, and Emile Peynaud, our specialist in Grands Crus, he created the Mas de Daumas-Gassac where he set himself apart by planting a Cabernet Sauvignon vineyard. His wines – administratively confined to the *'vin de table'* category – soon became famous. Henri Gault and Christian Millau, then at the height of their influence, described Daumas-Gassac as 'Château Lafite Languedoc'!

Philippe Courrian, owner of Château Tour Haut-Caussan, in Blaignan-Médoc, bought a property in the Corbières appellation, in Saint-Laurent-de-la-Cabrerisse, in the Aude. The vines were nestled along the banks of the Nielle River, in a wild and rugged setting. The turbulent course of the river inspired the name Château Cascadais for the newcomer.

Further north, in the Hérault region, the Montpellier-based Laurent Vaillé was experiencing a similar adventure near Aniane. Having identified promising terroirs in the Arboussas Massif, he created 'La Grange des Pères' where he planted, cultivated and vinified with passion. His wines were quickly noticed by wine lovers and his bottles soon reached prices that rivalled those of the Bordeaux Grands Crus.

The same spirit animated the owner of the *La Revue du Vin de France*, the dynamic Jean-Claude Le Brun, and his wife, the journalist Chantal Le Couty, who abandoned Parisian life and sold the magazine to become wine growers. Advised by their friend Michel Bettane, an experienced wine taster, the couple set their sights on the Prieuré Saint-Jean-de-Bebian, near Pézenas.

Jacques Ribourel, repatriated from Algeria like Robert Skalli, knew the Languedoc very well as he had built thousands of houses there. He turned to the vineyard, and fell in love with the Hospitalet estate – at nearly 1,000 hectares – situated on the spectacular Massif de la Clape, between Narbonne and the Mediterranean. Well assisted by his wife, he set about making it a wine paradise. After planting 100 hectares of varied grape varieties, he transformed the estate, adding a restaurant, a hotel, rooms for seminars and a series of astonishing collections: old cars, regional fossils, hives for bee keeping... with the intention of attracting thousands of visitors.

Following the example of the Englishman James Herrick, some Americans also tried the Languedoc adventure. Their initiatives were initially successful: John Goelet, who already owned the Clos du Val winery in Napa Valley, and his associate Bernard Portet, son of the former director of Château Lafite, bought some 60 hectares of promising terroir near Pézenas in 1997, where the vines were in very poor condition. The Franco-American duo created the Domaine de Nizas, combining French winemaking know-how with Californian viticulture techniques.

On the other hand, Robert Mondavi's venture at Aniane was a major American initiative that ended in resounding failure. At the same time John Goelet and Bernard Portet moved to Nizas in the Hérault, Mondavi was wanting to abandon its Californian brand Vichon, which was handicapped by the resurgence of phylloxera in the 1990s. It was eyeing the Languedoc as an alternative location, and it planned to launch new high-end varietal wines under the Vichon Mediterranean label.

Looking for the easiest way to enter the area, Mondavi first tried to acquire Daumas Gassac, which Aimé Guibert had made the most prestigious estate in the region, but the proposal was deemed insufficient and Mondavi was categorically refused. Instead, it turned to La Grange des Pères, a smaller but equally renowned estate.

Bob Mondavi and his sons Michael and Tim, guided by the French technician Thomas Duroux, now director of Château Palmer in Margaux, explored the *garrigues* of the nearby Arboussas Massif. They were convinced that the site, identified by Henri Enjalbert some 20 years earlier, would allow the establishment of a large quality vineyard.

Their plan was ambitious, involving clearing a vast, hilly area, which until then had been used mainly by the region's farmers to hunt wild boar... they came up against a steadfast refusal from hunters, wine growers and local elected representatives. Things quickly turned difficult. Notwithstanding the Mondavis' claim that they wanted to integrate into the Languedoc culture, they were called rude colonialists, financial monsters, capricious billionaires and greedy wine merchants...

Aimé Guibert, perhaps disappointed at not having been able to obtain the sum he was hoping for for Daumas Gassac, was the first to sound the charge.

In 2001, against the backdrop of municipal competition, at the end of a Marcel Pagnol-style tragicomedy, despite the support of the outgoing Socialist mayor and the president of the Hérault General Council, Mondavi capitulated to a coalition that brought together the new mayor (who was a Communist), Aimé Guibert, the local wine growers' union, the hunters who feared being deprived of their favourite territory and, for good measure, the actor Gérard Depardieu, who had just bought three hectares in Aniane!

AS THE YEAR 2000 approached, 'Châteaux & Associés', a company created to coordinate the management of the AXA-Millésimes properties and those of my family, grew. The structure managed several properties that were geographically distant from each other, as well as a trading company, the *Compagnie Médocaine des Grands Crus*. In addition, we had just broadened our activities by focusing on wine tourism and the opening of Cordeillan-Bages. Everywhere, the teams had been renewed and I felt the need to close ranks. I decided to bring us all together… in the Languedoc, which few of us knew.

In 1999, our team set off towards Toulouse, Carcassonne and Narbonne… to the Domaine de l'Hospitalet in the Massif de la Clape, on the shores of the Mediterranean, where we decided to hold our annual seminar. Since 1990, the scope of Châteaux & Associés had grown, with Villa Bel-Air in the Graves, Suduiraut in Sauternes, Quinta do Noval in Portugal and Disznókő in Tokaj. From 28 people nine years ago, we had now grown to around 40. When we arrived at our destination, Jacques Ribourel's warm welcome and the comfort of his facilities helped us to cope with the icy Tramontane wind that swept through the region during our stay.

We alternated between work meetings and field visits. The latter took us to Sète to Robert Skalli's winery, to Mas Amiel in Maury where the Dupuy family produced natural sweet wines of great originality, to our namesakes the Cazes in Rivesaltes, and to the discovery of the breathtaking Cathar castles of Peyrepertuse and Queribus. We came back from our stay cold, but seduced by the beauty of the landscapes and convinced by the quality and diversity of the wines we had discovered.

In the months that followed, I returned to the Languedoc on several occasions, most often with Daniel LLose. Originally from Argelès-sur-Mer, near Banyuls, Daniel knew the region intimately. In 2000, we contacted the services of SAFER Languedoc-Roussillon – the organization that oversees any potential vineyard purchases in the region – and we registered our interest. After a few contacts which we did not follow up, SAFER informed us that an interesting vineyard in the Minervois region had been put up for sale and suggested that we visit it. An appointment was immediately made.

It was about 20 hectares and located in the commune of La Livinière, at a place called La Gardiole, on the border of the departments of Aude and Hérault. The wine benefited from the name 'Cru Minervois-La Livinière' – as distinct from the regional appellation 'Minervois' – which for the local producers was a hoped-for step towards an independent communal appellation, like Pauillac or Margaux vis-à-vis the Haut-Médoc appellation which encompasses them geographically.

The seller was a wine grower from the neighbouring commune of Azille, Maxime Garcia, who wished to regroup his vineyard on plots closer to his home. At the foothills of the Black Mountain, La Livinière was a large village grouped around its church, the dome-shaped bell tower of which dominated the landscape. The exit of the village was marked by the large brick chimney of the old Saint-Joseph tile factory. The vineyard was omnipresent and dotted with old olive trees. A dirt road led to La Gardiole, a sort of promontory that seemed to stand guard over the plain. Here, there were about 20 hectares of vines, but other than these the place was isolated. In the distance, between two rows of plane trees, the Canal du Midi wound its way, and the only building, a small abandoned house, dominated a vast panorama which extended from the Black Mountain to the village of Azille.

The location was magical, the condition of the vines satisfactory, the price of the property reasonable. However, the absence of farm buildings was a difficulty. In any case, there was no hurry... A few weeks later, we were contacted by a well-known intermediary in the region, Michel Veyrier, who had heard about our visit to La Livinière. He wanted to show us a property that was one kilometre from La Gardiole and which he thought would be very complementary. The estate was called Vipur ('*vin puro*' in Occitan). Larger than La Gardiole, and in a single plot, it was located on a south-facing hillside, with 25 hectares of vines, unplanted vineyard land benefiting from the Minervois-La Livinière label, together with large areas of scrubland and an olive grove of 25 hectares (comprising 6,000 trees, it was the largest in the Languedoc). There were also two dwellings and a fairly large wine storehouse and vat house, all rather dilapidated. The owners, a family from the Paris region, did not live on site and obviously did not possess the wine-growing spirit.

In the Minervois, the village of La Livinière and the Domaine de l'Ostal set among the vines.

The Call of the Languedoc

Michel Veyrier was right, the whole area – about 150 hectares – would have allure and potential. Daniel LLose agreed, and immediately declared himself willing to give new life to La Gardiole and Vipur.

Through SAFER for La Gardiole and Michel Veyrier for Vipur, I concluded the transaction in the spring of 2001. The first thing to do was to unite the two estates under the same name. While reading *Montaillou, Village Occitan*, by Emmanuel Le Roy Ladurie (1975), a fascinating chronicle of a Cathar village at the time of the Inquisition, I discovered the word 'ostal' which designates 'house' in the Roman sense of the term, meaning the dwelling itself and all the people living under its roof. Our new Languedoc estate was a family property and I like teamwork. It was decided: La Gardiole and Vipur would become Ostal Cazes.

The most pressing thing now was to improve the quality of the plantings and to give unity to a vineyard planted with a little Syrah, a touch of Cinsault, Grenache and Mourvèdre and a lot of Carignan. To rebalance the whole, we extended the Syrah plantations and tore out a large proportion of the Carignan, keeping only the oldest vines. Several hectares of favourable land were planted with new vines. This was a long-term project that would take several years to complete.

The olive grove posed a particular problem. The vineyard that once occupied the site was ravaged by the cold in February 1956. The then owner obtained subsidies to uproot the vines and replace them with olive trees. This was the trend at the time. The trees, planted in 1957, had been totally neglected for 45 years. Never pruned, they had been invaded by the scrubland, and the olive trees had disappeared into an impenetrable bramble.

A decision had to be made. Wisdom suggested that a bulldozer should clear the way for a new vineyard. This would be the cheapest option. But we decided against it and instead called in a local contractor who, within three months, had cleaned up the land and preserved the trees. The resurrected olive grove was beautiful and inspiring, with its trees lined up like soldiers on parade, under a horizon dominated by the brilliant white snow on the Canigou mountain range.

We were welcomed with relative friendliness by our neighbours, most of whom were willing to help us get started. We established good relations with the local cooperative cellar where we sometimes vinified some plots. The Vipur vat room, roughly equipped, allowed us to process our first harvests, but it was clear we needed more modern facilities. The plans were almost complete when we learned that one of our neighbours, Robert Eden, wished to part with his cellars, a modern vat house and reception facilities that he had just finished installing in the old Saint-Joseph tile factory. Robert Eden explained that, influenced by a professor at the University of Montpellier, he had recently converted to bioclimatic architecture... and had suddenly decided to get rid of his brand-new equipment and the building that housed it in order to launch a new project.

The old building looked good, with a modern vat house and equipment. We could work there immediately in excellent conditions. Moreover, the location of the *tuilerie*, at the crossroads of the road from Carcassonne to Narbonne and the road leading to the village of La Livinière, would be ideal for Domaine de l'Ostal to position itself well in the regional tourist landscape. I was surprised by the decision of my neighbour Eden, as was Daniel LLose, but our disbelief was matched only by our enthusiasm and I quickly agreed to the purchase.

WE ALSO HAD TO TAKE CARE of the olives. I didn't know anything about olive growing and Daniel LLose didn't know much either. Local specialists and technical books told us that there were several varieties, some suitable for confectionery, others for oil production... so first we had to identify our trees. As we couldn't find any archives relating to the 1957 plantation, we turned to the experts: our olives were mostly 'Picholines', mixed with 'Ascolana' and some 'Lucques'. A perfect mix to produce an excellent oil.

We approached the Clermont l'Hérault olive-growing cooperative and signed an agreement which, after pressing, would allow us to recover the oil from our own olives. All we had to do was harvest. Choked by the undergrowth, the trees had suffered greatly, and experience taught us eventually that olive harvests are very irregular. The harvest, in December, is difficult to mechanize and is highly dependent on the weather conditions. However, we quickly managed to produce 10,000–12,000 50cl-bottles per year of a tasty oil that our customers liked.

It took us a little less than 10 years to transform the estate into a coherent wine-growing entity and to produce, year after year, wines of character which we entrusted to our Bordeaux trading company for marketing. In addition to the main production of red wine, we added a small amount of white wine and – in a particularly good move – a rosé wine of the 'Provence' type, which was an immediate success.

I often visit the Domaine de l'Ostal. I love the Mediterranean climate, the unspoilt landscapes and villages, the strolls along the shady banks of the Canal du Midi, the towering ramparts of the Cathar city of Minerve and... the roast guinea fowl of Madame Chabbert in Fauzan... I also sometimes meet Jancis Robinson, who has managed to convince her husband, Nick Lander, a renowned food writer, to leave the London fog for the sunny village of Marseillette, a few kilometres away.

The houses and buildings of Vipur have remained as they were. I was tempted for a while to transform this old Languedoc farmhouse into a holiday home. I even had detailed plans drawn up. Believing I had everything on my side, I took Thereza there on a beautiful summer day. The cicadas had obviously decided to discourage us invaders. Their deafening noise did not subside until nightfall and we had to shorten our walk in the scrubland to escape the aggressiveness of the insects that sprang up from all the bushes. The verdict was not long in coming: no holiday home here!

29 Return to the Douro

ON DECEMBER 31ST 2001, my assignment at Quinta do Noval, entrusted by AXA in 1993, was about to end. A few months before this, Thereza and I were invited to a reception organized by the port wine houses in honour of the King of Spain, Juan Carlos, who was visiting the Douro. The whole profession gathered together at the Vintage House Hotel recently opened in Pinhão by the Symington family, the most powerful wine production and trading company in port and owner of several quintas and famous brands (Taylor, Delaforce, Graham's… This was an opportunity for me to meet, perhaps one last time, the representatives of the Portuguese wine industry and trade.

Our table neighbours were Jorge and 'Tita' Roquette. Between the pear and the cheese courses, my neighbour described his career: a director of the Portuguese bank BPI, he now intended to devote more time to developing his family estate, Quinta do Crasto, located not far from there.

The history of the estate, which occupies a privileged position overlooking the river, was emblematic of the region. The vineyard took shape in the 19th century, and was bought at the beginning of the 20th century by Constantino de Almeida, an exporter of port wine and brandy.

Crasto became known for the quality of its wines and in 1923, when Constantino died, his son Fernando took over. In 1981, his granddaughter, 'Tita', daughter of Fernando and wife of Jorge Roquette, became the majority shareholder of the estate. Despite his responsibilities at the bank, he found time to assist his wife. With the help of their sons Miguel and Tomas, they implemented an ambitious programme to renovate and extend the vineyard and modernize the technical installations. They innovated, succeeded and produced Douro red wines of acclaimed quality.

This meeting with Jorge had long-term consequences. I visited him at Crasto, at his hillside winery, in the middle of the vineyards situated on a loop of the river, descending in terraces down to the banks. The house, perched on a

Above: Scouting in the Upper Douro: Thereza, Jean-Charles and I in the company of Jorge and Tita Roquette.

Below: Daniel Llose, Thereza, Marina, Catherine and Jean-Charles are well surrounded by the young generation of the Roquette family accompanied by the oenologist Manuel Lobo.

promontory, was typical of the Douro houses of the 19th century, with a spectacular location and breathtaking views over the valley – every bit as beautiful as the Noval terrace, which had impressed me so much a few years earlier.

As a good banker, Jorge had drawn up detailed business plans. And above all, ambitious. As his experience in wine growing was relatively recent, he was attentive to my remarks. We discussed his hypotheses. As we talked, I grew more convinced about the quality and the audacity of his proposals. One of his projects was the development of a new quinta, located further up the valley, near Vila Nova de Foz Côa, close to the Spanish border in the Upper Douro. During a visit with Daniel LLose, he showed us around 'Cabreira'. Its steep, difficult-to-access slopes plunged down to the river. As at Crasto, the site was astonishingly beautiful, but much wilder. Work on the vineyard had barely begun; the earth-moving machinery was making its first sculpting strokes to form the *patamares*, the terraces that would eventually support the rows of vines.

Jorge, who was far-sighted, was concerned about the future marketing of Cabreira's grapes. He was right to be so, as he planned to plant more than 100 hectares of vines. In 2002, he proposed that I set up a winemaking company with him, which could start immediately, using the method of buying grapes which is common in the Douro – a system similar to that used in Champagne. Initially, we would use Crasto's well-equipped winemaking facilities. We soon agreed and launched our association under the name of 'Roquette & Cazes', thus emphasizing the family character of our company.

We were convinced that the combination of the intrinsic qualities of the Douro grapes and the experience of our teams would produce wines that combined the sun of Portugal with the elegance of Bordeaux. Daniel LLose was put to work and developed our first vintages with the technicians of Quinta do Crasto. Despite the language barrier and the distance between them, the cooperation and exchanges between the Frenchman and the Portuguese team were a success. A name had to be chosen for the wine. During a long car journey from Boston to New York, I tested some ideas with an American friend. When I mentioned 'Xisto', which means 'shale' and refers to the rocks that form the soil of the Douro mountains, my travelling companion immediately exclaimed: 'That's the one! In the United States, no one will know how to spell it spontaneously. They'll ask you to spell it… and the name will be remembered!'

In 2005, Jorge Roquette and I presented the first vintage of our joint venture, Xisto 2003, at Vinexpo in Bordeaux, where we had the satisfaction of seeing our wine selected as one of the 'top 10' discoveries of the year.

Our project evolved rapidly. After producing three vintages of Xisto under the guidance of Daniel LLose and Manuel Lobo de Vasconcellos, a talented oenologist from Quinta do Crasto, we decided to create a different wine, thus giving birth in 2006 to the Roquette & Cazes Vintage. Elegant and harmonious, it was designed to be drunk on release. We cut back the production of Xisto, the big brother, to years when the sometimes extreme climatic conditions of the Upper Douro lent themselves to the production of superlatively structured wines.

As the teams learned to work together it soon became clear that we needed to become more directly involved in the production process, alongside our Portuguese friends. We explored the vineyards, mostly by river, which was the most convenient and spectacular route. From Pinhão, a three-hour sail led to the upper reaches of the Douro, through the gorges and locks of Cachão de Valeira. Near Villa Nova de Foz Côa, Rita – daughter of Jorge Roquette and sister of Tomas and Miguel – and her husband João welcomed us to their splendid guest house, Casa do Rio, surrounded by almond, olive and fruit trees. Each time we visited, Jorge and his children showed us the work they were doing in Cabreira, which was gradually becoming a spectacular quinta.

Located at a site called 'Meco', the property stood adjacent to steep, rocky, scrub-covered land overlooking the Douro which was dotted with olive trees: a position that had definite viticultural potential. At this time, it was only used by a few shepherds from Castelo Melhor, the neighbouring village, who made meagre pastures for their sheep there; many plots were for sale. Jorge took care of the contracts and acted as our interpreter with the owners. We succeeded in acquiring, in several stages, almost 25 hectares of well-exposed land, grouped together on the bank of the river, near Cabreira.

The soils, which were in a wild state, had to be prepared for planting, and bulldozers set to work on the sometimes dizzying slopes, playing a balancing act as they traced the *patamares* that would eventually receive the rows of vines. We prepared 11 hectares in 2010, then another 11 hectares in 2012, which we planted immediately using three of the main traditional grape varieties: the very Portuguese Tinta Roriz, Touriga Nacional and Touriga Franca, to which we add a hint of Tinta Francisca, a relative of Syrah.

All this confirmed our strong roots in the Douro Valley, and we have now given this newly born Quinta the name 'Quinta do Meco'.

Above: The dizzying slopes of the Quinta do Meco, on the left bank of the river Douro.

Below: Meco in spring: its steep vineyards neatly buffered by almond trees.

Return to the Douro

30 Shipping to Châteauneuf-du-Pape

IT WAS EARLY SUMMER 2006. Absorbed by my computer screen, I answered distractedly to the 'hello' that Jean-Charles threw at me as he entered my office, and continued to type on the keyboard. He flipped through the day's mail piled up in my basket and extracted a few pages: 'Opportunity to acquire vineyards in Châteauneuf-du-Pape.' The document was sent to us by Michel Veyrier, who had helped us set up in the Languedoc a few years earlier.

I have always had a weakness for the wines of Châteauneuf. I like the Beaucastel of the Perrin family and the Vieux Télégraphe of the Brunier family. A little further north, I appreciate the productions of Domaine Guigal in Ampuis and the Chave family in Hermitage. I also had a fondness for Gérard Jaboulet, from Tain l'Hermitage, a tireless promoter of wine, too soon deceased, whom I met several times during my travels. I must admit that I was nevertheless not very familiar with the Rhône Valley, of which, apart from these few stars, I knew little more than Anne-Sophie Pic's table in Valence. Which was still a good start.

Jean-Charles commented on the letter: 'Domaine des Sénéchaux? I don't know… The fact that Michel is looking for a buyer in Bordeaux means that no one wants it locally… it must not be a first choice!'

Without looking up, I heard myself reply: 'You never know…' and I grabbed a copy of the monumental 1997 edition of Parker's Guide (*Guide Parker des Vins de France*) from my shelf. For several years, the American critic had been an advocate for the wines of Châteauneuf and gave them a new and international visibility. I immediately found the information: Big Bob called the Sénéchaux wine 'excellent' and gave the estate four stars. I read aloud: '…a resplendent ruby colour, with a nose of sweet, ripe black cherries and smoky herbs, this Châteauneuf-du-Pape is soft, round and seductive on the palate…' As for Châteauneuf in general, Parker is wildly enthusiastic: '…rich and very full-bodied, with a dense, deep colour, they can be kept for at least 15–20 years and are characterized by aromas of leather, fennel, liquorice, black truffle, pepper, nutmeg and smoked meat. Stock up now!'

It was springtime, and the weather was fine. Jean-Charles and I exchanged glances. 'Let's go and see.'

No sooner said than done. I called Jean-Pierre Perrin to tell him that we would soon be passing near his house and that we would be happy to visit him at Beaucastel.

A few days later, we were in Châteauneuf-du-Pape. Jean-Pierre welcomed us and, of course, asked why we were there. I told him straight away. After touring the imposing Beaucastel cellars and tasting a few wines, we found ourselves in the dining room, grappling with an imposing salt crusted seabass. François, the family technician and Jean-Pierre's brother, was due to join us. But he was late and we started lunch without him. He finally arrived: 'We didn't wait for you; where did you come from?' asked our host. And François, to everyone's amazement, replied: 'I was in Châteauneuf, with the people from SAFER... I was visiting a vineyard for sale, the Domaine des Sénéchaux.'

After the surprise, Jean-Charles and I congratulated ourselves for not having kept the reason for our visit secret. It goes without saying that the Perrins would not stand in the way of a negotiation that they knew was already underway with us. The two brothers assured us that if the deal went ahead, they would do their best to ensure that we were well received by the wine growers of the appellation.

Michel Veyrier told us about the reasons for the sale. The Roux family, owners of Domaine des Sénéchaux, also owned Château Trignon in Gigondas, a vast 65-hectare vineyard. Its main activity centred around a pharmaceutical laboratory but, in 1990, the family decided to take a decisive turn and sold the laboratory to an American group. Pascal Roux, son of the company's founder, then devoted himself to the management of Château Trignon, following in his father's footsteps. He became interested in wine and bought the Sénéchaux vineyard in 1993.

In 1997, following the unfortunate dissolution of the National Assembly, the political wind shifted abruptly. No sooner had Jacques Chirac installed him at Hôtel de Matignon, the official residence of French prime ministers, than Alain Juppé had to give way to Lionel Jospin. The latter hastened to re-establish the wealth tax that had disappeared with the departure of François Mitterrand, and the Roux family felt that the time had come to distance themselves from the French tax authorities.

In 1998, it was done… the Swiss shores of Lake Geneva were welcoming. A few years later, in 2003–04, the wine-producing Rhône Valley experienced a severe economic crisis, aggravated by unfavourable weather conditions. The Roux's interest in their French wine heritage waned. They considered selling their vineyards in Gigondas and Châteauneuf-du-Pape. In 2006, the wine business picked up, and it was time to sell. Pascal Roux got in touch with Michel Veyrier, and put the family's vineyards up for sale.

Of course, Pascal Roux's decision did not go unnoticed by his neighbours in Châteauneuf-du-Pape. Nor did it go unnoticed by the *Société d'Aménagement Foncier et d'Etablissement Rural* (SAFER) in Vaucluse, which followed the matter closely from its headquarters in Avignon. The head of SAFER for the Châteauneuf-du-Pape appellation, urged on by the local wine growers, made no secret of his intention to use his right of pre-emption. Once the acquisition had been made, the vineyard would be cut up into pieces and divided among the neighbours. For SAFER, the intervention had the advantage of generating fees, and everyone was working hard to ensure that the matter was settled 'internally' and did not go beyond the boundaries of the appellation.

The professional climate in Châteauneuf-du-Pape was unusual, and the more we got to know the local life, the more we realized that there was a great distance between the Bordeaux wine world and the viticultural atmosphere of the Rhône Valley.

In Bordeaux, as elsewhere in France's appellations, the wine growers are organized into wine unions. But in Châteauneuf-du-Pape, a small war was going on between the traditional wine growers and the advocates of a more modern and qualitative viticulture. The professional organization had been in turmoil for a few years, leading to a split between the 'local union', guardian of traditions, and the 'Intercommunality', which counted among its members the best-known – and most qualitative – estates of Châteauneuf, which joined their counterparts in neighbouring communes. The stars of the appellation – Beaucastel, Vieux Télégraphe, Montredon, la Nerthe, and so on – supported the 'Intercommunality'. Apart from the mayor, to whom, at the request of Michel Veyrier, we paid a formal visit, we had no contact with the local union. And even less with SAFER…

The mayor's name was Jean-Pierre Boisson. He kindly received us into his office in Châteauneuf. We had a surprising conversation with him. After introducing ourselves, explaining our approach and setting out our ambitions, we listened to him talk about his commune. He complained about the current

Above: On the banks of the river Rhône, Châteauneuf-du-Pape sits snugly at the centre of its vineyards.

Below: One-time seat of the popes of Avignon, the ruins of Châteauneuf's castle sit atop its pretty village.

Above: In the cellar of the Domaine des Sénéchaux, Jean-Charles and the director Bernard Tranchecoste.

Below: Sénéchaux dates back to the 14th century and is one of the oldest estates in the region.

trend for prioritizing the sales of bottles, which are more qualitative, over bulk deliveries which until recently constituted the main way of marketing the wines of the appellation.

The mayor criticized the race for quality, which he considered excessive. He accused it of creating a spirit of competition between the wine growers, of generating rivalries and of creating a bad climate within the profession. On top of that, he noted, the tankers that used to take the wines from the town's cellars to the merchants' warehouses had been replaced by vehicles heavily loaded with bottles which, throughout the year, caused traffic jams and damaged the local roads… In short, the municipal welcome, without being openly hostile, was not particularly warm.

In the following weeks, a meeting with the local wine growers was proposed. The two rival unions agreed to a joint meeting. In the summer of 2006, Jean-Charles and I met in a large room, in front of an audience of about 25 people. A little intimidated, we did our best to present, in a religious silence, our activity in Bordeaux and our project. At the end of our presentation, we took part in a question-and-answer session. Several speakers showed open hostility towards us… which reminded me of what my father used to say to me at the time of the election campaign for the mayor's office in Pauillac: 'You mustn't fear your opponents. On the contrary…' We ended up enjoying the discussion and the assembly dispersed arm in arm.

At the same time, thanks to Michel Veyrier, the conversations with Pascal Roux were progressing. Knowing that SAFER's plans were already advanced, the deal had to be concluded as quickly as possible. A meeting was organized. For the sake of discretion, Pascal Roux, Jean-Charles and I met on the terrace of a café in Montmirail, in the shadow of the famous Dentelles, a spectacular rocky panorama of Haute Provence. We worked out the details of our agreement without difficulty.

The SAFER committee, pushed by a few wine growers, did everything it could to hold things up. The possibility of pre-empting the sale, which is sometimes used in similar situations, was often mentioned. But in the case of Sénéchaux, the principle came up against a legal impossibility. The right of pre-emption available to SAFER only applies to properties held as 'own property'. It does not apply to the 'transfer of shares' in a company. As the estate was owned by the Roux family through a limited company, the circumstances were therefore favourable for us. This restriction (which disappeared a few years later) allowed us to go ahead with the operation without a hitch.

Jean-Charles and I celebrated the signing of the deed of sale at the end of summer 2006. We now knew the region well and enjoyed its good restaurants. In Mondragon, we discovered the Auberge La Beaugravière, where truffles played a leading role, accompanied by wines from a cellar full of treasures. We visited our future neighbours, such as the Richard family at Château La Nerthe, and the Féraud family at Domaine du Pegau, whose wines are praised by Robert Parker. They all welcomed us kindly.

Now owners of the Domaine des Sénéchaux, we quickly took an inventory. The vineyard was well kept, the wines good. Since they took over, Pascal Roux and his manager, Bernard Tranchecoste, had done a great job. The soils, rich in gravel and pebbles (the alpine 'diluvium' of geologists), were typical of the Châteauneuf-du-Pape terroir. The property covered a total of 27 hectares. Red grape varieties (24 hectares) were in the majority. Grenache dominated, present on a little more than half the surface area, followed by Syrah at nearly 20 percent and a small number of Mourvèdre vines. The plots of white vines, which needed freshness, were located on a cooler northern slope and at altitude. The traditional local grape varieties were found here: White Grenache, Roussanne, Bourboulenc and Clairette. The vineyard was a few decades old, but had been regularly renewed, and the soils were worked without chemical weeding. Harvesting had all been done by hand.

For vinification and storage, the estate had modern and well-equipped premises in the village of Châteauneuf itself. There was not much to change in the working methods. The barrels needed to be renewed, as did the tuns, which were showing their age, and we got on with this immediately.

Our programme was simple: to continue to develop the estate by relying on the existing team. Daniel LLose supervised the technical management and was, once again, in his element. For several years, the vinification of Les Sénéchaux was overseen by the acclaimed – and now sadly late – Philippe Cambie, a renowned oenologist and expert in blending, who was known for his blunt approach and advised many of the local wine growers. Bernard Tranchecoste was used to working with him, and the trio soon established a good relationship and proved to be very efficient.

As we had done with Domaine de l'Ostal, we entrusted the marketing of our Châteauneuf to our trading company based near Bordeaux. It was delighted to see our portfolio strengthened by a quality label and a world-renowned appellation. Domaine des Sénéchaux now benefits from an efficient international distribution network.

The famous giant pebbles – galet roulés – of Châteauneuf, reflecting and radiating the sun to warm the vines.

31 Château Haut-Batailley

IN THE SUMMER OF 2016, my children and I met in Magescq, at the incomparable Relais de la Poste in Les Landes, with our friends Jacques and Jean Cousseau. The purpose of the meeting was to examine the renovation scheme for Lynch-Bages. Our project put in the developments that would meet our needs, seemed to fall within our budget, and was well advanced in its planning. Nonetheless, it represented a significant investment. Throughout September, my son Jean-Charles and our financial director Pierre Doumenjou had been working hard to answer questions about all aspects of the construction, both technical and financial.

For several months, Jean-Charles had been in contact with BNP and LCL. Both banks had given us their agreement, thus showing their confidence in the figures we had given them and in the future of our company.

In the meantime, in October 2016, Alexis Weill, a specialist in the wine sector and senior banker at the Rothschild bank, made a sensational entry into our daily professional life by communicating to us the elements of a file that bore the code name 'ASPIS'. It concerned the sale of Château Haut-Batailley, an 1855 Cru Classé, by the Des Brest-Borie family.

Located in Pauillac, just one kilometre from Lynch-Bages, Haut-Batailley's founding was the result of the division of Château Batailley between Marcel and Francis Borie, sons of Eugène Borie, a wine merchant who left his native Corrèze to settle in Pauillac at the end of the 19th century. A specialist in the northern French and especially Belgian markets, Borie-Frères established itself firmly in the Bordeaux landscape (Marcel Borie was mayor of Pauillac for a time), and the two brothers acquired Château Batailley together after World War I, before dividing the property between them in 1941.

They divided the vineyard in half, with the road from Pauillac to Saint-Laurent acting as a border. Marcel Borie kept the Batailley house and his brother Francis organized his vines around the old existing buildings. To

Château Haut-Batailley – one of 18 'Fifth Growths' decreed by the 1855 Classification – is situated in the very south of the Pauillac appellation. It became the property of our family in 2017.

differentiate it from his brother's, Francis Borie gave his estate the name Château Haut-Batailley. The Tower of Aspic monument built in the 19th century on the Batailley plateau by the pious Mademoiselle Marie-Louise Averous, a landowner in Pauillac, has today become the symbol of the château.

After the division of their estates, the paths of Marcel and Francis Borie also diverged. Marcel, owner of Château Batailley and head of the trading company, died in 1958, leaving the place to his son-in-law Emile Castéja who made Batailley his home in Pauillac. Emile Castéja was succeeded by his son Philippe, who today runs the family business, which became 'Borie-Manoux'. Philippe Castéja lives between Bordeaux and Batailley, where his son Frédéric assists him in managing the vineyard.

In 1942, Francis Borie, owner of Haut-Batailley, increased his hold on the Médoc wine industry by acquiring Château Ducru-Beaucaillou in Saint-Julien, which became his family's base. His son, Jean-Eugène, lived at Ducru-Beaucaillou.

When Francis Borie died in 1953, Château Haut-Batailley was given to his daughter Françoise Des Brest-Borie. Françoise, who had lived outside Bordeaux, leased the estate to her brother Jean-Eugène.

Some 25 years later, during the great crisis of the 1970s, I welcomed at my insurance agent's office in Pauillac my neighbour Raymond Dupin, owner of the neighbouring property Grand-Puy Lacoste. A hardened bachelor with a Landes beret on his head, he announced his decision to sell Grand-Puy and asked me about the price he could get for it. I put forward a figure, almost at random. He obviously expected me to show interest and make him a higher offer, but I knew for a fact that my father and I didn't have a penny in our pockets at the time.

A few days later, I learned that the deal had been done with my friend Jean-Eugène Borie of Ducru-Beaucaillou in Sain-Julien – and at pretty much the exact price I had named. After Jean-Eugène Borie's death in 1998, his properties were shared between his three children. Ducru-Beaucaillou went to Bruno and Sabine, and Grand-Puy-Lacoste to François-Xavier, who also took over the lease of his aunt Françoise Des Brest's property, Château Haut-Batailley.

To complicate matters further, new family ties brought Grand-Puy-Lacoste and Batailley, immediate neighbours, closer together: François-Xavier Borie's daughter married Frédéric, son of Philippe Castéja.

Haut-Batailley has an excellent terroir, some 40 hectares in all, only half of which was planted with vines, and the technical facilities were impeccable. There was little stock, apart from the 2016 harvest, but this was offered at cost price. Since the death of Jean-Eugène Borie, the Des Brest family had never been directly involved in the management. Haut-Batailley had all the makings of a 'sleeping beauty'.

For us, the opportunity to buy this property held a double interest. Obviously, it was an important plot of vines in our Pauillac appellation and a *cru* listed in the 1855 Classification. But, above all, the integration of an estate of this quality into our family business could facilitate future asset reorganizations. We were determined to study the case.

Once the decision to sell had been taken, the owners wanted to move quickly and quietly. We had to hastily show our interest by making an initial offer. All business aside, Jean-Charles contacted his banker friends to establish the basis for financing our proposal. At the beginning of November 2017, we sent Alexis Weill a letter of intent and I convened a family meeting for the 12th.

On the morning of November 11th, Jean-Charles, Kinou, Catherine and I (Marina, on a trip to China, could not be with us) visited Haut-Batailley, under the guidance of Emeline, daughter of François-Xavier Borie, who welcomed us warmly. The impression was as we expected. The technical equipment, well sized, was in perfect condition. The vines were well kept. The yields were low – a guarantee of good quality. Our conclusion was clear: Haut-Batailley was an attractive prospect and we wanted to do everything in our power to succeed with the deal.

A few days later, we learned that we had been selected for the final negotiation. We had to submit a final offer on November 23rd. Jean-Charles worked hard to obtain the 'comfort letters' by which our bankers would guarantee our financial commitment. For months, Jean-Charles, assisted by Pierre Doumenjou, had been working hard with our financial backers to put in place the financing for the reconstruction of Lynch-Bages and had won their confidence. They were now reaping the benefits of their efforts in this new case. Obtaining bank guarantees in such a short time is a tour de force.

On November 23rd at 5.15 pm, we sent our proposal by email. Four offers were made. Alexis Weill suggested that ours was fairly well placed. He asked us to clarify a few things, as the Des Brest family was due to meet the following weekend to decide what to do. We held our breath…

SUNDAY NOVEMBER 27th 2016. Second round of the presidential polls to select a candidate for the Centre-Right Republican party. Goodbye Juppé… Hello Fillon! The day ends with no news from ASPIS. Nothing has filtered out of the Des Brest family meeting. Tension was mounting.

On the afternoon of the next day, November 28th, Thereza and I are at Charles de Gaulle, on a flight to Bangkok. As we were about to take off, my phone, which I had not yet put into 'flight mode', displayed a simple text message from Jean-Charles: 'IT'S US!'

We had to wait until we arrived in Thailand to get more details.

During our stay in Asia, I remained in contact by telephone with Jean-Charles and Pierre Doumenjou who were preparing the next steps with Alexis Weill. The aim was to sign a promise of purchase before the end of December, so as not to increase the time taken by the two official bodies that control agricultural transactions in France: SAFER, which has a right of pre-emption and can redirect the sale as it sees fit, and the *Commission des Structures Agricoles* (CDOA) that issues – or not – the 'authorization to farm', according to complex rules of preference. Like a double-bladed razor…

There was a small grain of sand in the mechanism: Haut-Batailley owned a parcel of vines in the Saint-Julien appellation, run by Bruno Borie, and in turn he owned a parcel of Pauillac vines that were part of Ducru-Beaucaillou. Perhaps we could envisage an exchange… although the two plots were not comparable. We would have to negotiate…

Everything was progressing well. An appointment was made for the signing of the preliminary sales agreement, which was to take place in the neutral ground of Saint-Emilion on December 22nd, a Thursday. The weather was fine in the Bordeaux region. The Des Brest and the Cazes families had arranged to meet at the notary's office, and the atmosphere was friendly. Everyone expressed their satisfaction with the way the transaction was being carried out. Each one of us insisted that the old relations between our two families be maintained. Around midday, the *compromis de vente* was finally signed, and the group dispersed.

We were aware that there were still obstacles to overcome before we could finalize the procedure. We now had to pass our project through the mill of SAFER and the CDOA before the final deed could be signed – in two to three months, if all went well. We also had to work out the details of the financing of the operation with our bankers. The needs relating to the acquisition of Haut-Batailley would be added to the cost of the reconstruction work at Lynch-Bages.

In Bages, in the early days of 2017, about 50 Chinese armed with cameras descended on the village to photograph Juliette Binoche as she filmed for an episode of a television series that took place in the Bordeaux vineyards. After a few days of great excitement, we were brought back to reality: rumours were circulating that some people were trying to derail our project… Had Philippe Castéja been disappointed in his hopes of reconstituting the historical Batailley? Was Bruno Borie unhappy at having been pushed out of the project by his own family? And who were the other candidates?

Jean-Charles met Bruno Borie and managed to obtain his agreement to proceed, after the sale, with an exchange of the Saint-Julien and Pauillac parcels. In mid-January, Bruno Borie seemed to back out. The finalization of the exchange protocol was laborious. Finally, Bruno Borie suggested an oral agreement, which was sufficient between people of good company. We would proceed with the exchange once the deal was done…

We were assured that no one would push SAFER to intervene. Nevertheless, the regional president of the organization, who we did not know, may have had other intentions. On January 19th, while I was in Portugal, I received a call from Jacky Lorenzetti, owner of Château Pedesclaux in Pauillac.

Above: The Virgin Mary, at the top of the Aspic Tower, watches over the vineyards of Haut-Batailley.

Below: The Haut-Batailley vat room, renovated by François-Xavier Borie, has what it takes to make great wines.

The sun is shining, it's spring: Jean-Charles and Kinou celebrate the end of the long negotiations that led to our arrival at Château Haut-Batailley in April 2017. At the top of this tower, a statue of the Virgin Mary depicts her stepping on the devil, represented by a venomous snake, the asp... Hence the unusual name for this landmark, 'La Tour L'Aspic'.

I knew that he was among the list of potential buyers of Haut-Batailley. He told me that he had just received a visit from the head of SAFER for the Médoc, who told him that SAFER could still scupper the sale. The visitor mentioned the possibility of a 'butchering' of Haut-Batailley which would allow SAFER to redistribute the vines to deserving young farmers. But SAFER did not have sufficient means and needed the support of an outside investor… whose intervention would, of course, be rewarded by the allocation of part of the vineyard. On the phone, Jacky Lorenzetti showed the greatest fair play. As far as he was concerned, the game was up… He was not interested in the operation.

Who triggered this intervention by SAFER? Did a third party intervene to derail the current transaction? I would later learn that the pressure came from a local notary who had been excluded from the transaction by the Des Brest family. Did he act on his own initiative, or was he pushed by a client of his office who wanted to be a spoilsport?

Jean-Charles and I asked for an audience with the regional president of SAFER. He received us with a slightly forced bonhomie, and began by explaining his mission: to encourage land consolidation whenever possible in order to 'optimize farms'. He added that he was obliged to intervene. No one, in particular the commission, the famous CDOA, should be able to reproach SAFER for not having done its duty.

We pointed out to him that, in this case, there is no regrouping to be done. Haut-Batailley, a Cru Classé in 1855, forms a whole. It cannot be dismantled without making it disappear. We did not give up. We urged the president to be clearer. He confessed that he did not have a young farmer on hand, but admitted that he had received 'strong pressure'. He mentioned some of our important neighbours. We were surprised: SAFER's mission could not be to give preference to these owners and we would not understand if this were the case. Did we convince him? Finally, the president reassured us… SAFER would not pre-empt the deal, neither totally nor partially. We parted as good friends.

The signing of the final deed was scheduled, subject of course to the agreement of the Commission. We still had to cross the last hurdle, but the risk of refusal was now reduced. For two months, Jean-Charles had steered the family boat with precision and perseverance. The financing was complete, SAFER had been neutralized, the CDOA had been convinced and the competitors had been contained. In this cold and wet Médoc winter, the sun began to shine through the clouds and we signed the final notarial deed on the scheduled date, March 28th 2017.

Under the leadership of Daniel LLose, our team immediately took charge of the property. The planting rights corresponding to the available land were obtained without a hitch, and were implemented in 2018. We immediately started the soil studies to choose the most suitable grape varieties and began the preparatory work. Not surprisingly, the technical installations – vat room and cellar – proved to be faultless and the 2017 harvest went off without a hitch.

We planted 17 new hectares, bringing the vineyard of Haut-Batailley to around 40 hectares. In parallel, the construction was starting at Lynch-Bages at the beginning of the year. During the first quarter of 2018, the new buildings gradually began to take shape.

In the spring of 2018, determined to showcase our first Haut-Batailley vintage without waiting for the market to establish itself, we announced our En Primeur sale. On April 25th 2018, we posted our slightly higher release price and launched a modernized Haut-Batailley label. The Bordeaux trade did not welcome our initiative with cries of joy, but sales were quickly established. Export sales were satisfactory and we noticed that our French and foreign customers trusted us. This first campaign was a success.

The bulk of the En Primeur sales of the 2017 vintage took place in May 2018. As every year, most of the properties sent their usual brokers lists of potential buyers, specifying the volumes offered, which varied greatly in this vintage from one property to another, and real successes were rare: less than 10 percent of the properties saw their initial sales proposals validated by all of their allocated buyers. Our estates, in particular Lynch-Bages, were part of this minority, with a price that was hailed by all, in Bordeaux and abroad.

32 In Pursuit of Quality, 1995–2021

FROM 1975 ONWARDS, for about 15 years, Lynch-Bages was a permanent construction site. By 1990, we had caught up with the majority of the delays. Our technical equipment now met the requirements of modern oenology. The Fête de la Fleur in June 1989 marked the end of this busy building period.

But in the vineyard, too, things were constantly evolving.

After the postwar years, which saw the continuation of ancient cultivation methods, the terrible frosts of February 1956 destroyed vast areas of vines and prompted a move towards more modern vineyard arrangements, with priority given to replanting. The wine growers at this point largely adopted 'clonal selection' which sought out the best possible plants and contributed to the general improvement of the vineyard stock.

For the plantations of the 1960s and 1970s, emphasis was placed on production potential, with high-yielding clones favoured. Gradually, wine growers learned to use more qualitative plants and to choose them according to the characteristics of their soils. At the same time, they tried to better control the diseases and insects that attacked the vines. They succeeded in bringing grapes more regularly to maturity and there was an improvement in the quality of the fruit brought to the winery. From the 1980s onwards, there were no more truly bad vintages.

In the 1990s, we tried to optimize the maturity of the grapes and to balance the production of each plot and each vine. We experimented with various natural approaches: control of the vegetation by leaf removal, grassing between the vine rows and green harvesting, and we began to sort the grapes seriously at harvest time.

At Lynch-Bages and Pichon-Longueville, mobile manual sorting tables were set up for the first time for the 1993 harvest. At the end of the row, grapes were poured onto a conveyor belt where a team of sorters checked their condition before sending them onwards to the vat room. For good measure, a second wave of sorting was carried out in the vat room, after destemming. The transformation in quality that resulted was spectacular.

Year after year, progress in the technical environment has resulted in more precise vinification and continuous improvement of the wines. As the potential issues are better controlled, weak years are rarer and less catastrophic – but exceptional vintages still exist. Thus, the 2000 vintage benefited from ideal weather conditions, and thanks to all the good fairies bent over its cradle, this first vintage of the new century will be remembered as one of the great years of Bordeaux.

At AXA and in the companies of the group, 65 is the age limit for an operational position and the rule applies to everyone – so this 2000 vintage coincided with my leaving the company. To replace me at the head of 'Châteaux & Associés', I proposed Christian Seely, who had proved himself highly capable at Quinta do Noval.

The team that I had assembled over the previous 15 years in 'Châteaux & Associés' to manage the AXA properties and the Cazes properties was redistributed between the two entities, and all went smoothly.

Malou le Sommer remained attached to Lynch-Bages, as did my sister Sylvie, who remained in charge of communications. Pierre Doumenjou constructed an accounting and financial centre for Lynch-Bages. Daniel LLose was a special case. His intimate knowledge of the AXA companies as well as our own led us to entrust him with a technical supervisory position, and, at first, he shared his time between the two groups.

His actions were decisive for the study and start-up of the Languedoc, Châteauneuf-du-Pape and Portuguese estates which our family company acquired from 2002, but we also strengthened our production unit by recruiting a full-time technical director. At Lynch-Bages, after Stephen Carrier, who left us for a Californian project, we recruited Nicolas Labenne in 2005, a highly qualified young oenologist. Son of a family of wine growers from Gers, he was also a man of the field who, after having worked at Lafite, directed Calon-Ségur in Saint-Estèphe for 10 years.

With our new team in place, we turned our attention to the maintenance and renewal of the vineyards.

All plants age and the vine is no exception. In the first few years after planting, some vines die and disappear, and must be replaced immediately. This is called 'complantation' – and the number of victims obviously increases as the years go by. As long as the annual rate of disappearance remains moderate, this method makes it possible to keep quality high without compromising quantity – but it cannot continue forever, and at some point, for the sake of plot management, larger sections of a vineyard have to be grubbed up and replanting done.

A vine has a hard life. Like any living being, it is subject to multiple external attacks. It is the target of various diseases, various moulds, micro-organisms or aggressive insects. In terms of longevity, not all grape varieties are equal. The most fragile is Cabernet Sauvignon, which is subject to numerous diseases. It is difficult to extend the life of a Cabernet plot beyond 50 years, whereas Merlot can withstand another two or three decades. In any case, the thinking must be long term.

In the first decade of the 21st century, Jean Cordeau, an agricultural engineer from Montpellier and former head of the vine department at the Gironde Chamber of Agriculture, who had 60 vintages to his credit, agreed to share his experience with us. He spent the best part of three years surveying our vineyards with Daniel LLose and Nicolas Labenne. The 'clonal selection', favoured after the frost of 1956 and the new plantations of the 1960s and 1970s, had certainly improved our situation, but it had led to uniformity. The old plant material, the bearer of the history of the vineyard, had little by little disappeared as the vines were uprooted and replanted. Not only is clonal unity a threat to the diversity of the vineyard and the durability of its identity, but it also makes the vines more vulnerable to disease. We needed to rectify this…

Together, LLose, Labenne and Cordeau defined a replanting strategy based on 'massal selection'. In our oldest plots of land, they selected beautiful vines of each variety to create our own collection of Petit Verdot, Cabernet Sauvignon and Merlot. For each variety, we created a reserve of 400 to 800 'individuals', plants that we could multiply at will. This method guaranteed the durability of the vineyard and its genetic diversity. At Lynch-Bages, we selected Petit Verdot from the last plot that was not replanted, just before it was pulled up. The vines there were 80 years old. By keeping them, we were preserving the diversity of our Petit Verdots in Pauillac which had almost disappeared.

Before planting, it was necessary to rid the soil of nematodes, unwanted hosts that feed on the roots. These micro-organisms are carriers of viruses that endanger future plantings. To combat phylloxera – a voracious insect that has been present in wine-growing soils for more than 120 years – the only remedy is to graft our French grape varieties onto plants (rootstocks) of American origin.

To prepare the soil, we chose to give up all chemical treatments, preferring to let the soil rest and wait four to five years between uprooting and replanting.

While we waited, we sowed carefully selected plants (vetch, oats, phacelia) to help enrich the soil by adding organic matter. As a bonus, in spring, the flowers in the fields transformed the plot into a colourful carpet.

In the vineyards, we adopted new methods to combat butterflies and the 'grape worm', which likes to attack the flowers in June and pierce the berries in the course of the summer, causing the fruit to rot. Abandoning insecticides, we fought this plague by relying on 'sexual confusion'. Discovered by an inventive agronomist, this technique consists of deceiving male butterflies in search of a female by disrupting their hormonal system. The production of eggs, and therefore caterpillars, is reduced. The wine growers install small capsules in the vineyard that diffuse 'female' pheromones. They hang them from the trellis wires, at a rate of 500 traps per hectare. And it works! Panicked by the enticing smells coming from all sides, the male butterflies are desperately looking for their soul mate, without finding one!

We now combine these 'soft' methods with the creation of an efficient system for treating wine-growing effluents. We take advantage of the network set up, with the help of the mayor of Pauillac, for almost the entire territory of the commune. It allows us to evacuate to a collective purification station the water loaded with organic matter from the vats, the cellars and the cleaning of agricultural equipment.

We remain mindful of the impact of our wine growing on the local population, so we maintain contact with our neighbours and use organic farming methods for the vineyards near our houses. We opt for safer equipment, plant hedges and install drift nets to carefully prevent bird damage wherever useful.

IMPROVING QUALITY ALSO requires precision in the way the vineyard is managed. For 25 years, we have adopted and pushed to the limit the so-called 'parcel selection', which consists of vinifying separately the grapes coming from each physical parcel. In a vineyard like Lynch-Bages, there are about 100 of them. As it is rare that the grapes from one plot are enough to fill a tank, and we did not have a hundred tanks at the time, we mixed grapes from different plots and tried to group together grapes of comparable quality. The cellarmaster knows his terroir inside out and took on the delicate role of assigning a tank to each load of grapes, depending on their origin. In Bordeaux, where the approach is different from that of other wine regions, small, single-variety vintages are rare. The talent of the winemaker is expressed in the blending.

Above: Nicolas Labenne observes the vineyard of Lynch-Bages: meticulous plot selection in the vineyard and the modern equipment of the vat room make vinification extremely precise.

Below: The technical directors of our three Médoc properties (left to right): Raphaël Destruhaut (Ormes de Pez), Nicolas Labenne (Lynch-Bages) and Julien Galland (Haut Batailley) work as a team and enjoy comparing their judgements of the new vintage.

The wine that bears the name of the château reflects the character of the vineyard as a whole.

The soils of the Bordeaux region have been shaped over the geological eras by the ocean, which deposited its sediments before withdrawing. Then by the Garonne and the Dordogne, which removed debris (sand, pebbles, etc) from the mountains of the Pyrenees or the Massif Central. If we add the diversity of the reliefs created by erosion to that of the soils, it is easy to understand that a Médoc *cru*, whose average surface area is quite vast, unlike other regions, is in fact made up of a multitude of micro-terroirs.

A number of years ago, we launched a detailed analysis of all our vineyards, starting with Lynch-Bages. A resistivity study revealed the texture and profile of the soils on the surface and at depth (and reminds me of the time when I was interested in oil deposits). These observations made it possible to determine homogeneous zones which we then analyzed in greater detail. We dug 300 two-metre-deep pits that allowed direct observation of the subsoil. In addition to this visual observation, we carried out detailed analyses of organic matter, potassium, phosphorus, nitrogen, boron, zinc, manganese, and so on. The mass of information gathered allowed us to reorganize the plots of land according to their real quality potential and their vigour.

For new plantings, this information continues to guide us in the choice of the most suitable grape varieties. Grape varieties have always been chosen according to the geological and geographical characteristics of the plots and their texture: Merlot is adapted to colder, more clayey, lower-lying soils. Cabernet Sauvignon is best suited to very stony, well-drained, sunny plots.

In the course of the growing year, we supplement these measurements with various techniques, including satellite photography of the plant cover. The colours show the evolution of the ripening grapes. We also use a GreenSeeker, a tractor-mounted camera that films the vegetation in each row of vines. Once the images have been processed by a computer, it is possible to define a plot zoning of the ripening progress that is even more precise than satellite photography. This detailed knowledge of the vineyard and the soil also helps us to define the best fertilization methods and to better manage the grassing of the plots and the leaf removal and thinning operations.

Thanks to this painstaking work, we have been able to define about 200 homogeneous zones and adopt a finer 'intra-cellular selection' for harvesting, which allows the precise harvesting of smaller and more homogeneous batches. Of course, this complex organization of grape collection is incompatible with mechanical harvesting. It requires a great deal of preparation and the total involvement of harvesting teams.

By 2006, we realized that our modern winery was already out of step with the progress we were making in vineyard management. Intra-cellular selection doubled the number of batches of grapes, an inflation that we had not foreseen. If we wanted to achieve the same high standards in the vinification as in the vineyard, we needed twice as many vats, smaller and of different sizes. We needed to review the organization of our vat house from top to bottom.

We soon realized that a simple change of vat house would not be enough. Our winery was simply not suitable, having evolved over the years from a disorderly group of old buildings. It would be impossible to install 80 tanks, especially of a smaller size than our current 44 tanks. Furthermore, our four barrel cellars did not have enough space to house two harvests side by side, which forced us to carry out complicated handling and, as a result, to limit barrel ageing to about 15 months.

Did we need to fit out and extend the existing building or start from scratch? For several months, we weighed the pros and cons and evaluated the cost of each approach. Little by little, we came to the conclusion that we had to wipe out the past.

Who should be entrusted with the work? Twenty years earlier, in 1986, at the Ban des Vendanges dinner at Château Lagrange, my table neighbour had been Chien Chung Pei, alias 'Didi', son of Ieoh Ming Pei, architect of the Louvre pyramid. A young architect himself, he was then based in Paris where he was assisting his father. We hit it off. Two or three years later, faced with the reconstruction of Pichon-Longueville, I got in touch with him again. He showed interest, but was not available. We then crossed paths several times in New York where he was a regular at the local Commanderie de Bordeaux. The time had come to reach out again. My son Jean-Charles agreed – as he should, he is now in charge.

Jean-Charles and I met Didi shortly afterwards in New York, during the New York Wine Experience, a major event organized by Marvin Shanken, the head of the *Wine Spectator* magazine. In September 2008, an initial agreement was made. Its purpose was to outline the project and draw up specifications. The work was to be spread over several years and would involve our technicians, led by Daniel LLose and Nicolas Labenne. The Bordeaux architect Arnaud Boulain, who we used for the reconstruction of the village of Bages, was also involved. Arnaud has a great deal of experience in wine construction, having been involved in the building of several important cellars: Châteaux Cos d'Estournel in Saint-Estèphe and Pédesclaux in Pauillac, in collaboration with Jean-Michel Wilmotte, not to mention the Château Beychevelle cellars which he designed and built alone.

Over a four-year period, we carried out a comprehensive review of the options and then determined the general principles of the project. There would be no alterations to the existing building, no tinkering with it. Everything would be razed to the ground to allow for total reconstruction. Our choice of the Pei firm obviously implied that the style of the building would be resolutely modern. We gave the signal to start in 2014. Didi and his team immediately set to work with Daniel LLose and Nicolas Labenne. It took a good two years to produce detailed plans and a model to show the finished building.

In December 2016, it was time to start. Before demolishing, we had to clear the premises. We left our offices with a heavy heart and moved to a different space in the village of Bages. All the technical equipment in the vat house also had to be moved. A temporary building was constructed in record time near our agricultural equipment garage as the temporary vat house, where we would vinify at least two harvests. For the barrels, new air-conditioned storage facilities, just built in the port area of Pauillac, provided the solution. Our wines in cask would be safe there while we built their new refuge.

Didi Pei and his deputy, the Mexican Rossana Gutteriez, closely followed the work and made frequent visits to Pauillac. Arnaud Boulain was also regularly present on the site. Rossana's precision and intransigence with all the different companies involved would prove invaluable. On our side, Malou Le Sommer coordinated the operations, assisted by our warehouse manager in Macau, Anne-Sophie Giambi, who maintained permanent contact with the companies. With the arrival of Michel Barthes, overall site coordinator, the team was complete. The demolition phase began in February 2017, with ranks of bulldozers having a field day…

We wanted the buildings to be functional above all else, with everything at the service of the wine. The improvements therefore focused on the following areas:

- Maximum use of daylight
- Ease of cleaning
- Vat room with a capacity for 80 stainless-steel, truncated, cone-shaped, isothermal vats

Malou le Sommer, our architect Chien Chung Pei ('Didi'), Marina and Jean-Charles on the construction site launched in 2017.

The new winery buildings at Lynch-Bages viewed at dusk... Everything was ready for the harvest of 2020...

In Pursuit of Quality, 1995–2021   295

In our new wine cellar: Jean-Charles watches, as if at the prow of a ship...

- Vat room and offices on two floors
- Large underground barrel cellar that can accommodate two harvests simultaneously
- Six lift tanks on three levels to avoid pumping and take advantage of gravity
- Water- and energy-efficient installation
- Retrofitting of solar panels for energy independence
- A large reception area that can accommodate three simultaneous grape arrivals
- Use of the above courtyard for bottling
- Cellar for the 'property' stock
- Enhancement of the historic 19th-century vat house
- Tour circuit and reception areas
- Tasting rooms for professionals and visitors
- Panoramic terrace with views over the town and the vineyards of Pauillac.

In the spring of 2017, once the land was cleared, our village became a huge building site. The objective was to be finished in time for the 2019 harvest. But, as was only to be expected, we had to deal with a number of problems that put us four months behind schedule. Then, in the spring of 2020, Covid emptied the site of its workers. We planned instead to be ready for the 2020 harvest, with the landscaping and moving into our new offices postponed until the following winter and spring: 'After the harvest', as my grandfather used to say when he wanted to postpone something. It was his way of telling us that there was no rush…

The year 2020 will be remembered as 'The Year of Coronavirus'. For several weeks, the epidemic threatened the smooth running of the harvest. The fear of contagion was everywhere. In the vineyard, of course, where three picking teams operated, but above all in the cellars where the appearance of a *cluster* could paralyze operations… and lead to consequences that were difficult to predict. At Lynch-Bages, about 300 people live together for a fortnight during the harvest, most of them are regular team members, coming each year – some from within the region, some from farther afield. A large group arrives by special bus from the villages around Mirandela, in northern Portugal; others arrive from Spain, Morocco and Eastern Europe. In the rows of vines, all languages are spoken. A dozen or so cooks are hard at work, 12 hours a day, to feed the hungry.

We prepared very carefully and took every possible precaution. First of all, we tested everyone for Covid-19. In Mirandela, a local pharmacy tested the Portuguese team before they embarked for France. The Lynch-Bages staff were also tested at the Pauillac laboratory. For the other seasonal workers, the Regional Health Agency, an official body, delegated two nurses to test each of the arrivals. Everyone played the game. Aware of what was at stake, the health services were mobilized to provide the results within 24 hours. We had just one positive case among our potential grape pickers.

Unfortunately, in that most unusual of years, we had to sacrifice the atmosphere to safety: wearing a mask was compulsory, both in the vat room and in the vineyard. Everything was disinfected at all times… hands washed… no more big communal meals. Some received single-use boxes or bags for picnics. Others gathered in small groups, in rotation, under a large refectory tent where they could maintain the necessary distance. No visitors were allowed in the vat room, and no invitations were made to the harvest kitchen either. It was only a postponement… We would meet again in the future!

For all of us at Lynch-Bages, 2020 was a year like no other. We were finally using our new facility. We had to get used to the premises and master the new equipment. After one or two days of starting up and learning, it was done. Our equipment worked perfectly and met expectations. The grapes are handled gently, without pumping, using gravity and the differences in level. The 200 batches harvested separately thanks to the intra-cellular selection were easily distributed in the 80 vats. The cellarmaster prepared an individualized programme for each tank (pumping over, with or without aeration, *délestage*). The vinification process was now electronically controlled and extremely precise. No pumps or hoses were left in the aisles. The atmosphere in the vat room was completely different from the one we knew. It was quiet, clean and bright. I couldn't help but think of Emile Peynaud, who once said: 'The quality of wine is the result of an accumulation of useless precautions.' His remark takes on its full meaning today.

Above: The carefully preserved 1866 vat house. Integrated into the new facility, it is a link to the estate's history.

Below: In the new underground barrel cellar we wanted to make the maximum use of daylight – here we can house two harvests simultaneously.

In Pursuit of Quality, 1995–2021

Above: An aerial shot of the village of Bages and Lynch-Bages, as seen today from the northeast.

Below: An aerial shot of the village from the southwest.

33 A Family Affair

THE ACQUISITION OF Lynch-Bages by my grandfather in 1939, followed two years later by that of the *Société Civile des Ormes de Pez*, is where our family's involvement in the wine business began. Maintaining the family character of this heritage, to which successive generations have remained attached for more than six decades, is a difficult exercise in navigating a sea strewn with legal and fiscal reefs.

Originally, and during the war years, Lynch-Bages and Ormes de Pez were the personal property of my grandfather, Jean-Charles Cazes. It was only in 1946, after my father's return from captivity, that two Sociétés Civiles were created for the properties. Jean-Charles, who had a large majority in the management, split the rest with his four sons.

When Henri, the eldest of the children, died in 1955, his shareholding was divided between the partners. During the 1960s, my grandfather gradually passed on his shares in the company to his three surviving sons. But, company or not, he remained the only one in charge and his sons had no say in the matter. And the sons didn't really care.

For 30 years, their father demonstrated his skills as a vigneron. Moreover, all three of them followed a path far removed from wine growing: Marcel and Gilbert in the general management of Crédit Lyonnais; André, my father, in the insurance business.

From 1965 onwards – by which time he was 88 years old, although still manager of the two non-trading companies of Lynch-Bages and Ormes de Pez – Jean-Charles handed over the day-to-day running to André, who was living in Pauillac. He took on this job alongside the cellarmaster, and in agreement with his brothers – a sometimes delicate situation. I have recounted the story of how my father, overloaded with work in his agency, absorbed by his mandates as mayor of Pauillac and general councillor, had in 1971 thought about selling the properties. I offered to come and help him.

My father immediately started a discussion with his brothers about the future. Marcel, the eldest, summarized their commitment in a one-page handwritten note, which concluded: 'With the idea that the properties should remain in the family, under the name of Cazes, and in order to avoid disputes among the grandchildren, later on, Gilbert and Marcel agree to transfer their shares to André, who will then be the manager with Papa. André will pay back Gilbert and Marcel, as and when he can... Later, Jean-Michel will settle in Pauillac as he has expressed his intention to do. Thus, three generations are assured of owning the properties under the Cazes name.'

In the summer of 1973, I took the plunge and moved to Pauillac with my family. What would have happened if I had continued my Parisian career? Given my father's state of mind at the time and the distance from his brothers, it is not impossible to think that they would have agreed to sell. It is all the more likely since the decade of the 1970s was not a path strewn with rose petals.

Very early on, my father was concerned about transferring the properties to the next generation. The first concrete operation followed the accidental death of my mother in 1975. As our parents were married under the community regime, her titles were divided between her three children: Jean-Michel, Jacqueline and Sylvie, from oldest to youngest.

As early as the 1980s, we worked together to determine the most economical way to carry out future transfers. We carried out numerous studies in order to untangle the complex legal and fiscal web we had to face. We then took action and implemented the necessary structural changes. The process took several years and was completed at the end of 2004. At the same time, the partners agreed on the operational organization to be put in place when the time came: the management of the company would be entrusted to my son, Jean-Charles.

It has been a long process, but we have succeeded in passing on the family properties between four generations and have set up a new structure capable of standing the test of time. We have given it the name 'PAGAMO', found in the Pauillac vineyard register. This is the plot of vines where the calvary marking the entrance to Lynch-Bages was built almost two centuries ago. In this new company, we have brought together the staff and resources of all the entities of our group, Lynch-Bages and Ormes de Pez, but also our properties in the Languedoc, Châteauneuf-du-Pape, Portugal and Australia, as well as our wine trading company and our activities in the field of tourism, catering and hotels. The new scheme streamlines the management of the whole.

Above: In 2006, my son Jean-Charles and I with my younger sister Sylvie, our partner.

Below: Many good things… with us, the girls are in the majority!

A Family Affair

Above: *Jean-Charles is now in charge of our family business, under the watchful eye of his three sisters.*

Below: *In 2018, the whole family gathered with Thereza and I to celebrate our 50th wedding anniversary.*

In 2006, health problems forced me to take a break for a few weeks. This kind of break is always conducive to reflection. It was now 33 years since I returned to Pauillac to settle down with my wife, who was willing to follow me, and our children.

The good fortune of our new life was that we started at a time when the wine business was going to undergo more changes in a few years than in the whole of the previous century. Our children are now grown. Jean-Charles, after starting out as a management controller in the Brazilian subsidiary of a large French industrial company, changed careers. In 2001, he joined our trading company, where he worked to promote Bordeaux wines in all markets around the world.

When he was 32, he seemed to be tempted by the many opportunities that were opening up to him. This was at the beginning of 2007, and I felt the time had come for me to take a step back and hand over the management of our business to him. I knew that he had prepared himself for this new responsibility and that he would be well surrounded by the very efficient trio that had accompanied me for many years: Daniel LLose, technical director; Malou Le Sommer, commercial director; and Pierre Doumenjou, financial director. A solid team that Nicolas Labenne reinforced in 2005 by taking over the technical management at Lynch-Bages.

A few years later, in 2011, I gave up my beautiful office to my son and took refuge in the nice room on the village square, opposite the terrace of the Café Lavinal, where I collected some of my books and memories. I had full confidence in Jean-Charles' ability to run our family business, and had the feeling that I had succeeded in carrying out, at the right time, a peaceful generational transfer and avoided the temptation to fight the 'battle of too many', the classic enemy of the end of one's career, in all professions.

Today, I am no longer subject to the pressure of daily professional life, but I am happy to give my opinion when I am asked, which sometimes happens. I get involved in the action, see people and visitors frequently knock on my glass door. I enjoy these meetings and they keep me in touch with the life of the vineyard.

I sometimes try to imagine what would have happened if we had not made these profound changes to the structure of our company. I am convinced that sooner or later we would have ended up in a deadlock from which it would have been impossible to escape. And that the only option would have been to sell the whole thing to the highest bidder... This is the outcome I wanted to avoid. This was only possible thanks to the cooperation of my sisters: Jacqueline and Sylvie, who approved the plan that was proposed to them. I remain deeply grateful to them.

Since the 1930s, our company has developed through the efforts of four successive generations. I am happy to have participated in the construction of the edifice and I hope with all my strength that my children will be able to maintain the family character of our company... and will have the necessary means at their disposal.

What does the future hold for us? Perhaps the ill winds – the taxman, financial crisis, division – will one day get the better of us. However, I can't help hoping that together, our successors will be able to find solutions to the difficulties that will inevitably arise on their way.

34 And Then…

I HAVE LIVED IN PAUILLAC since 1973. I had, so to speak, the 'chance' to start my new professional career with a crisis that was difficult to overcome. This experience taught me the fragility of our wine economy. It was a lesson I have not forgotten. I then had the good fortune to live through the 1980s, which were much more favourable, thanks to the opening of the markets and the improvement in quality resulting from the progress of modern oenology. We were able to renovate our production facilities, which were in a sad state due to a lack of maintenance and technical investments.

I think of a sentence spoken by my father: 'During my studies, I was taught in political economy that there were crises every 10 years. For me, the alternating between good and bad times is natural. When there is an upturn in wine for a year or two, we wait for the crisis. Those who, like me, have experienced difficult years always say: it won't last!' Experience has taught me to share this point of view. In the long term, I see the history of my profession as the ripples of a stormy sea: periods of growth and prosperity have been followed regularly by profound crises that have damaged the vineyard. The wine business, by its very nature, is vulnerable. We operate under the constant threat of external events.

The path of the last 50 years has not been smooth. The uncertainties caused by the oil crises, the Gulf War a little later and the financial crisis of 2008 have had serious consequences. The events that are shaking Eastern Europe as I write these lines and the anxiety that is being felt around the world raise the spectre of a new downturn…

In truth, I was very lucky to have returned to the country where I had spent my youth at the right time. Favourable conditions made it possible everywhere in Bordeaux, and here in particular, to renovate and extend production facilities that were more than a century old, and to put them in perfect condition. By the turn of the year 2000, our Bordeaux wineries and cellars were already on a par with those of California, Australia and other newly producing countries. This effort has continued over the last 20 years. Our vineyards are now leading the way and are well equipped to face the challenges ahead. In addition to technology, at Lynch-Bages and the wider region, Bordeaux has a history that continues to set us apart.

The 'Place de Bordeaux', a unique commercial organization, inseparable from the success of our wines in the world, has changed. The organization, the methods and the mentalities are no longer those of previous centuries. I am convinced that it will continue to evolve in the future, thanks to the efforts of all concerned and the strengthening of an intelligent cooperation between the production and the trade.

In the vineyard, the evolution of the climate is the essential factor of change. However, I remain convinced that the Bordeaux grape varieties will be able to adapt and will not change significantly over the next 50 years. Viticulture will continue to progress. The methods of cultivation, treatment and maintenance of the soil are already evolving towards increasingly 'clean' techniques. Driven, it must be said, by consumers, wine growers will be inspired more and more by the treatment methods advocated by organic agriculture, without resorting to the nonsense of biodynamics. This is the direction we have taken. We already cultivate 40 percent of our vineyards in Bordeaux according to these principles, and almost all of those in the Languedoc and the Rhône Valley, where the climate is more favourable.

In the cellars and vats, the working methods will follow similar trends. The very taste of wine, which has changed over time, may one day be different again. Since the 18th century, the safety of winemaking has been based on the use of sulphur, nicknamed the 'friend of the cellarmaster'. The evolution towards more neutral methods, if technically possible, will lead to changes to be taken into account at the time of harvesting and during ageing. As in the vineyard, the organic movement is happening in the cellar. We must prepare ourselves for it.

I LIVE IN THE MEDOC, a land blessed by the gods, bordered to the west by the ocean and to the east by the majestic Gironde Estuary. The vineyards have settled here in a gently undulating landscape. Some of the world's greatest wines are produced here. The names of these wines, scattered all along the châteaux route, are a delight to visitors. I personally had the privilege, after my

Above: The house in the middle of the vineyards where I spent my childhood has become my home again.

Below: Visitors are welcome at Lynch-Bages.

And Then... 309

Above: The Médoc landscape, vineyards and river.

Below: The vines of Bages are beautiful in autumn…

grandfather and father, year after year, to bring one of these wines to life. And I hope that my children will continue to do so long after me.

The most important thing is the wine. Each bottle contains a universe which, like the genie in Aladdin's lamp, is ready to escape at the first opportunity. Everything is contained in it: geography and history, fruit, climate, soil, tradition, know-how, but also friendship and shared pleasure.

Index

Page numbers in *italic* refer to the illustrations

1855 Classification 20, 72–3, 120, 154, 165, 166, 280

A

Abeillé, Jacques 94, 96
Acers, Maurice *47, 49*
Achille-Fould, Aymar 93, 95
Agrellos, Antonio 220–2, 224
Air Force 52, 113–14
Algerian war (1954–62) 45, 52, 53
Alibert, Marcel 13, 18, 19
Alvarez, Gabriel 72
Alvarez family 239, 242
Amat, Jean-Marie 102, 103, 110–12, 123, *129*
Les Amis de l'Ecole du Bordeaux 176
Andrus, Gary 244–5
appellation contrôlée 71, 201–2
Arangoïts, Dominique 235, 238
Arcaute, Jean-Michel 239, 247, 248
Argentina 245–50
Argerich, Juan 248, 249
aszú 226, 233–4, 237, 238–9
Austin, Texas 45–8
Australia 250–5, 302
Averous, Domaine 71
AXA 96, 119, 158, 161–2, 288
AXA-Millésimes 151–6, 209–10, 212–13, 215, 219, 232, 239, 240, 250–1, 259

B

Bacsó, András 229–32, 234, 236, 239–40, 242
Bages 8, 20, 31, 63, 70, 178–83, *180–2, 184–5, 300*
Bages, Domaine de 20–7
Baillenx, Aymar de 230
Balaresque 78, 90
Bamford, Martin 107–8, 109–10, *109*
Barbier, Jean-Paul 173
Baronchelli, Elie 94, 96
'La Baronnie' 120
Barsalou, Yves 256–7
Barton, Anthony 103, *104, 125,* 127
Bass Charrington 87, 109
Baudry, Patrick 8, 139–41, *140,* 148

Bébéar, Claude 151–4, *152,* 156, 158, 162, 163, 194, 210, 212–15, 219, 225, 230, 238
Béhéretche, Ignace 32
Beijing 8, 189, 190
Bel Air, Château 203–8, *205*
Benegas, Tiburcio 246
Bérard, Gabriel 57, 114
Bercoff, André 102–3
Bergey, Guy *134*
Bernard, Olivier 127, *129*
Bert, Pierre 90
Bettane, Michel 168, 257
Beychevelle, Château 78, 93, 95, 152–3, 197, 216, 225, 294
Bizot, Xavier 255
Blanc, Georges 179
Blanc de Lynch-Bages 200–2
Blanchy, Alain 77, 88
Bocuse, Paul 102, 112
Bodnar, Sandor 229, 232, 242
Bofill, Ricardo 162, 163, *192*
Boissenot, Eric 83, *160*
Boissenot, Jacques 83, 162, 213
Boisson, Jean-Pierre 272–5
Bollinger 253–5
Bolter, William 109
Bordeaux, Henri, Duke of 23–4
Bordeaux Institute of Oenology 73, 74, 79, 80–3, 85, 113, 135
Borie, Eugène 75, 278
Borie, Jean-Eugène 72, 83, 95, 99, 100, 107, 279–80
Borie family 278–82
Borkombinat 227, 228–9, 231–4, 237, 239, 242
Boulain, Arnaud 178, 293–4
Boulud, Daniel 128
Bouteiller, Bernard 156
Bouteiller, Bertrand 95, 158
Bouteiller, Jean 165
Bouteiller family 154–6, 157
Boutemy, Francis 204
Bras, Jean-Claude 225–6, 229
Broadbent, Michael 104–5, 167

C

Cabernet Sauvignon   71, 289, 292
Calem, Maria Ascunção   222, 224
California   244–5
Calvet   76–7, 91, 210
Cambodia   199
Cantenac-Brown, Château   78, 150, 153–4, 156, 209–12, *211*, 216
Caribbean   50–1
Carroget, Jacques   239
Castéja, Philippe   279, 280, 282
Castel, Pierre   164, 197, 206
Cathay Pacific   186–7, *188*
Cayrou, Jérôme   27
Cazes, A and J-M (insurance agency)   10, *95*
Cazes, André (JMC's father)   37, 42, 55–6, 59, 60, *61, 101, 133*, 307
   early life   28
   marriage   28–9
   in war   30, 35–6, 240
   in Bordeaux   41
   at Lynch-Bages   63, 69, 71–2
   financial problems   88, 93, 97–8
   and Claudine's death   91–2
   tourism and gastronomy   100
   Fête de la Fleur   148
   and future of vineyards   301–2
Cazes, André and Bernard (Rivesaltes)   256, 259
Cazes, Andréa (JMC's grandmother, *née* Gimbert)   14–17, 31–7, 43, 58
Cazes, Anne-Christine (Kinou, JMC's daughter)   9, *65*, 126, *165, 182*, 280, *284, 304*
Cazes, Catherine (JMC's daughter)   9, *165*, 266, 280, *304*
Cazes, Claudine (JMC's mother, *née* Lavinal)   28–30, 32, 34, 41, 91, 302
Cazes, Gilbert (JMC's uncle)   15, *16*, 28, 30, 43, 55, 56, 94, 301–2
Cazes, Henri (JMC's uncle)   13, 17, 55, 60, 301
Cazes, Jacqueline (Jacotte, JMC's sister)   29, 30, 34, 36, 37, 40, 302, 306
Cazes, Jean (Lou Janou, JMC's great-grandfather)   12–13
Cazes, Jean-Charles (JMC's grandfather)   *12*, 13–19, *15–16*, 27, 28, 31–2, *33*, 35–6, 55–8, 62, 63–4, *65*, 69, 71, 72, 301
Cazes, Jean-Charles (JMC's son)   8, 85, *165*, 250, 251, 255, 266, 270–1, 274, 275–6, 280–5, *284, 293, 295–6*, 302, *303–4*, 305
Cazes, Jean-Michel   25, 37, 46, 49, *101, 104, 121, 125, 130, 133, 165, 191, 195, 236, 249, 252, 303–4*

childhood   29–37
education   39–42, 43–5
studies in US   45–50
and IBM   52–5, 61–2
becomes interested in wine   55–6
marriage   59–60
returns to Pauillac   60–2
works for La Providence   62, 83
first harvest   79–85, *86*
and CMGC   94–7
financial problems   97–8
tourism and gastronomy   99–106
in US   120–39
and AXA-Millésimes   151–6
and Pichon-Longueville   157–66
and Cordeillan-Bages   173–8, 183–4
renovates Bages   178–83
in Asia   186–99
in Portugal   217–24, 265–8
Hungarian venture   225–43
retirement   305–6
see also Lynch-Bages, Château
Cazes, Marcel (JMC's uncle)   13, *16*, 28, 43, 55, 56, 301–2
Cazes, Marina (JMC's daughter)   9, *65, 165*, 166, 240, *266*, 280, *295*, 304
Cazes, Sylvie (JMC's sister)   *133*, 288, 302, *303*, 306
Cazes, Thereza (JMC's wife)   9, 59–60, *121–2*, 123, 130, *152, 165*, 187–8, 217, 248, *249*, 266, *304*
Chabalier, Hervé   89
Chaban-Delmas, Jacques   89, 124
Chan, Johnny   8, 188, 189–90
Chan, Judy   193–4
Chandou, François   128
Chapel, Alain   102, 112
Charasse, Michel   205–6
Charmolue, Jean-Louis   72, 95, 99
Château & Estate Wines Co   126–7
Châteauneuf-du-Pape   270–6, 273, 277, 288, 302
Châteaux & Associés   156, 210, 259, 288
Chauvet, Serge   213–14, 233–4
Cheung, Vincent   8, 188, 194, *196*
China   8, 188–97
Chirac, Jacques   115, 171, 271
Christie's   105, 203
Chroman, Nathan   105, 122
Clinvest   225, 230, 231
Club des Cent   112
Commanderie du Bontemps de Médoc et des Graves   77, 106, 108, 113, 141, 145, 147, *149*, 171, 198, 211–12

Compagnie Médocaine des Grands Crus (CMGC) 94–7, 208, 238, 259
Compagnie du Midi 209–10
Conolly, Jacqueline and Thurloe 110
Conseil Interprofessionnel des Vins de Bordeaux (CIVB) 10, 90–1, 100–2
Cordeau, Jean 289
Cordeillan-Bages, Château 173–8, 177, 183–4, 259
Cordier, Jean 72, 113, 156
Corrèges, André 139
Cos d'Estournel, Château 78, 95, 136, 216, 294
Cottin, Philippe 74, 120, 132
Courrian, Philippe 257
Covid-19 pandemic 130, 184, 195, 297–8
Crasto, Quinta do 265–8
Crédit Agricole 88, 97
Crédit Lyonnais 55, 88, 94–8, 230, 301
Croser, Brian 251–5, *252*
Cruse, Emmanuel 77
Cruse & Fils Frères 19, 76
'Cruse Affair' (1973) 88–91
Cruse family 67, 74
Cuba 50
Cullen, Vanya 253–4

D

Daguin, André 123, 128, 171
Daguin, Ariane 128, *130*
Davies, John 109
de Gaulle, Charles 45, 59
Déjean, Bernard 20–1, 23, 27
Déjean family 8, 20–1
Delmas, Jean 73, 83
Delon, Michel 95, 127, *129*, 136, 157, 165
Delor 76, 91, 132
Deroye, Louis *155*
Des Brest family 278, 280–2, 285
Desai, Bipin 123
Desseauve, Thierry 232, *234*
Dessewffy, Château 230
Destruhaut, Raphaël 291
Dethier, Jean 162–3, 235
Deutsch, Sherwood 99, 100
Dillon, Patrick *159*, 163
Disznókő 231–43, *241*, 259
Dora, Miklos Sandor (Miki) 120–4, *122*, 127, 130, 244
Doumenjou, Pierre 249, 278, 281, 288, 305
Dousson, Robert 107, 108
Doutrelant, Pierre-Marie 103
Dreyfus-Ashby 10, 78, 93
Drouillard, Pierre 21–2, 23

Dubœuf, Georges 179
Ducellier, Alain 72
Ducru-Beaucaillou, Château 83, 95, 99, 100, 279–80, 282
Dulhoste, Claude 231
Dupin, Raymond 280
Durousseau, André 98

E, F

Ecole des Mines, Paris 44, 48
Eddington, Rod 187
Ekler, Dezső 235–7, 240, *241*
Elizabeth, The Queen Mother 105
En Primeur market 10, 58, 78, 79, 87, 94, 131–2, 137, 138, 142–5, 170, 286
Engrand, Jean-Pierre 55–6, 111
Enjalbert, Henri 105, 257, 258
Eugénie-les-Bains 179
Evans, Len 251–3
Faith, Nicholas 104, 110
Ferreira, João-Maria Carregal 135
Fêtes de la Fleur 145–50, *149*, *152*, 218, 212
Finigan, Robert 105, 168
First Growths 120–7
Fouquier, Georges 77, 88
Fournier, Henriette 103, *104*
Franc-Mayne, Château 153, 209
French Revolution 24, 146

G

Galard, Hector de 225–6, 229–31
Galland, Julien *291*
garage wines 170–1
Garantie Mutuelle des Fonctionnaires (GMF) 152–3, 225, 230, 239
Garcia, Francis 102, 136
Gardère, Jean-Paul 73
Gardinier, Xavier 174–5, 231
Garin, Georges 55
Gastines, Jean de *159*, 163
Gault, Henri 103, 108, 112, 257
Gausset, André 102
Gauthier, Pierre 161
Gilbeys Ltd 107
Gimenez, André 64, 72, 117, 141
Ginestet (company) 76, 78, 212
Ginestet, Bernard 77, 91
Giscard d'Estaing, Valéry 89, 115
Giscours, Château 78, 108, 216
Gloria, Château 18, 73, 95, 105, 132
Godebski, Nicolas 233, 234
Goelet, John 258
Goguel, Jean 45

Index 315

Gouin, Léon 55
Gounel, Jean-Jacques 161–2
grapes 71, 200, 289–90, 292
Great Wall Winery 192
Guérard, Michel 102, 112, 123, 179
Guevara, Ernesto (Che) 22, 246
Guibert, Aimé 257, 258–9
Guillard, Michel 108, 162–3
Guillot de Suduiraut, Dominique 202–3

H, I

Haïrabedian, Lionel 141, 163
Haut-Batailley, Château 278–86, *279, 283*–4
Harvey's 73, 105, 107
Haushalter, Georges 96
Haut-Bages Averous, Château 115–17
Haut-Brion, Château 73, 83, 120, 229
Herrick, James 256, 258
Hétszőlő 230, 239, 243
Hong Kong 186–9, 193–5
Horgan family 254
Hungary 225–43
IBM 8, 52–5, *57*, 61–2
India 199
International Distillers and Vintners (IDV) 78, 107–8, 110

J, K

Japan 197–8
Jauffret, Jean-Paul 100–2, 132, 207
Johnson, Frank 100
Johnson, Hugh 104, 108, 110, 167, 214, 228, 242–3
Johnson, Lyndon 48
Johnson-Hill, Sue and Alan 109
Juppé, Alain 171, 207, 212, 271, 281
Jurine, Sébastien 27
Kauffmann, Jean-Paul 232, *234*

L

La Gardiole 260–3
La Lagune, Château 77, 216
La Livinière 260, 261, 263
Labenne, Nicolas 288–9, 291, 293–4, 305
Lafite, Château 72–4, 120, 162, 201
Lagrange, Château 197–8, 216, 229
Lalande family 211, 211
Lan Chi Pat 194–7, 196
Languedoc 256–64, 288, 302
Lardat, Pierre 173–4
Lascombes, Château 109, 216
Latour, Château 72–3, 105–6, 115, 120, 214–15, 229
Launay, Château de 200

Lavinal, Arthur 29–30, 38, 39–41
Lavinal, Berthe (*née* Delbrel) 29, 40
Lawton, Daniel 77, 88, 210
Le Brun, Jean-Claude 257
Le Collen, Eric 146–50, 218
Le Collen, Michel 146, 150
Lecouty, Chantal 103, 257
Le Saux, Arnaud 177, 184
Le Sommer, Christian 161
Le Sommer, Marie-Louise (Malou) 160, 161, 210, 288, 294, 295, 305
Lefebvre, Julien 184
Leibovich, Bernard 197
Leibovitz, Mo and Loretta 110
Léoville-Las Cases, Château 95, 136, 157
Lévignac, Michel 94, 96
Lichine, Alexis 50, 58, 75, 77, 87, 103, 104, 105, 109, 167, 173
Lillet, Pierre 108
LLose, Daniel 116, 119, 131, 134, 160, 212, 266, 286
  at Lynch-Bages 114–19, 293–4, 305
  fermentation problems 134–5
  Pichon-Longueville 157–8, 162
  Villa Bel-Air 200–1, 204, 207
  Château Suduiraut 213
  in Portugal 222, 224, 267–8, 288
  Hungarian venture 230–1, 233–4, 237–8, 240, 242
  in California 244–5
  and Argentinian vineyard 247–9
  in the Languedoc 259–63, 288
  Domaine de Sénéchaux 276
  selection of vines 289
Loudenne, Château 107–12, 202
Lur Saluces, Alexandre de 103, 104, 201
Lurton, André 206
Lurton, Lucien 72, 202
Luze 78, 91, 153
Luze, Simone de 210–11
Lycée Louis-le-Grand, Paris 42, 43–5, 151
Lynch, Federico Benegas 245–50
Lynch, Jean-Baptiste 23–4, 27
Lynch, Michel 8, 23–7
Lynch, Patrick 246
Lynch-Bages, Château *169, 185, 309*
  Cazes family buys 18–19
  early history 20–7
  under JMC's grandfather 56–8
  animal traction 63, *65*
  in 1970s 63–71, *68, 84*
  'real' tax regime 69–70
  migrant workers 70–1
  André Cazes takes over 71–2

JMC's first harvest 79–85, *86*
modernization 85
financial problems 87–8, 93–4, 97–8
tourism and gastronomy 99–100, 126
employs oenologist 113–19
second wine 115–17
modernization programme 131–9, 141–2, *143, 144*
fermentation problems 132–5
wine taken into space 139–41, 147–50
Fête de la Fleur 145–50, *149*, 218
Asian market 186–99
white wine 200–2
renovation scheme 278, 286, 293–8, *295–6, 299–300*
pursuit of quality 287–93
Lynch family 22–7, *25*

M

Macao 179, 188, 199, 294
malolactic fermentation 79–80
Manoncourt, Thierry 103, *104*, 127, 128, *129*, 136, 203
Margaux, Château 72, 77, 83, 91, 115, 120, 202, 216, 229
Martin, Henri 10, 18, 73, 90–1, 95, 105, 131–2, 141, 148, 198
Marx, Thierry 178, 180, 183–4, 198
Matignon, Jean-René 158, *160*, 162
Mau, Gaston 79–80
Mau, Roger 10, 56–7, 72, 80, *81*, 83, 113, 114, 118
Meco, Quinta do 268, *269*
Mendes, Sérgio and Gracinha 110–11, 123, *137*
Mentzelopoulos, André 83
Mészáros, László 237–8, 240
Miguel, Zé 217–18
Millau, Christian 103, 108, 112, 257
Ministry of Aviation 52
Mitterand, François 171, 271
Mondavi, Robert 7, 121, 125–6, *125*, 170, 244, 258–9
Montagnac, Pierre 96, 176, 189, *191*, 193, 194
Montrose, Château 95, 99, 100, 216
Morin, Christian 139, 148
Moses, Alain 78, 90, 97
Moueix, Christian and Marie-Laure 108
Moueix, Jean-François 129, 170
Moueix, Jean-Pierre 75–6
Mouton Rothschild, Château 72–3, 74, 120

N, O

Napa Valley 121, 123, 124–6
Napoleon I, Emperor 26

National Institute of Designations or Origin (INAO) 205–6, 207
New York 45–7
Noval, Quinta do 217–24, 221, 259, 265, 288
oil crisis (1973) 10, 78, 79, 85, 307
Olazabal, Francisco (Vito) de 220
Les Ormes de Pez, Château 13, 18, 19, 55, 72, 94, 117–19, 142–5, *143, 147*, 150, 183, 301, 302
Ostal, Domaine de l' 260–4, 276
Overstreet, Dennis 121, 124

P

PAGAMO 302
Pagézy, Bernard 154, 210
Paillardon, Pierre and Danielle 175–6
Palladin, Jean-Louis 128
Parker, Robert 167–72, *169*, 270–1, 276
Pascaud family 213
Pauli, Georges 113, 114, 156
Pearson Group 73, 214
Pei, Chien Chung (Didi) 293–4, *295*
Penning-Rowsell, Edmund 100, 104
Perrin, Jean-Paul 270, 271
Perromat, Jean 202, 203
Pétain, Philippe 30–1, 69
Petaluma Winery 252–3
Petit-Village, Château 212–13
Peynaud, Emile 74, 79, 80–3, 82, 85, 94, 108, 112, 129, 134–7, 162, 168, 170, 213, 257, 298
Pez, Château de 78, 108
Phélan Ségur, Château 174, 231
Philip, Prince 105
phylloxera 12, 14, 27, 71, 155, 227, 258, 289
Pibran, Château 161–2
Pichon-Lalande, Château 154, 158, 165, 216
Pichon-Longueville (Pichon-Baron), Château 95, 150, 152, 154–6, 157–66, *159–60*, 215, 216, 235, 287, 293
Pichou, Dominique 147–8
Pijassou, René 7, 105–6
Pinault, François 215
Pine Ridge Vineyards 244–5
'Place de Bordeaux' 75–8, 308
Planchou, Jean-Paul 94–5
Polaert, Jean-Paul *144*
Pommery 174–5
Pontet-Canet, Château 73, 74, 90, 216
Poon, Wai Lin (William) 110–11, *112*
port wines 217–24
Portet, André 73
Portet, Bernard 244, 258
Portugal 217–24, 265–8, 288, 302
Pouyalet, Léonard 27

Prats, Bruno   95, *104*, 127, *129*, 136, 207, 212–13
Présence insurance group   154
Prial, Frank   105, *152*, 247
La Providence insurance company   10, 18, 36, 56, 60, 62, 83, 93–4

R
Rabier, Alain   176–8
Rahoul, Château   110, 227
Raskó, György   228, 229
Rauzan-Ségla, Château   95, 215, 216
Relais & Châteaux   175, 176
Renaud, Serge   189
Ribéreau-Gayon, Jean   79, 80
Ribourel, Jacques   257–8, 259
Ricard, Claude   *104*, 127, *129*, 136
Robertson, 'Sandy' Irvine   110
Robin, Bernard   153–6, *155*, 213, 219, 225–6, 230–2
Robinson, Jancis   104, 110, 256, 264
Rocha, Jean-Luc   184
Roger, Bruno   214, 215
Rolland, Lt Colonel   113–14
Rolland, Michel   83, 169, *212*, 213, 247–9
Roquette, Jorge   *252*, 265–8, *266*
Roquette & Cazes   267–8
Rotary International   45, 47, 50
Rothschild, Eric de   74, 162
Rothschild, Philippe de   74, 76, 99, 105, 120–1, 244
Roux, Pascal   271–2, 275, 276
Rouzaud, Jean-Claude   186
Royal Masonic Senior School, Bushey   41–2
Royal Tokaj Wine Company   228, 239, 242–3
Rugus, Nancy   127, 130

S
SAFER   259–62, 271, 272, 275, 281–5
Saji, Keizo   197–8
Salvi, John   109
Sauternes   213–14
Schneider group   61–2
Seagram   126–7
Seely, Christian   222, 224, 288
Seely, James   222
Sénéchaux, Domaine de   270–1, *274*, 275–6
Shanghai   189, 190, 193
Shanken, Marvin   138, 150, 293
Shell oil   92
Shi, Cindy   194, *195*
Sicet, Hélène   218
Sichel, Peter Allan   108–9
Simon, Ab   126–7, *126*, 139, 202

Singapore   172, 186, 198
Skalli, Robert   256–7, 259
Skawinski, Pierre   *67, 68*
Société Civile de Bel-Air   203–8
South Africa   60
Space shuttle   139–41, *140*, 147
Spurrier, Steven   175, 244
Stavisky, Alexandre   90 and n
Suckling, James   138
Suduiraut, Château   213–14, 259
Suntory   197

T
Tapanappa   253–5
Tari, Nicholas   108
Tari, Pierre   *104*, 107, 108
Tasaki, Shinya   197
Thailand   198–9, 281
Thillier, Jean-François   176
Tibur, Xavier   57, *68*, 69
Tinon, Samuel   228, 242
Tokaj vineyards   225–43
Tokyo   197
Toso, Mario   248, 249
La Tour Carnet, Château   95
Trefethen, John and Janet   124
Tuil, Jean-Paul   102–3

U, V
United States of America 45–50, 120–30, 244–5
University of Texas, Austin 45–8
Vaillé, Laurent   257
Van Zeller, Cristiano   218–20, 223
Veyrier, Michel   260–2, 270–5
Vial, General Félix de   18–19, 27, 75
Villa Bel-Air   203–8, *205*, 259
Vinding-Diers, Peter   110, 227–8
VINIV Bordeaux   183
Vipur   260–4

W, X, Y, Z
Wallace, Steve   124
Waugh, Harry   104, 105, 167, 214
Weill, Alexis   278, 280–1
The Wine Advocate   167, 168, 170, 172
Wine Spectator   138–9, 150, 162, 184, 245, 293
World War II   19, 30–7, *33*, 301
Wright, Michael   253
Xiradakis, Jean-Pierre   102, 110–11, 123
Xisto   267–8
Yan Chai   195
Yquem, Château d'   201, 213

Acknowledgements

Front cover: Tim Foster
Inside pages: all images from the archives of Château Lynch-Bages except: p81, p84 (b), Michel Guillard; p101 Sara Matthews; p159, p221 (t), Serge Chapuis; p.181 (t), p181 (b), Jérôme Mondière and Pierre Grenet; p185 Jérôme Mondière; p205 Alan Benoît; p241 (t), (c), (b), Furmint Photo.

Other books from Académie du Vin Library we think you'll enjoy:

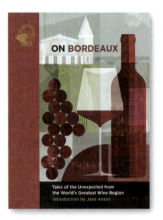

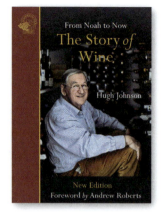

ON BORDEAUX
Tales of the Unexpected from the World's Greatest Wine Region
Susan Keevil
Why these wines are the most talked about.

ON CHAMPAGNE
A Tapestry of Tales to Celebrate the Greatest Sparkling Wine of All
Susan Keevil
The thoughts, opinions and conclusions of the world's finest champagne writers.

THE STORY OF WINE
From Noah to Now
Hugh Johnson
The new edition of Hugh Johnson's captivating journey through the history of wine.

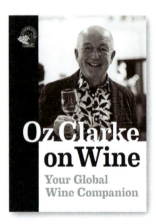

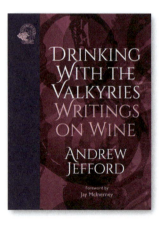

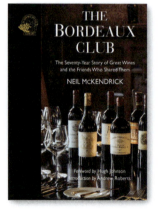

OZ CLARKE ON WINE
Your Global Wine Companion
A fast-paced tour of the world's most delicious wine styles with Oz.

DRINKING WITH THE VALKYRIES
Writings on Wine
Andrew Jefford
Celebrating the limitless beauty of wine difference.

THE BORDEAUX CLUB
The Seventy-Year Story of Great Wines and the Friends Who Shared them
Neil McKendrick
Bordeaux's finest vintages explored.

www.academieduvinlibrary.com